MAGNA CARTA AND ITS MODERN LEGACY

Magna Carta is celebrated around the world as a symbol of limited government and constitutionalism. But in 1215 Magna Carta was a failure, abrogated within months. Why then do we celebrate this piece of parchment? To mark its 800th anniversary, this book brings together top scholars from the United Kingdom, the United States and Australia to answer this question and analyse Magna Carta's historic and contemporary influence.

Using a political science framework, *Magna Carta and Its Modern Legacy* draws from scholarship on influence and constitutional design to explain how parchment can contain executive power. Individual chapters on Britain discuss such topics as socio-economic rights in Magna Carta; Magna Carta and the British constitution; and public understanding of the charter. Internationally focused chapters look at Magna Carta and jury trial in America, slavery in the Caribbean, court delays in the Pacific, the proportionality principle and judicial supremacy.

ROBERT HAZELL is Professor of Government and the Constitution at University College London. He is the founder and director of the Constitution Unit, an independent think tank specialising in constitutional reform that has published detailed reports on Britain's constitutional reform programme. Professor Hazell frequently appears on the BBC and other media to talk about constitutional issues, and he has received the Political Studies Association's Communication award.

JAMES MELTON is Senior Lecturer in Comparative Politics at University College London. His research focuses on comparative constitutional design, investigating the origins, stability and enforcement of formal constitutional texts. He is a principal investigator on the Comparative Constitutions Project and co-author of the project's first book, *The Endurance of National Constitutions* (Cambridge, 2009).

Comparative Constitutional Law and Policy

Series Editors:

Tom Ginsburg, University of Chicago
Zachary Elkins, University of Texas at Austin
Ran Hirschl, University of Toronto

Comparative constitutional law is an intellectually vibrant field that encompasses an increasingly broad array of approaches and methodologies. This series collects analytically innovative and empirically grounded work from scholars of comparative constitutionalism across academic disciplines. Books in the series include theoretically informed studies of single constitutional jurisdictions, comparative studies of constitutional law and institutions and edited collections of original essays that respond to challenging theoretical and empirical questions in the field.

Volumes in the Series:

Magna Carta and Its Modern Legacy

Edited by

ROBERT HAZELL
University College London

JAMES MELTON
University College London

CAMBRIDGE
UNIVERSITY PRESS

CAMBRIDGE
UNIVERSITY PRESS

32 Avenue of the Americas, New York, NY 10013-2473, USA

Cambridge University Press is part of the University of Cambridge.

It furthers the University's mission by disseminating knowledge in the pursuit of education, learning and research at the highest international levels of excellence.

www.cambridge.org
Information on this title: www.cambridge.org/9781107533103

© Cambridge University Press 2015

First published 2015

A catalog record for this publication is available from the British Library.

ISBN 978-1-107-11277-3 Hardback
ISBN 978-1-107-53310-3 Paperback

Contents

List of Contributors

Vernon Bogdanor is Research Professor at the Institute of Contemporary British History, King's College London.

David Clark is Professor of Law, Flinders University.

Robert Hazell is Professor of Government and the Constitution and Director of the Constitution Unit in the School of Public Policy, University College London.

Anthony King is Professor of Government, University of Essex.

Craig S. Lerner is Professor of Law and Associate Dean for Academic Affairs, George Mason University School of Law.

Renée Lettow Lerner is Professor of Law, George Washington University.

James Melton is Senior Lecturer in Comparative Politics in the School of Public Policy, University College London.

Victor Menaldo is Assistant Professor of Political Science, University of Washington, Seattle.

Roger Mortimore is Professor of Public Opinion and Political Analysis, King's College London, and Director of Political Analysis, Ipsos MORI.

Derek O'Brien is Reader in Law, Oxford Brookes University.

Natalie Riendeau is an independent researcher.

Geraldine Van Bueren is Professor of International Human Rights Law, Queen Mary University, University of London, and Visiting Fellow, Kellogg College, University of Oxford.

Nora Webb Williams is a PhD student at the University of Washington, Seattle.

Preface

The idea for this book came from the Political Studies Association (PSA), which wanted political science to play its part in the 800th-anniversary celebrations of Magna Carta. Professor Justin Fisher of the Magna Carta Institute at Brunel and Jennifer Hudson of the PSA Executive asked me to organise a conference and a book, and I willingly agreed. It could have been a challenge to find something new to say about Magna Carta, but thanks to the contributors to this volume, I am confident that we have succeeded. So my first thanks go to them, for finding the time to write very interesting chapters and for coming to the United Kingdom to discuss their contributions with each other at a workshop held at the Constitution Unit in the School of Public Policy at UCL in June 2014.

Thanks must also go to the others who attended the workshop – Conor Gearty, Clodagh Harris, George Jones and Colin Munro – for their comments on the draft chapters; and thanks to our administrator, Ben Webb, for organising it with his usual enthusiasm and efficiency. We also express special thanks to the interns who have supported this project: Annabelle Huet, Daniel Helen and Chrysi Kalfa. Daniel's expertise as a medieval historian was particularly valuable.

For including the book in the Cambridge University Press series on comparative constitutional law and policy, we thank the editors, Zachary Elkins, Tom Ginsburg and Ran Hirschl. Our thanks also go to the anonymous reviewers of our book proposal and to John Berger, our editor at Cambridge. And we thank the PSA for funding the project and paying for the workshop in 2014 and the conference to launch the book in 2015. Without the PSA's foresight and support, this book would not have happened.

I reserve my last but warmest thanks to my colleague and co-editor James Melton. He has done all the hard work and ensured that everyone delivered on time (a first in my experience of edited books); he did so throughout with tact, good humour and quiet efficiency. It has been a real pleasure working with him on this project, and I hope that we find the opportunity to work together again.

Robert Hazell
Constitution Unit
School of Public Policy
University College London

INTRODUCTION

1

Magna Carta ... Holy Grail?

James Melton and Robert Hazell

Magna Carta is revered by citizens and human rights activists all over the world. It has become a symbol for limited government and constitutionalism used by political theorists, constitutional drafters, political elites and even ordinary citizens to justify constraining political power. Thus, when Jay-Z entitled his most recent album *Magna Carta ... Holy Grail*, he was signalling his aspiration to constrain the power of the recording industry, just like Magna Carta was meant to constrain King John. The irony is that '[i]n 1215 Magna Carta was a failure'.[1] King John completely ignored the edicts set forth in the Charter, which led England into the very civil war that the Great Charter was meant to prevent. Why, then, do we celebrate this historic piece of parchment? Put differently, how has the significance of Magna Carta come to be equated with that of the Holy Grail?

This volume sets out to answer the question. In doing so, it makes two contributions to the extant literature. First, it commemorates Magna Carta's 800th anniversary by detailing its influence in the United Kingdom and abroad. The book reviews the existing historical and legal literature on Magna Carta as well as providing some new insights about its influence. These new insights are generated by moving to a more systematic conceptualisation of influence. Second, the volume begins a dialogue with the literature on constitutional design. This is a quickly evolving, interdisciplinary literature that spans economics, history, law, political science and sociology. We believe that those interested in constitutional design have much to learn from modern understandings of Magna Carta, and we therefore provide some examples of how reflecting on Magna Carta can provide lessons for those interested in modern constitutions.

[1] J. C. Holt, *Magna Carta*, 2nd ed. (Cambridge: Cambridge University Press, 1992), 1.

This introductory chapter proceeds in three sections. The first provides a bit of history about the making of Magna Carta and its contents. The second defines what we mean by influence and provides a typology for analysing the influence of Magna Carta. The third sketches out the plan for the rest of the volume.

THE MAKING AND CONTENTS OF MAGNA CARTA

There are two accounts of the making of Magna Carta. Traditionally, the story of Magna Carta paints King John as a tyrant who oppressed his people and deserved the insurrection that led to the Charter. This is the account told by Sir Edward Coke in his many writings, including the *Petition of Right* (1628) and the second volume of the *Institutes of the Lawes of England*. In these works, Coke used Magna Carta in his fight against King Charles I to argue that the Great Charter served as a repository of ancient common law rights that all English monarchs must respect. Coke was essentially drawing a parallel between his own dispute with King Charles I and the dispute between King John and his barons in 1215, so it is little wonder that he describes Magna Carta as a victory for the righteous barons over the tyrannical King John.[2]

Coke's version of the events surrounding Magna Carta has been retold many times. His narrative can be found in historical accounts of the writing of Magna Carta and has even found its way into children's literature. For instance, the story of *Robin Hood* pits righteous Robin against a greedy, oppressive King John, and the history of Magna Carta in *Our Island Story* not only tells our children that Magna Carta 'is the foundation of all our laws and liberty' but also that '[n]o king of England has ever been so bad as John'.[3] This is the narrative of Magna Carta that gives the Great Charter its symbolic power. It is a narrative that is engrained in us during childhood and gives us hope that a simple piece of parchment delineating the legal limits of executive power can tame even the most oppressive tyrants.

More recently, a revisionist narrative has arisen to describe Magna Carta's creation. This alternate account is more sceptical (and probably more accurate) both about Magna Carta itself and about the villainy of King

---

[2] Take, e.g., these words from ch. 15 of the second volume of Coke's *Institutes*: '. . . that in the raigne of King John, and of his elder brother King Richard, which were troublesome and irregular times, diverse oppressions, exactions, and injuries, were incroached upon the Subject in these Kings names, for making of Bulwarks, Fortresses, Bridges, and Bankes, contrary to Law and right'. Here, Coke explicitly notes the oppression of King John and his brother Richard.

[3] Henrietta Elizabeth Marshall, ch. 36, 'The Story of the Great Charter', *An Island Story: A History of England for Boys and Girls* (New York: Frederick A. Stokes Company, 1920). Available at: http://digital.library.upenn.edu/women/marshall/england/england-36.html.

John.[4] According to this version, King John was a victim of circumstance. He had inherited a host of problems from his father and older brother. To start, both King Henry II and King Richard I expropriated large sums from their citizens. By the time of King Richard I's death in 1199, the King's 'exploitation of England for funds [had] reached unprecedented levels'. Given the early English state's financial obligations, King John had few options but to continue to exploit its resources.[5]

There were also changes in the structure of the state during the rule of the Angevin kings. As the state became larger and more complex, it became necessary for the royal household to employ a full-time, educated staff and to lay down new rules and regulations to manage the affairs of state.[6] These innovations formed the foundation for the common law institutions that we recognise in the United Kingdom today.[7] They were necessary to enable efficient governance of the growing nation, but they angered the aristocracy, which felt excluded from the new modes of governance created by the Angevin kings.[8] Not only did the barons have to compete with the King's new staff members for royal favour, and all of the benefits such favour entails, but the King had stronger control over the state, leaving the aristocratic class with fewer freedoms than under previous monarchs. The noble classes became acutely aware of the implications of this new form of government during the reign of King John because, after the loss of Normandy, he was forced to rule from England. This put him in a better position to enforce the rules of Angevin government than had been the case with his father and brother, who spent most of their respective reigns abroad, and formed one of the key grievances that led to Magna Carta.[9]

Lastly, King John inherited the wrath of Philip Augustus of France, who had vowed to unite all of France. At the time, Normandy was under the rule of the Angevin kings, so in order to unite France, Philip Augustus needed to take back Normandy. Philip Augustus's war with the English started during the reign of King Richard I, but he was unable to wrestle Normandy and other English-held French territory away from England until 1204. His success was a

---

[4]   See in particular, Holt, *Magna Carta* (1992). See also Ralph Turner, ch. 2, 'Young John in His Brothers' Shadows', *King John: England's Evil King* (Gloucestershire: History Press, 1994); Alicia Mavor, 'Magna Carta: A Bitter Indictment of King John's Rule?' *History Today* (2013), available at: http://www.historytoday.com/alicia-mavor/magna-carta-bitter-indictment-king-johns -rule; Graham E. Seel, 'Good King John', *History Today* 62(2) (2012).
[5]   Ralph V. Turner, *Magna Carta: Through the Ages* (2003), 34.
[6]   Ibid. at 17.
[7]   Holt, *Magna Carta* (1992).
[8]   Holt, *Magna Carta* (1992).
[9]   Turner, *Magna Carta: Through the Ages* (2003), 32; Holt, *Magna Carta* (1992).

major loss of both territory and resources for King John, who spent most of the rest of his reign preparing for and launching a campaign to retake Normandy. To finance this campaign, King John had to acquire even larger sums than his brother, King Richard I, had levied.

In short, King John faced three major obstacles at the start of his reign: (1) a financially drained state, (2) an angry aristocratic class and (3) a war with France that he eventually lost. According to this account of Magna Carta, the three circumstances put King John in an impossible position. He had to raise large sums of money to pay the state's debts and to finance his campaign in France, but the aristocracy had already been heavily exploited by his father and brother and was unlikely to pay more willingly. Fortunately for John, his predecessors had already built a foundation for him to raise these funds: through a combination of even higher taxes; increasing amercements – penalties for wrongdoing; and taking full advantage of 'feudal incidents' – opportunities that allowed the king to levy additional revenue, such as payments to the king to recognise an heir's succession.[10]

These are the events that eventually led to the barons' insurrection against King John and the writing of Magna Carta. This revisionist account of Magna Carta is quite different from the traditional view. Instead of a righteous group of barons trying to restrain a tyrannical king, it sees Magna Carta as an attempt by self-interested barons to take advantage of a relatively weak king with few allies in Continental Europe.[11] In 1215, King John had just lost his campaign to retake Normandy against Philip Augustus, and only two years before that he had made peace with Pope Innocent III after the Pope imposed a five-year-long interdict on England for King John's insubordination. Thus, in 1215, the timing was ripe for King John's barons to try to lift the more oppressive taxes which had been introduced and to reclaim some of their ancient rights.

The revisionist version is generally accepted today as providing the background and historical context for Magna Carta. Not only does such an account correspond better with what we know of the historical context in 1215, but it also helps explain Magna Carta's text. The vast majority of the Charter is about ancient rights and duties, fees and taxes, comprehensible now only to medieval historians (the full text is reproduced in the Appendix). For instance, Articles 3–8 protected the inheritances of minors and widows from abuse by their guardians, limiting the damage that could be done to an estate in a feudal incident; Articles 12–16 regulated the use of scutages, fees paid by knights in lieu

[10]   Ibid. at 16.
[11]   Ibid. at 61.

of service to the king; Articles 20–22 limited the size of amercements. Feudal incidents, scutages and amercements are but a few examples of the means used by King John to raise revenue. Magna Carta was the barons' attempt to limit his ability to raise funds through such methods – at least without their approval. Thus, it is unsurprising that about two-thirds of Magna Carta's provisions were concerned with setting limits on the use of the King's fiscal powers.[12]

Even Magna Carta's most famous provisions – Articles 39 and 40 – can be read as a way for the barons to remove their financial well-being from the will of the King. These articles state that:

> (39) No free man shall be seized or imprisoned, or stripped of his rights or possessions, or outlawed or exiled, or deprived of his standing in any other way, nor will we proceed with force against him, or send others to do so, except by the lawful judgement of his equals or by the law of the land.
> (40) To no one will we sell, to no one deny or delay right or justice.[13]

Articles 39 and 40 have been interpreted to mean that the criminally accused have the right to be tried by a jury of their equals, to protection from unjustified restraint, to due process of law and to a timely trial. However, in 1215, the meaning of these two articles was much more limited.[14] Although guised in the language of the free man, Articles 39 and 40 were primarily meant to transfer the settlement of disputes involving the barons from the king, who might use criminal accusations to extort them, to communal inquests, which were used throughout England at the time.[15]

As should be clear from the aforementioned discussion, the main beneficiaries of Magna Carta were the barons. Even Articles that claimed to protect all free men, such as Articles 39 and 40, where primarily meant to insulate the barons from the king. But Magna Carta soon acquired a wider, symbolic importance, being re-issued and re-confirmed many times in the thirteenth and fourteenth centuries before its resurrection by Sir Edward Coke in the seventeenth century.[16] It is Magna Carta as a charter of liberties, with those few

---

[12] Paul Halsall, 'The Text of Magna Carta', *Internet History Sourcebooks Project* (2014), available at http://www.fordham.edu/halsall/source/magnacarta.asp, see the introductory note.

[13] British Library, 'English Translation of Magna Carta' (accessed 13 November 2014), available at http://www.bl.uk/magna-carta/articles/magna-carta-english-translation; Articles 39 and 40 were eventually combined into Article 29 in the 1225 reissue of Magna Carta.

[14] Holt, *Magna Carta* (1992), 6.

[15] Holt, *Magna Carta* (1992), 331.

[16] The original Magna Carta was only in force for a few months before being set aside by King John. It was subsequently reissued in 1216, 1217, 1225 and 1297; see Holt, *Magna Carta* (1992), 1–2. The 1297 reissue is still in force in the United Kingdom today, although most of its provisions have been repealed; see http://www.legislation.gov.uk/aep/Edw1cc1929/25/9/contents for the statutes currently in force.

provisions that have been interpreted to enshrine wider legal principles, that has reverberated down through the ages, giving the Great Charter its mythical status. It is because Magna Carta has come to be seen as a declaration against arbitrary rule and a defence of the principles of freedom and equality before the law that it acquired its subsequent importance.

MODES OF INFLUENCE

The world is poised to celebrate the 800th anniversary of Magna Carta in 2015. One reason for such a celebration is the Great Charter's 'influence'. In the words of Sir Robert Worcester – writing on behalf of the Magna Carta 2015 Committee – Magna Carta 'has influenced constitutional thinking worldwide including in France, Germany, Japan, the United States and India as well as many Commonwealth countries, and throughout Latin America and Africa'.[17] According to the celebration committee, then, Magna Carta has shaped theories of constitutionalism, and perhaps even the contents of constitutions, in virtually every corner of the world.

Despite the claims of the celebration committee, Magna Carta's influence is unclear, because the term *influence* itself is unclear. By claiming that Magna Carta is influential, is the celebration committee suggesting that the Charter's famous Article 39 has been copied into constitutions all over the world? Is the committee suggesting that the rights entrenched in Magna Carta have become prevalent in modern constitutions, albeit in different terms? Or is it suggesting an even more elusive (and tenuous) form of influence: that the principle of constitutionalism has been widely accepted? It is easy to speculate that Magna Carta has been influential all over the world, but it is far more difficult to pinpoint precisely how it is has been influential. In order to do so, one must first define influence and the modes through which it operates.

By influence, we mean that Magna Carta has shaped those countries' constitutions in some way. However, this definition is still quite vague because it does not tell us *what* has been influenced. Magna Carta might affect the *actual* contents of a country's constitution, or its influence might be more *symbolic*, merely affecting the principles underlying the text. These different types of influence, then, tell us what aspects of a constitution have been affected by Magna Carta – its contents or the underlying principles. One

---

[17] Robert Worchester, 'Why Commemorate 800 Years?' *Magna Carta Today* (2013), available at http://magnacarta800th.com/magna-carta-today/objectives-of-the-magna-carta-800th-com mittee/; see third paragraph.

	Direct	Indirect
Actual	United Kingdom and New Zealand, where Magna Carta is still in force; early English statutes	United States Bill of Rights; legal protection for the accused in modern constitutions
Symbolic	Debate over the United States Bill of Rights; constituent assemblies in Brazil	General references to constitutionalism or the rule of law

FIGURE 1 – Modes of Magna Carta's Influence in the United States Constitution

can also differentiate influence by the degrees of separation between Magna Carta and the text being influenced. Was Magna Carta or its text a direct source of influence, or did it influence a given text via another document? In the former case, its influence is *direct*, and in the latter, its influence is *indirect*. Together, one can think of these alternatives as two distinct dimensions of influence (as illustrated in Figure 1) leading to four modes of influence: (1) direct, actual influence; (2) indirect, actual influence; (3) direct, symbolic influence; and (4) indirect, symbolic influence.

As one might expect, it is difficult to identify examples of direct, actual influence of an 800-year-old document originally written in Latin. The best examples of Magna Carta's actual, direct influence come from the United Kingdom. Not only are some provisions of Magna Carta still in force in the United Kingdom, but Magna Carta was highly instrumental in the writing of numerous early English statutes, many of which are still in force today.[18]

Examples of Magna Carta's direct, actual influence outside of the United Kingdom are harder to find. There are some places where Magna Carta is actually used as law. For instance, in New Zealand, the Imperial Laws Application Act (1988) lists a number of British laws, including parts of the Magna Carta, which remain in force in New Zealand.[19] As another example, Renée Lerner notes in her contribution to this volume that many U.S. states – for example, Delaware (1776), Maryland (1776), Massachusetts (1780), New Hampshire (1984), New York (1777), North Carolina (1776), South Carolina (1778) and Virginia (1776) – borrowed language directly from Articles 39 and 40 of Magna Carta when writing their first constitutions. Remnants of the language

---

[18] See the Observance of Due Process of Law Act (1368), the Petition of Right (1628), the Habeas Corpus Act (1679) and the Bill of Rights (1689).

[19] New Zealand Parliamentary Counsel Office, *Imperial Laws Application Act* (1988), available at: http://www.legislation.govt.nz/act/public/1988/0112/latest/whole.html#DLM135091.

from Magna Carta remain in many of those states' constitutions.[20] All of these are examples where the language from Magna Carta is in force in modern constitutions, demonstrating its continued direct, actual influence.

Instances of indirect, actual influence are easier to find than instances of direct, actual influence. Perhaps the best example is the United States Bill of Rights. More than half of the articles in the U.S. Bill of Rights can be traced to documents influenced by Magna Carta. For instance, we know that James Madison relied on both early English statutes – for example, the English Bill of Rights – and early U.S. state constitutions when crafting the American Bill of Rights, and we have already noted that those documents were, in turn, directly influenced by the text of Magna Carta.[21] We can plainly see this influence when looking at the text of the first ten amendments to the United States Constitution. Take, for example, the Fifth Amendment to the U.S. Constitution. It provides for 'due process of law' and that 'private property shall not be taken for public use, without just compensation'.[22] These phrases are present in a number of early English statutes as well as in U.S. state constitutions, but the roots of this language can be traced to Articles 28 and 39 of Magna Carta.[23]

[20] Massachusetts' constitution still states that 'no subject shall be arrested, imprisoned, despoiled, or deprived of his property, immunities, or privileges, put out of the protection of the law, exiled, or deprived of his life, liberty, or estate, but by the judgment of his peers, or the law of the land' (Article 12). New York's constitution still states that '[n]o member of this state shall be disfranchised, or deprived of any of the rights or privileges secured to any citizen thereof, unless by the law of the land, or the judgment of his or her peers' (section 1). North Carolina's constitution still states that '[n]o person shall be taken, imprisoned, or disseized of his freehold, liberties, or privileges, or outlawed, or exiled, or in any manner deprived of his life, liberty, or property, but by the law of the land' (section 19). Virginia's constitution still states that no man 'shall not be deprived of life or liberty, except by the law of the land or the judgment of his peers' (section 8).

[21] Amar, Akhil Reed, *The Bill of Rights: Creation and Reconstruction* (New Haven: Yale University Press, 1998).

[22] Zachary Elkins, Tom Ginsburg and James Melton, 'United States of America 1789 (rev. 1992)', *Constitute: The World's Constitutions to Read, Search and Compare* (2014), available at: https://www.constituteproject.org/constitution/United_States_of_America_1992#139.

[23] Due process of law is simply 'law of the land' from Article 39 of Magna Carta rephrased into more modern terminology; see Eric T. Kasper, 'The Influence of Magna Carta in Limiting Executive Power in the War on Terror', *Political Science Quarterly* 126(4) (2011): 547–78. The phrase 'due process of law' originates in the Observance of Due Process of Law Act (1368) of the United Kingdom, which spells out the meaning of 'law of the land' in Article 39 of Magna Carta. Thus, the framers of the American Constitution borrowed 'due process of law' indirectly, because the phrase was from an act that was inspired directly by the Magna Carta.

Article 28 of Magna Carta states that '[n]o Constable nor other Bailiff of ours shall take the corn or other goods of any one without instantly paying money for them, unless he can obtain respite from the free-will of the seller.' The sentiment of Article 28 is almost identical to that of the Fifth Amendment, even though Article 28 is specific to 'goods' rather than the broader wording of 'private property' in the Fifth Amendment.

The Sixth Amendment to the United States Constitution can also be traced to Magna Carta. This amendment states that 'the accused shall enjoy the right to a speedy and public trial, by an impartial jury of the State and district wherein the crime shall have been committed . . .'.[24] Notions of timely jury trials can be traced to Articles 39 and 40 in Magna Carta. There are also links between the Seventh and Eighth Amendments to the U.S. Constitution and Magna Carta, albeit through other English statues and U.S. state constitutions. In total, then, the rights guaranteed by four out of the ten amendments contained in the U.S. Bill of Rights were indirectly influenced by the text of Magna Carta.

Thus far, we have only considered the indirect, actual influence of Magna Carta when such influence is mediated by a single text. Given the afore-mentioned claim of the Magna Carta 2015 Committee, it is worth at least considering how far Magna Carta's influence reaches. To do so, Figure 2 illustrates the prevalence of the four legal process rights most commonly

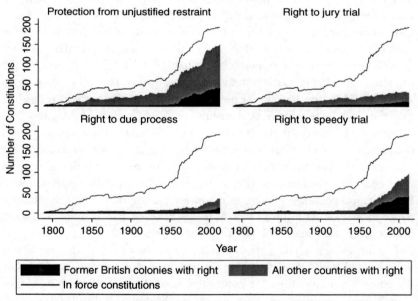

FIGURE 2 – Prevalence of Select Magna Carta Rights in National Constitutions, 1789–2013[25]

[24] Elkins, Ginsburg and Melton, 'United States of America 1789 (rev. 1992)', *Constitute* (2014), available at: https://www.constituteproject.org/constitution/United_States_of_America_1992#141.
[25] Data is from the Comparative Constitutions Project (CCP) and is available to download from http://comparativeconstitutionsproject.org/. The following variables are used in Figure 2: hab-corp, jury, dueproc, speedtri.

associated with Magna Carta – that is, protection from unjustified restraint, the right to a jury trial, the right to due process and the right to a speedy trial – in all national constitutions written from 1789 to the present. Each panel in the figure illustrates the prevalence of a different right. Within the panels, the solid line indicates the number of constitutions in force from 1789 to 2013, the grey-shaded region indicates the number of constitutions with a given right from 1789 to 2013, and the black-shaded portion indicates the number of constitutions in former British colonies with a given right from 1789 to 2013.

Figure 2 suggests that the actual text of Magna Carta may not be as influential as the Magna Carta 2015 Committee would lead us to believe. Of the four rights analysed in the figure, only protection from unjustified restraint has consistently been found in more than half of the world's constitutions. The right to trial without delay has become more popular over time, with its rise in popularity starting after the World War II. One could argue that this increased popularity is the result of the inclusion of this principle in the International Covenant on Civil and Political Rights (ICCPR),[26] not its existence in Magna Carta. However, since more than half of the constitutions that include the right to trial without delay are former British colonies, the prevalence of this important common law principle is probably (at least in part) due to the influence of Magna Carta on overseas territories. The other two rights included in Figure 2 have never been very common. Of course, it is possible that the data in the figure underestimates the influence of Magna Carta because, by focusing strictly on the constitutional text, we are ignoring other domestic sources of law that may entrench Magna Carta's principles. That said, since the constitutional text is the centre of the constitutional order in most countries, the fact that three of the four rights typically associated with Magna Carta are relatively rare in countries' constitutional texts should give pause to anyone who thinks that Magna Carta has had widespread *actual* influence on the contents of national constitutions.

The foregoing analysis suggests that the actual influence of Magna Carta is quite limited. Thus, if Magna Carta has had the global influence suggested by the 2015 Committee, then the committee is most likely referring to Magna Carta's symbolic influence. Here, we are mostly concerned with direct, symbolic influence, because it is too hard to track indirect, symbolic influence.[27]

[26] Article 14(c) of the ICCPR states that all persons should 'be tried without undue delay'; see http://www.ohchr.org/en/professionalinterest/pages/ccpr.aspx.

[27] To illustrate indirect, symbolic influence, consider the Anti-Federalists' use of the English Bill of Rights (1689) to justify the need for a bill of rights in the United States. Since Magna Carta was used to justify the limits placed on the Crown in the English Bill of Rights (1689), one

Since Magna Carta is associated with principles such as constitutionalism and the rule of law, one could extend its indirect, symbolic influence to any mention of these principles. However, it is nonsense to suggest that modern-day notions of constitutionalism are the same as in 1215, and there are too many intervening legal statutes and events to suggest that Magna Carta is responsible for the evolution of modern conceptions of constitutionalism.[28] Perhaps modern-day notions of constitutionalism can trace their roots to Magna Carta, but even this is a bit of a stretch, especially considering that similar charters were adopted throughout Europe in the thirteenth century.[29]

Fortunately, instances of direct, symbolic influence are frequent. They are also less tenuous because, for this type of influence, Magna Carta is directly invoked. The debates surrounding adoption of the United States Constitution and Bill of Rights are a good example of the direct, symbolic power of Magna Carta. A key issue in the adoption debate was the Constitution's lack of a bill of rights. Magna Carta was used symbolically by both proponent and opponents of a bill of rights. In Federalist No. 84, Alexander Hamilton argued that bills of rights, like Magna Carta, were simply 'reservations of rights not surrendered to the prince.' For the Anti-Federalists, Brutus argued in his second essay that Magna Carta has 'long been the boast, as well as the security', of England. Ultimately, the Anti-Federalists' argument was more convincing, and a bill of rights became a precondition for adoption of the United States Constitution. This is an example of direct influence because Brutus explicitly mentioned Magna Carta.

Magna Carta continues to be referenced by constitutional drafters. For instance, Table 1 provides the number of mentions of Magna Carta, and several other symbolic texts, in six Brazilian constituent assemblies. Early in the modern constitutional era, constitutions of the United States, France and Portugal were the most referenced texts; Magna Carta was barely mentioned. However, over time, mentions of Magna Carta became more prevalent, and by the drafting of the 1967 and 1988 Brazilian constitutions, the Great Charter was mentioned more than any other document listed. Table 1 provides evidence that Magna Carta not only has great symbolic influence, but that its symbolic influence may have increased over time.

might say that its use by the Anti-Federalists constitutes an indirect influence on the United States Constitution. We do not consider this example in the text for two reasons. First, Magna Carta was referenced by the Anti-Federalists as well, and second, the English Bill of Rights (1689) had actual influence on the United States Bill of Rights too.

[28] See Holt, *Magna Carta* (1992).

[29] The best example is Hungary's Golden Bull (1222), sometimes referred to as Hungary's Magna Carta, but there are others. See Menaldo and Williams's chapter in this volume (Ch. 9) or Holt, *Magna Carta* (1992), 519.

TABLE 1. *Mentions of Select Symbolic Texts during Brazilian Constituent Assembly Debates*

Symbolic Text	Brazilian Constituent Assembly					
	1823	1890–1891	1933–1934	1946	1966–1967	1987–1988
Magna Carta	0.01	0.06	1.27	2.11	8.24	6.94
Bible	0.01	0.03	0.05	0.06	0.13	0.60
UDHR	–	–	–	–	0.18	0.47
United States Constitution	0.13	2.23	3.68	4.51	6.18	6.70
French Constitution	0.24	0.81	2.61	2.23	3.82	4.69
Portuguese Constitution	2.28	0.51	1.24	2.65	2.34	6.10
Number of days	149	70	165	167	38	306

Note: Cells represent the number of times per day each text was mentioned.[30]

In summary, there is little doubt that Magna Carta has been influential. However, unless one is willing to accept that Magna Carta is responsible for modern beliefs in constitutionalism and the rule of law, it is probably over-claiming the case to argue that Magna Carta has 'influence[d] constitutional thinking worldwide'. Based on Figure 2, it would seem that the actual influence of Magna Carta on modern constitutions is pretty limited, especially outside of former British colonies. Magna Carta's modern influence seems to be mostly symbolic. As seen in Table 1, it is not uncommon for Magna Carta to be invoked during periods of constitutional change to support formally limiting political power, and it may even be more common to invoke Magna Carta today than it was at the start of the modern constitutional era. However, we suspect that today's symbolic invocations of Magna Carta are no different than Coke's, or the barons' invocation of Henry I's Charter of Liberties in 1215 – a politically convenient distortion.[31]

THE PAST, PRESENT AND FUTURE INFLUENCE OF MAGNA CARTA

The previous section offered a superficial look at Magna Carta's influence. The remainder of this volume digs deeper into the Great Charter's influence, both in the United Kingdom and abroad. The first section explores how Magna Carta has shaped the United Kingdom's evolution from a feudal

[30] Data from Zachary Elkins, 'Magna Carta Abroad', presentation at the National Archives in Washington, DC, on 17 February 2012. Reused with permission of Professor Elkins.

[31] Holt, *Magna Carta* (1992), 20.

monarchy to a constitutional one. The second looks at Magna Carta's influence outside of the United Kingdom. The third section considers Magna Carta from an academic perspective, asking what academics can learn from reflecting on Magna Carta. Here, we briefly describe each of these themes.

Influence in the United Kingdom

In the United Kingdom, Magna Carta continues to shape constitutionalism. For centuries, the Great Charter has been evoked to check the power of the Crown. Magna Carta was used against King Charles by Sir Edward Coke in the Petition of Right (1628) and is referenced in the Bill of Rights (1689) to delineate King James II's abuses of power. Its success in constraining successive generations of monarchs may even explain the country's lack of a codified constitution, which is often attributed to the fact that the United Kingdom has never experienced a revolution in modern times.[32] One could argue that the principles of Magna Carta made a revolution unnecessary and enabled the United Kingdom to gradually, and peacefully, transition into a constitutional monarchy.

The first part of the book provides a careful analysis of Magna Carta's history in the United Kingdom. It starts with a chapter by Vernon Bogdanor, who explains how Magna Carta has shaped the evolution of the United Kingdom's constitution. The next two chapters explain the place of Magna Carta today. Anthony King evaluates the legitimacy of the United Kingdom's constitution, assessing whether or not it is still an elite bargain between the monarch and his or her barons. The final chapter in this section, by Roger Mortimore, evaluates modern support for Magna Carta and the values that underpin it, using Ipsos MORI survey data on public knowledge and attitudes about the rights in Magna Carta.

Influence Abroad

Magna Carta has been at least as influential outside of the United Kingdom's borders as within. Very few domestic laws achieve international recognition, and Magna Carta is one of those laws.[33] In part, the Charter's international influence is attributable to Britain's imperial success. Nearly a third of the

---

[32] Anthony King, *The British Constitution* (Oxford: Oxford University Press, 2007).
[33] Other examples include the United States Constitution and French Declaration of the Rights of Man.

world's independent states are former British colonies,[34] and more than half of its former colonies are still formally connected to Britain through the Commonwealth. The de jure rights entrenched in many of these countries' constitutions can be linked directly to Magna Carta. This is certainly true in the United States. As noted in the previous section, drafters of the Constitution drew heavily on Magna Carta, and judges continue to use it to understand the motivation underlying some of the rights set forth in the United States Constitution.[35] Elsewhere, the influence of the Great Charter is still present but less direct. For instance, the United States Constitution continues to influence constitutional drafters throughout the world.[36] Given that many of the de jure rights in the United States Constitution can be traced back to the Great Charter, or other British statutes that were inspired by it, one could argue that Magna Carta has indirectly influenced almost all modern constitutions.

The second section of the book systematically evaluates the influence of Magna Carta outside of the United Kingdom. The section contains three chapters on the influence of Magna Carta in former British colonies. The first, by Renée Lerner, evaluates the role that Magna Carta played in perpetuating jury trials in civil disputes in the United States, even after these had been abandoned in many other jurisdictions, including the United Kingdom. Her chapter perhaps provides an explanation of why, as illustrated in Figure 2, the right to jury trials has never been very popular in national constitutions. The next chapter, by Derek O'Brien, looks at the role Magna Carta played in justifying slavery in the Commonwealth Caribbean and the continued role it plays in judicial interpretation in those jurisdictions. Lastly, David Clark looks at the problems states in the Commonwealth Pacific have had implementing Magna Carta's promise of justice without delay.

Reflecting on Magna Carta

The third, and final, section is more prospective than the former two. It explores what we can learn from reflecting on our knowledge of Magna

---

[34] Thierry Mayer and Soledad Zignago, 'Notes on CEPII's Distance Measures: The GeoDist Database', *CEPII Working Paper Series* (2011), available at http://www.cepii.fr/CEPII/en/bdd_modele/presentation.asp?id=6.

[35] See Craig Lerner's chapter in this volume (Ch. 8). In addition, see Eric T. Kasper (2011); Justin J. Wert, 'With a Little Help from a Friend: Habeas Corpus and the Magna Carta after Runnymeade', *PS: Political Science* 43(3) (2010): 475–78; Kent Worcester, 'The Meaning and Legacy of the Magna Carta', *Political Science* 43(3) (2010): 451–56.

[36] Zachary Elkins, Tom Ginsburg and James Melton, 'Comments on Law and Versteeg, The Declining Influence of the U.S. Constitution', *NYU Law Review* 87(6) (2012): 2088–101.

Carta. For a variety of reasons, the Great Charter is a remarkable piece of parchment. Although every detail has been scrutinised by historians and lawyers,[37] there is still much to be learned from its edicts. In part, this is because political scientists have largely ignored the Great Charter.[38] As a result, there is significant room for future research that tests theories developed in political science against the vast body of historical research surrounding the Great Charter. For instance, the events surrounding Magna Carta's creation are a clear example of the credibility problem facing executives.[39] King John had abused his royal privilege in the years leading up to Runnymede. He used a combination of bribery, blackmail and sometimes plain theft to acquire the financial and political power necessary to battle the French. These abuses of power not only violated the oaths King John had previously sworn but also created a latent demand for the restoration of peoples' customary rights.[40] The result of this demand was Magna Carta, which was sufficient to convince some of the barons to join him in the civil war to be fought over the next year.[41] Comparison of the events in 1215 England to similar events in other European countries during the thirteenth century or in other eras in English history might allow one to test Albertus and Menaldo's[42] hypotheses about the ability of parchment to solve the credible commitment problem facing authoritarian leaders.

There are other lessons to be learned from Magna Carta as well. For instance, the edicts set forth in the Great Charter are a combination of customary Anglo-Saxon law, canon law and invention.[43] As a result, studying Magna Carta may allow political scientists to say something about the

---

[37] David V. Stivison, *Magna Carta in America* (Gateway Press, 1993), 118–81.

[38] Worcester makes this same point; see Worcester, 'The Meaning and Legacy of the Magna Carta' (2010). We have only identified a couple of studies that really use Magna Carta as a case in their research. Eric T. Kasper (2011) reviews all of the recent mentions of Magna Carta in United States Supreme Court cases. Lisa Blaydes and Eric Chaney, 'Feudal Revolution and Europe's Rise: Political Divergence of the Christian West and the Muslim World before 1500 CE', *American Political Science Review* 107(1) (2013): 16–34, use Magna Carta as anecdotal evidence to demonstrate the relative weakness of European monarchs in the Middle Ages compared to their Islamic counterparts in the Middle East, p. 22. In addition, there was a review of the historical and legal literatures on Magna Carta in *PS: Political Science* in 2010; see various authors in *PS: Political Science* 43(3) (2010).

[39] Michael Albertus and Victor Menaldo, 'Dictators as Founding Fathers? The Role of Constitutions under Autocracy', *Economics & Politics* 24(3) (2012): 279–306; Roger Myerson, 'A Field Manual for the Cradle of Civilization: Theory of Leadership and Lessons of Iraq', *Journal of Conflict Resolution* 53(3) (2009): 470–82.

[40] Holt, Magna Carta (1992), 196–97.

[41] Ibid., 375–76.

[42] Albertus and Menaldo, 'Dictators as Founding Fathers?'

[43] R. H. Helmholz, 'Magna Carta and the Ius Commune', *University of Chicago Law Review* 66(2) (1999): 297–371; Holt, *Magna Carta* (1992).

development of law[44] or about the mechanisms through which customary and canon law diffused into Magna Carta.[45] Yet another fruitful area of research on the Magna Carta is the efficacy of constitutional rights. Magna Carta is a rare example of parchment barriers that worked. Although the barriers set forth in the Great Charter were insufficient to constrain King John, in the decades following his rule, the de jure rights in the Magna Carta grew into something far greater. Studying the process through which this occurred may offer insights into creating more efficacious domestic and international human rights instruments.

In the third section, we provide some examples of the lessons that Magna Carta has to offer. Craig Lerner provides an argument about the meaning of proportionality in Magna Carta, which has implications for modern jurisprudence in the United States. Victor Menaldo and Nora Williams evaluate theoretical arguments of judicial empowerment against English and United States history to assess whether or not they explain the relative weakness of the judiciary in the United Kingdom. Geraldine Van Bueren explains how the Charter of the Forest (originally part of Magna Carta) can be seen as a forerunner of economic and social rights. She suggests that the modern labelling of such rights as 'second generation' rights creates a spurious distinction. Lastly, Natalie Riendeau will explain the myths surrounding Magna Carta, how those myths are perpetuated and how they contribute to Magna Carta's modern-day relevance.

CONCLUDING REMARKS

There is no question that Magna Carta has been, and still is, influential. The question is, how has the Great Charter been influential? Here, we offer a slightly more questioning take on Magna Carta's legacy than that of others who will be celebrating Magna Carta in 2015. Our account is more questioning in two respects. First, we find that Magna Carta's influence is primarily symbolic. This symbolic influence stems from the traditional account of Magna Carta and is called upon to build support for placing formal limits on political authority. Such symbolic influence can be seen in the use of Magna Carta in constituent assembly debates – for example, in Brazil – in analogies between Magna Carta and the Universal Declaration of

---

[44] Gillian K. Hadfield and Barry Weingast, 'Microfoundations of the Rule of Law', *Annual Review of Political Science* (2014), forthcoming.

[45] Graham, Erin R., Charles R. Shipan and Craig Volden, 'The Diffusion of Policy Diffusion Research in Political Science', *British Journal of Political Science* 43(3) (2013): 673–701.

Human Rights,[46] and even in calls for constitutional reform in the United Kingdom.[47] Notably, the symbolic influence of Magna Carta is perpetuated largely by elites, which is supported by the evidence presented in Mortimore's chapter (Chapter 4) that the general public has little knowledge of Magna Carta.

The actual influence of Magna Carta seems to be limited to the United Kingdom and the countries of the British Commonwealth. All of the examples of actual influence noted in this volume are from the United Kingdom or its former territories. We have found little evidence that Magna Carta's provisions affected the contents of constitutions in other jurisdictions. Furthermore, when Magna Carta has been influential outside of the United Kingdom, the influence has not always been positive. In fact, in each chapter on Magna Carta's influence abroad, the actual influence of the Charter has had negative repercussions. In the United States, Magna Carta was used to perpetuate the inefficient use of jury trials in civil disputes. In the Caribbean, Magna Carta was used to perpetuate discrimination against minorities. In the Pacific, Magna Carta has created impossible expectations about the timeliness of justice.

Thus, the contribution of this volume is largely to point out that Magna Carta's influence is not as clear and not always as positive as the traditional account of the Great Charter would lead us to believe. We are not the first to point this out, but in a year when the traditional account will be the focus, we feel that it is a point worth remembering.[48] Does this mean we should not celebrate Magna Carta or its 800th birthday in 2015? Absolutely not! The Great Charter serves as an important symbol for the principles of constitutionalism and the rule of law, and at a minimum, it is worth celebrating to help reinforce those principles. However, we should not forget that parchment alone was not sufficient to constrain executive authority in 1215 and, by itself, parchment remains unlikely to serve as such a constraint in 2015.

---

[46] At the 50th Anniversary of the UDHR in 1998, the UDHR was promoted by suggesting it was a 'Magna Carta for all humanity'; see the United Nations Department of Public Information page on the UDHR's 50th Anniversary at http://www.un.org/rights/50/carta.htm.

[47] The UK Parliament Political and Constitutional Reform Committee's 2014 report recommending constitutional reform in the United Kingdom was entitled 'A New Magna Carta?'; see http://www.parliament.uk/pcrc-constitution.

[48] For instance, see Holt, *Magna Carta* (1992) and Turner, *Magna Carta: Through the Ages* (2003).

PART 1

INFLUENCE IN THE UNITED KINGDOM

2

Magna Carta, the Rule of Law and the Reform of the Constitution

Vernon Bogdanor

I

On 13 July 2013, an article in *The Economist* referred to Magna Carta, in the context of the supposed Arab spring. It declared:

> When you say that it takes decades not years, to bring about democratic change, you are off by a factor of 10. It takes centuries. The imperfect democracy we enjoy in the West has its roots in the Middle Ages. The signing of the Magna Carta in 1215 by the English King John can be held as a good starting point.

This is of course quite anachronistic. Magna Carta has all too often been interpreted not in terms of what it said, but of what interpreters believed or hoped that it said. Our understanding of it has evolved through time, not because we discover new evidence about it, but because our perspective alters. Our understanding of the past is, perhaps inevitably, influenced by our present standpoint. Historians, it has been suggested, remember the future and imagine the past.

Yet, although Magna Carta is by no stretch of the imagination a democratic document, it does contain one fundamental principle, which resonates throughout British history: the principle that government must be subject to law.

Of course, very little of Magna Carta survives today. Of its sixty-three clauses, just three remain. The rest have been repealed, and most have been superseded. The two most important clauses of the original document are 39 and 40:

> (39) No free man shall be seized or imprisoned, or stripped of his rights or possessions or outlawed, or exiled, or deprived of his standing in any other

way, nor will we proceed with force against him, or send others to do so, except by the lawful judgment of his equals or by the law of the land.

(40) To no one will we sell, to no one deny or delay right or justice.

In addition, the Charter insists that the king cannot arbitrarily tax his subjects without their consent. The implication is that only a body properly summoned for the purpose – in other words a parliament – can legitimately give consent; and, indeed, a parliament did come into existence in the 1250s. Of course, the principle of no taxation without representation played an important role in the revolt of the American colonists against British rule in the eighteenth century, and the political philosopher Edmund Burke, who supported the colonists, declared that the Americans were absolutely entitled to 'sit down – to the feast of Magna Charta'.

It is the clause on taxation and the two clauses quoted previously that express the fundamental principle which makes Magna Carta so important: that government must be subject to law. Under Magna Carta, the executive – that is, the king – is put under constraint by the barons. He can no longer do what he likes.

This principle laid down in Magna Carta played a vital role in the seventeenth century in the attack on the theory of the divine right of kings. The parliamentarians argued that Magna Carta had laid down principles so fundamental that no king could ever override them. It was in terms of these fundamental principles that Charles I was to be accused of treason. In 1649, the House of Commons declared that 'Charles Stuart, the now King of England – had a wicked design totally to subvert the ancient and fundamental laws and liberties of this nation, and in their place to introduce an arbitrary and tyrannical government.' Later, in 1681, Parliament sought to impeach the Chief Justice. He was charged with having 'traitorously and wickedly endeavoured to subvert the fundamental laws and the established religion and government of this kingdom'. Finally, as is well known, when the Commons condemned James II in 1689, one of the charges against him was that of 'having violated the fundamental laws'.[1]

Whigs and radicals were frequently to refer to the Magna Carta in opposing the claims of royal absolutism, the theory of divine right. Nevertheless, the content of these fundamental principles remained somewhat obscure. When, in 1641, the Earl of Strafford was being impeached for breaking the fundamental laws of the kingdom and the Commons was about to vote on the issue, the MP and poet Edmund Waller asked what these fundamental laws actually were. There was an embarrassed silence. But then a fellow MP – perhaps

[1]   J. W. Gough, *Fundamental Law in English Constitutional History* (Clarendon Press, 1955), 1–2.

significantly a lawyer – rose and said that if Mr Waller did not know what the fundamental laws of the kingdom were, he had no business to be sitting in the House of Commons at all!

Many of those who preached the doctrine of fundamental law believed it to be embodied in the common law, a body of judicial doctrine based upon principle. For those who thought in this way, a statute declared what the law was; it did not create it. The task of the common law judges was 'to act as ultimate court of appeal in constitutional matters, as a supreme court. The law itself was sovereign; and the judges alone understood its mysteries'.[2] There was a common law constitution, an idea resurrected in our own time, most notably by Lord Justice Laws.

In the seventeenth century, therefore, Magna Carta came to be 'transformed from a baronial charter of privileges into a declaration of the rights of all free Englishmen'.[3] It became a myth, perhaps a necessary myth.[4] Indeed, in the seventeenth century it became 'something of a cult'.[5] Both Whigs and radicals drew upon it in order to give strength to their view of constitutionalism. They argued that, in doing so, they were merely appealing to principles of Anglo-Saxon freedom, principles which had been reaffirmed in the Magna Carta. Thus radicals could argue that, far from seeking to break with the past, they were seeking to resurrect it, by appealing to principles already enshrined in English history and, in particular, in Magna Carta. 'The appeal to the past, to documents (whether the Bible or Magna Carta) becomes a criticism of existing institutions, of certain types of rule. If they do not conform to the sacred text, they are to be rejected.'[6]

Of the various groups who used Magna Carta as a weapon against the king in the seventeenth century, the Levellers were the most radical; and it is to the Levellers that we owe the idea of a written constitution designed to protect the fundamental law.[7] In 1647, they drew up the first of three Agreements of the People, according to which Parliament was to be limited by fundamental law, which was unalterable. Under the terms of this first Agreement, Parliament could not legislate against the freedom of religion, it could not exempt anyone from the due process of the law, it could not abridge the freedom to trade abroad, and it could not impose the death penalty except for

[2]   Christopher Hill, *The Century of Revolution* (1961) (Routledge, 2002), 66.
[3]   Christopher Hill, *Intellectual Origins of the English Revolution Revisited* (Clarendon Press, 1997), 211.
[4]   Hill, *Intellectual Origins*, 225.
[5]   J. P. Kenyon, *Stuart England*, 2nd ed. (Penguin, 1985), 38.
[6]   Christopher Hill, *The World Turned Upside Down: Radical Ideas during the English Revolution* (1972) (Penguin edition, 1991), 95.
[7]   Hill, *Intellectual Origins of the English Revolution*, 225.

murder. Above all, it could not abolish trial by jury. A third Agreement of the People, drawn up in 1653, went further and declared that 'all laws made, or that shall be made contrary to any part of this Agreement, are thereby made null and void'. This third Agreement can perhaps justifiably be regarded as the first real constitution in modern European history.

That title of the first written constitution is often given to Oliver Cromwell's constitution of 1653, the Instrument of Government. Cromwell indeed told the first parliament of his protectorate, in 1654, that 'In every government there must be somewhat fundamental, somewhat like a Magna Carta, that should be standing and be unalterable'; and the Instrument did certainly contain unalterable provisions, such as that providing for freedom of conscience in religion. Another such provision was that 'parliaments should not make themselves perpetual'. For, as Cromwell argued, 'Of what assurance is a law to prevent so great an evil if it lie in one and the same legislator to unlaw it again?'[8]

Yet, the Instrument of Government gave supreme power to Parliament, if not to the Lord Protector himself, who had abolished the House of Lords and was later to refuse to summon the Commons. It provided no mechanism by which limitations upon the power of Parliament or the Lord Protector could be enforced upon them; and the judges declared their acceptance of the actions of Parliament as manifestations of sovereign authority.

In fact, during the great constitutional struggle, which preceded the civil war, the parliamentarians, although they appealed to fundamental laws, were not – contrary to appearances – really questioning the doctrine of sovereignty. Their quarrel with the king concerned not the existence of sovereignty, but its location; they believed that it lay with the king in Parliament, not with the king alone. They were seeking to achieve what we would now call responsible government – control of the Crown by Parliament – rather than to limit the sovereignty of Parliament. The struggle was over who should hold undivided power, not whether it should be divided; and today we can perhaps see that what the king and the parliamentarians had in common was more important than what divided them.

Under the terms of the Agreement of the People, by contrast, the people themselves would create their government by means of a constitutive act.[9] Declared John Lilburne, the Leveller leader,

> An Agreement of the People is not proper to come from Parliament, because it comes from thence – with a command – it ought not so to do, but to be

8   Gough, *Fundamental Law*, 129–30.
9   Perez Zagorin, *The English Revolution: Politics, Events, Ideas* (Ashgate, 1998), x.

voluntary and free. Besides, that which is done by one Parliament – may be undone by the next – but an Agreement of the People begun and ended by the People, can never come justly within the Parliament's cognizance to destroy.[10]

The Levellers, however, faced the problem of who was to judge that a law was contrary to the Agreement. They implied that there should be judicial review. However, they believed that judges could not be relied upon to undertake such review. They could not be relied upon to be impartial, since they were likely to be subject to improper influence, and would be fearful of losing their jobs. Therefore, the task of review should fall to 'the whole People of England', to juries who were, for this purpose, to act as judges.[11]

After the Restoration, the idea of fundamental law receded. Nevertheless, it was to be resurrected across the Atlantic by the American revolutionaries, and some of the ideas of the Levellers were to be embodied in the American constitution. In Britain, however, following the Glorious Revolution of 1689, the Whig triumph was symbolised by the Bill of Rights. This Bill of Rights was very different from the American Bill of Rights. It did not serve to entrench fundamental rights against legislative majorities. Instead, it was a statute guaranteeing the rights of Parliament against the king. No limitations were placed upon the king, whose powers were to remain unlimited, in Parliament, but the balance of power was altered, in favour of Parliament and against arbitrary rule by the king. The Bill of Rights secured the power of the legislature against the king. It emphasised the doctrine of the undivided sovereignty of Parliament. Perhaps the time has now come to de-emphasise it.

In the eighteenth and nineteenth centuries, ideas of fundamental law and natural rights came to be superseded by Utilitarianism. The Utilitarians were heirs of a scientific age for which the whole idea of rights as a standard by which to judge positive law was a superstition – 'nonsense on stilts' in Jeremy Bentham's famous words. But in the latter part of the twentieth century, Utilitarianism found itself in headlong retreat. Rawls, Nozick and, perhaps especially, Dworkin – who were the dominant philosophers of law – all repudiated it and found themselves more sympathetic to older ideas of funda-mental rights. These thinkers were all champions of human rights. It is difficult, however, to accommodate rights within the Utilitarian scheme of things. And, indeed, as Bentham noticed, if Parliament is sovereign, how can individuals have rights against Parliament? There is a conflict between utility

[10] Perez Zagorin, *A History of Political Thought in the English Revolution* (1954) (Thoemmes Press, 1997), 14.

[11] T. C. Pease, *The Leveller Movement: A Study in the Historical and Political Theory of the English Great Civil War* (1916) (Peter Smith, 1965), 317–18.

and rights, and, for the thinkers I have just mentioned, the claims of human rights trumped those of utility. The intellectual climate in which we live today makes it easier to understand what perhaps neither Hobbes nor Dicey ever quite understood: how the ideas of parliamentary sovereignty and the rule of law could come to be in opposition to each other.

The principle, expressed in no doubt a primitive way in Magna Carta, that government must be subject to the law is a more important principle than that which lies behind democracy, of majority rule. The difficulty with the demo-cratic principle is the assumption sometimes made that a majority that has won power in a free election has the right to govern as it wishes, to do as it likes. That was a view held by Adolf Hitler. In December 1931, before he came to power, he declared that '... if we come to power legally we could then break through legality. ... the fundamental thesis of democracy runs: "All Power from the People"'. No wonder that, in January 1941, Hitler could say that 'the National Socialist Revolution defeated democracy through democracy'. It is worth noting too that, in 1980, Iranians voted in a free election for a theocratic republic in which human rights have come to be non-existent. We now know what nineteenth-century thinkers such as Tocqueville had predicted: that a democracy can be as despotic as, if not more despotic than, a traditional authoritarian government. For believers in the rule of law, however, ultimate power should lie neither with parliament nor with the people, but with the constitution.

Government under the law means much more than elections. It means also that there must be respect and freedom for opposition parties, free access to the press and other media, an independent judiciary with the power to check arbitrary government, civilian control of the armed forces, the removal of the military from politics and, above all, respect for human rights. A well-functioning democracy cannot exist without respect for the rule of law.

Both Britain and the United States had governments subject to the law long before they became democracies. Indeed, Britain became a full democracy comparatively recently, in 1928, when women over age twenty-one were given the vote on the same basis as men. But, long before Britain was a democracy, government had been regulated by the rule of law.

One of the signs of a constitutional democracy is that no one is above the law. In the United States, President Richard Nixon said in 1974, when accused of criminal offences after the Watergate break-in, that if a president does something, it cannot be illegal. The Watergate prosecutors proved him wrong, and he was forced to resign the presidency to avoid impeachment. In Britain, Lord Denning, as Master of the Rolls, reminded a minister in the 1970s: 'Be you ever so high, the law is above you.'

II

This principle, that no government is above the law, is embodied in most democracies in a written constitution. Britain of course has no constitution. Britain is one of just three democracies without one. Someone once said that the British constitution is not worth the paper it isn't written on.

Why does Britain remain almost unique in not having a written constitution? There are, I believe, two reasons, one historical and the other doctrinal.

The historical reason is that there is a sense in which Britain never began as a society. Most countries adopt constitutions to mark a break in their development, such as a revolution or the end of colonial rule. The British system of government, however, is marked by evolution and adaptation, without sharp breaks except during the civil war of the seventeenth century. But, significantly, after the experiment of the republic, 1660 was referred to as a restoration, as if the break was something of little importance. Since 1689, there has not been a real constitutional moment. France, by contrast, has had sixteen constitutions since the revolution began, and there is some talk today of a seventeenth. The story is told of someone who, in the 1950s, went to a shop in Paris to ask for a copy of the constitution and was told, 'I am afraid that we do not sell periodicals here.' There used to be an advertisement in the Paris metro that said, in effect, Republics come and go – Soudee paint lasts. The British constitution, by contrast, is what Dicey called a historic constitution. By that he meant not merely that the British system of government was very old, but that it was a product of evolution – no one ever designed or planned it. It developed, as it were, spontaneously.

But there is also a reason of principle why Britain has never had a written constitution. It is because, until recently at least, the only constitutional principle that Britain recognised was that Parliament was sovereign, that Parliament could do what it liked. If that was so, it was pointless to have a constitution, for the whole point of a constitution is to establish certain fundamental laws which lie beyond the reach of Parliament. In Britain, however, it seemed that there could be no such fundamental laws. In the eighteenth century, one constitutional theorist said that Parliament could do anything it liked except turn a man into a woman and a woman into a man. But, in fact, if Parliament said that a man was a woman, then, for the purposes of the law, a man would be a woman! Given that Parliament was sovereign, the British constitution could be defined in eight words: what the Queen in Parliament enacts is law. There seemed no need for anything more.

One might argue that Magna Carta has little value if its basic principle is at the mercy of Parliament – or, in effect, of government, since of course most governments enjoy a majority in the House of Commons. But governments in Britain have been limited not by a constitution, but by non-legal rules called conventions. By convention, there are certain things that no government would ever do. In theory, Parliament could pass an enactment providing that all red-headed people were to be executed next Monday; in practice, it would never do so.

But the trouble with conventions is that their precise scope and nature are not always clear. More than a hundred years ago, one constitutional theorist declared that Britain was governed by a system of tacit understandings, but that these understandings were not always understood. That is still to some extent true today.

However, the last forty years – and in particular the years since 1997 – have seen a constitutional revolution in Britain. The revolution began with our entry into the European Community, as the European Union was then called, in 1973. It continued with the devolution legislation of 1998 and the Human Rights Act of the same year.

These changes have fundamentally altered the British constitution. In eighteenth-century America, Rip van Winkle fell asleep for twenty years. Before he went to sleep, he knew of a pub called The George. It had a picture of George III outside it. When he woke up after twenty years, the pub was still there, still called The George, but the picture was of George Washington, not George III. Someone who went to sleep in 1996 and woke up today would find that the British constitution remains unwritten but has been radically altered. However, these changes are insufficiently noticed by the general public, who witnessed them occur, precisely because the constitution is unwritten. As Bagehot said in *The English Constitution*, 'An ancient and ever-altering constitution [such as the British] is like an old man who still wears with attached fondness clothes in the fashion of his youth; what you see of him is the same; what you do not see is wholly altered.'

Britain's entry into the European Community in 1973 marked a very fundamental change. For the European Community was not simply another international organisation like the United Nations or NATO. It was a legal order superior to that of the Westminster Parliament, with the right to pass laws which had direct effect in the United Kingdom *and* which superseded the laws of the United Kingdom. This is in direct conflict with the principle of the sovereignty of Parliament, which declares that there can be no law-giving body superior to Parliament. In an important case in 1991 (the *Factortame* case), however, the courts refused to apply part of a statute (the Merchant Shipping Act) because it was contrary to European law.

We can see clearly how the European Union limits sovereignty by looking at the issue of immigration. There is currently much discussion about immigration from ex-Communist countries that have recently joined the European Union, such as Poland, Romania and Bulgaria. Many would like to see immigration restricted. But Parliament cannot restrict it, since the free movement of peoples is guaranteed by European Union treaties. This is a clear example of the restriction of sovereignty. It is a striking illustration of the fact that Parliament can no longer pass any law that it likes.

Devolution has established the constitution of a quasi-federal state in the non-English parts of the United Kingdom – Scotland, Wales and Northern Ireland. Since 1999, Parliament is no longer responsible for the domestic affairs of the non-English parts of the United Kingdom – in matters such as health, education, housing and transport. They are now the responsibility of the devolved bodies in Scotland, Wales and Northern Ireland. On these matters, Westminster is now, in effect, an English Parliament – although of course MPs representing constituencies outside England can still vote for legislation affecting England only, something which many people believe to be an anomaly and which gives rise to the famous West Lothian Question. So Westminster has been transformed into a parliament for England, and a federal parliament for Scotland, Wales and Northern Ireland. In consequence, the general election of 2015 will not decide matters of housing, health, transport, or education for Scotland, Wales or Northern Ireland – those matters will be decided by elections for the devolved bodies, but only for England.

The Human Rights Act of 1998 alters our understanding of rights. Previously rights were residual – one could do whatever the law did not prohibit one from doing. But the Human Rights Act sets out a list of positive principles, based on the European Convention of Human Rights, that determine our rights. This is a positive statement of what our rights are; it is for the judges to interpret legislation in the light of this higher law, the principles enshrined in the European Convention of Human Rights.

But on the traditional understanding, there can be no higher law in the British constitution. There can be no law which Parliament cannot change, no fundamental or so-called constitutional law. Formally that remains the case. Judges, if they believe that legislation contravenes human rights, can do no more than issue a declaration of incompatibility. Such a declaration has no legal effect, and it is up to Parliament whether or not to alter the legislation. The courts cannot declare a statute void, as, for example, the United States Supreme Court can do with laws that contravene the American constitution. Parliament can still, if it wishes, maintain a law which offends against human rights – although so far it has not done so. Even so, the Human Rights Act makes the European Convention in effect part of the fundamental law of the land. It is the first step on what may perhaps prove a long journey towards a written or codified constitution.

The Human Rights Act proposes what in essence is a compromise between the two doctrines of the sovereignty of Parliament and the rule of law. But until recently the rule of law in Britain was interpreted comparatively narrowly, as a check upon the abuse of Crown or executive or police powers. It meant that no claim to authority would be recognised unless there was some legal backing for it. Only Parliament could confer that backing. There could therefore be no conflict between parliamentary sovereignty and the rule of law.

But in our own times, *rule of law* has come to have a much broader meaning. It has come to mean explicit recognition of those basic human rights which ought to be acknowledged in any liberal society; and in this sense of the term, there can of course be a conflict between parliamentary sovereignty and the rule of law. This compromise depends upon a sense of restraint on the part of both the judges and Parliament. Were the judges to seek to invade the political sphere and make the judiciary supreme over Parliament – something which critics of the Human Rights Act allege is already happening – there would be considerable resentment on the part of ministers and MPs. Conversely, were Parliament ever to ignore a declaration of incompatibility on the part of the judges and refuse to repeal or amend the offending statute or part of a statute, the Human Rights Act would prove of little value.

Thus the Human Rights Act seeks to secure a democratic engagement with rights on the part of the representatives of the people in Parliament. But, of course, the main burden of protecting human rights has been transferred to the judges, whose role is bound to become more influential. Many human rights cases concern the rights of very small minorities that are too small to be able to use the democratic machinery of party politics and pressure groups very effectively. Many of these minorities are highly unpopular – suspected terrorists, prisoners, asylum-seekers and suspected paedophiles. Life would no doubt be simpler if the victims of injustice were always attractive characters or nice people like ourselves. However, our legal system was probably already fairly good at securing justice for nice people. The Human Rights Act seeks to provide rights for all of us, whether we are nice or not. Perhaps, indeed, there is no particular virtue in being just only to the virtuous.

The compromise on which the Human Rights Act rests may be a tenuous one, dependent as it is upon self-restraint by judges, ministers and MPs. I once asked a senior judge what would happen if there were to be a conflict between the principles of the sovereignty of Parliament and the rule of law. He replied with a smile: 'That is a question that ought not to be asked.'

The radical implications of the Human Rights Act have not been noticed largely because Britain does not have a codified constitution. In a country with a codified constitution – such as, for example, France or Canada – the Act might have required a constitutional amendment or some special process of legislation to enact it. In a country with a codified constitution, the Act would almost certainly have given rise to a great deal of public debate and discussion, for such a country would have become accustomed to the idea that legal modalities are of importance in the public affairs of the state.

The Human Rights Act presupposes a basic consensus on human rights between judges on the one hand, and the government, Parliament and the people on the other. The Act assumes that breaches of human rights will be inadvertent and unintended and that there will therefore be little disagreement between the government and the judges.

But there is clearly no such consensus when it comes to the rights of unpopular minorities. Two matters in particular – issues concerning asylum-seekers and issues concerning suspected terrorists – have come to the fore since the Human Rights Act came into force. Of course, the problem of asylum long predated the Act, but it has grown in significance since the year 2000 and is now a highly emotive issue, capable, so politicians believe, of influencing many voters in a general election, and so determining the political character of the government.

Terrorism also has taken on a different form since the horrific atrocity of 9/11. The form of terrorism to which Britain was accustomed, that of the IRA, was, in a sense, an old-fashioned form of terrorism with a single specific and concrete aim – namely the reunification of the island of Ireland. Global terrorism, by contrast, of the kind championed by Al-Qaeda or Isis, is quite different. It is a new and more ruthless form of terrorism, with wide if not unlimited aims, amongst which is the establishment of a new, Islamic empire and the elimination of the state of Israel. To deal with this new form of terrorism, governments argue, new methods are needed, and these new methods may well infringe human rights. The judges, however, retort that we should not compromise our traditional principles – habeas corpus and the presumption of innocence – which have been tried and tested over many centuries and have served us well.

Some senior judges, however, have gone further. They have suggested that a natural consequence of the Human Rights Act should be an erosion of the principle of the sovereignty of Parliament. They argue that the sovereignty of Parliament is but a judicial construct, a creature of the common law. If the judges could create it, they can now, equally justifiably, supersede it. In *Jackson v. Attorney-General*, 2005, the case that dealt with the validity of the Hunting Act, judges for the first time declared, obiter, that Parliament's ability to pass primary legislation is limited in substance. Lord Steyn declared, obiter, that the principle of the sovereignty of Parliament, while still being the '*general* principle of our constitution', was 'a construct of the common law'. Further:

> The judges created this principle. If that is so, it is not unthinkable that circumstances could arise where the courts may have to qualify a principle established on a different hypothesis of constitutionalism.

He then went on to say in words, which have been much quoted:

> In exceptional circumstances involving an attempt to abolish judicial review of the ordinary role of the courts, the Appellate Committee of the House of Lords or a new Supreme Court may have to consider whether this is a constitutional fundamental which even a sovereign Parliament acting at the behest of a complaisant House of Commons cannot abolish.[12]

Lord Steyn later elaborated on these obiter by saying that 'For my part the dicta in *Jackson* are likely to prevail if the government tried to tamper with the fundamental principles of our constitutional democracy, such as 5 year Parliaments, the role of the ordinary courts, the rule of law, and other such fundamentals. In such exceptional cases the rule of law may trump parliamentary supremacy."[13]

In another obiter dictum from *Jackson*, Lady Hale of Richmond said, 'The courts will treat with particular suspicion (and might even reject) any attempt to subvert the rule of law by removing governmental action affecting the rights of the individual from all judicial powers."[14]

In another obiter dictum in the same case, another law lord, Lord Hope of Craighead, declared:

> Parliamentary sovereignty is no longer, if it ever was, absolute. It is not uncontrolled – It is no longer right to say that its freedom to legislate admits of no qualification whatever. Step by step, gradually but surely, the English principle of the absolute legislative sovereignty of Parliament – is being qualified.

---

[12] [2005] UKHL 56. Para. 102.
[13] The Attlee Foundation Lecture: 11 April 2006: 'Democracy, The Rule of Law and the Role of Judges', 20.
[14] Para. 159.

He then said: 'The rule of law enforced by the courts is the ultimate controlling factor on which our constitution is based."[5]

It may be significant that Lord Hope is a Scottish law lord, for the Scots have
always shown more scepticism than the English towards the absolute sovereignty of Parliament, which they find difficult to reconcile with the Acts of
Union of 1707.

The implication of these remarks by the three law lords is that the sovereignty of Parliament is a doctrine created by the judges which can also be
superseded by the judges. At present, the rule of recognition of the British
constitution – its ultimate norm, ignoring complications arising from the
European Communities Act of 1972 – remains the sovereignty of
Parliament. But some senior judges might prefer to see the sovereignty of
Parliament supplanted by an alternative rule of recognition – the rule of law.

It is clear, then, that there is a conflict between these two constitutional
principles: the sovereignty of Parliament and the rule of law. This conflict, if
not resolved, could generate a constitutional crisis. What I mean by a constitutional crisis is not simply that there are differences of view on constitutional matters. That is to be expected in any healthy democracy. What I mean
by a constitutional crisis is that there is a profound difference of view as to the
method by which such differences should be settled. There is a profound
difference of view as to what the rule of recognition is, or ought to be; perhaps
the two are indistinguishable.

In any society, a balance has to be drawn between the rights of the
individual and the needs of society for protection against terrorism, crime,
etc. But who should draw the balance – the judges or the government?

Senior judges would, I suspect, claim that they have a special role in
protecting the rights of unpopular minorities – such as, for example, asylum-
seekers and suspected terrorists. They would say that in so doing they are
simply applying the Human Rights Act as Parliament has asked them to do.

The government and, one suspects, most MPs and much of the press would
disagree. They would say that it is for them, as elected representatives, to weigh
the precise balance between the rights of the individual and the needs of
society. For they are elected and accountable to the people, but the judges are
not. They will admit that the Human Rights Act allows the judges to issue
declarations of incompatibility. But this, they argue, should not be made an
excuse for the judges to seek judicial supremacy. If the judges, or indeed
anyone else, believe that there is a case for a supreme court along American
lines, they should, such critics suggest, make that case publicly and seek the

---

[5] Paras. 107 and 120.

explicit approval of Parliament and the people. The judiciary should not seek to expand its role by stealth – although both the American Supreme Court and the French *Conseil Constitutionnel* did in fact acquire their powers in such a way, since in neither case are their powers explicitly laid down in the constitution. Neither the American constitution of 1787 nor the Fifth Republic constitution of 1958 has anything to say about the judicial review of legislation.

There is thus a profound difference of view as to how issues involving human rights should be resolved. The government believes that they should be resolved by Parliament. The judges believe that they should be settled by the courts. Because they are coming to disagree about the rule of recognition, both government and the judges may also suppose that the other has broken the constitution. Government and Parliament say that judges are usurping power and seeking to thwart the will of Parliament. Judges say that the government is infringing human rights and then attacking the judiciary for doing its job in reviewing legislation for its compatibility with the Human Rights Act. The British Constitution is coming to mean different things to different people – something different to the judges from what it means to government, Parliament and the people. The argument from parliamentary sovereignty points in one direction, while the argument from the rule of law in another. There will therefore be a conflict and a struggle. How will it be resolved?

There are, clearly, two possible outcomes. The first is that Parliament succeeds in defeating the challenge of the judges, and parliamentary sovereignty is preserved. But the logical corollary of such an outcome would be that Parliament might well, on some future occasion, refuse to take notice of a declaration of incompatibility. The second possible outcome is that the Human Rights Act comes to trump Parliament, and that in practice a declaration of incompatibility by a judge comes to be the equivalent of striking down legislation. It is too early to tell which outcome is more likely to prevail. But it may be that the compromise embodied in the Human Rights Act cannot in the long run survive.

III

The crucial consequence of the various constitutional reforms we have seen since 1997, together with our membership in the European Union, means that Britain is beginning to develop fundamental laws. The British constitution is no longer historic, but is becoming something deliberately designed and planned. Britain has been doing something almost unique in the democratic world by converting an unwritten constitution into a written one. But this has been done in a typically British unplanned and pragmatic way, by piecemeal means.

One reason for this state of affairs is that there is no real political will to do more. Constitutional reform lies low on most people's list of priorities. Shortly before the 1997 general election, when one of the main policies of the Blair government was constitutional reform, the survey research organisation MORI asked people for their priorities. In a list of fourteen, constitutional reform came in at fourteenth! The British people, perhaps wisely, are interested not in constitutional procedures but in political substance.

There is a further obvious reason why Britain's progress towards a constitution has been unplanned and pragmatic. It is that there is simply no consensus on what the final resting place should be. There is no consensus, for example, on whether Britain should remain in the European Union, on the electoral system for Westminster, on the future of the House of Lords, or on Scotland's place in the United Kingdom.

Nevertheless, the constitutional reforms already enacted have had very radical consequences. The most profound of these is that they have limited the power of government. In the 1970s, a leading Conservative, Lord Hailsham, declared that the system of government in Britain was an elective dictatorship. But the reforms have undermined it. They have limited the power of government. Governments now have to ask about their legislation: is it compatible with our membership of the European Union, is it compatible with human rights, will the judges accept it, will it be operative outside England? Britain is now much less of an elective dictatorship than it was. The scope of government is now much more limited.

Power has been dispersed – to the European Union, to the judges and to devolved bodies in Scotland, Wales and Northern Ireland. Someone once defined liberty as power cut into pieces. The constitutional reforms since 1997 have indeed cut power into pieces.

Britain is therefore moving away from a constitution based on the sovereignty of Parliament to one based on the dispersal of power – indeed a separation of powers – both at the centre where there is a new separation of power between government and the judges and territorially within the United Kingdom, in the non-English parts of the United Kingdom, and between the United Kingdom and the European Union.

All this of course leads some to think that it is time we had a written or codified constitution. It is said that former prime minister Gordon Brown wanted Britain to adopt a codified constitution on the 800th anniversary of Magna Carta in 2015. In principle there is perhaps a strong case for a constitution. But there are two reasons why it is possible the time is not yet ripe.

The first reason is that there is much constitutional uncertainty, a sense of incompleteness. There is no real finality. When the National Assembly of Wales was being set up, the Welsh Secretary, Ron Davies, declared that devolution in Wales was a process, not an event. The same can be said of constitutional reform in general. It is an ongoing process rather than an event. All the reforms so far enacted leave questions open. Britain's future in the European Union is obviously uncertain with the promise by the Prime Minister of a referendum by 2017. In addition, the future of the Human Rights Act is uncertain. The Conservative manifesto of 2010 proposed to repeal it, and there is much talk of a British Bill of Rights. The Scottish Parliament is to be given much wider powers. Will there be a consequential reaction in England? Will England seek devolution? These questions all remain unsettled.

Britain is at a transitional stage – halfway between a state in which Parliament is sovereign and one in which the constitution is.

But there is a more fundamental reason why the time may not yet be ripe for a written constitution, for the reforms are incomplete in another sense. The form of a constitution, if it is to be effective, must reflect social forces. A constitution must in some sense reflect society. The British (unwritten) constitution today does not. It reflects a top-down model of government inherited from the past in which the role of the people is essentially reactive and passive. The constitutional reforms that have occurred so far have done little to alter this situation. This can be seen if we ask what difference the changes have made to the ordinary person living in England, who does not want devolution and who, while she may welcome the Human Rights Act, hopes never to have to use it. The reforms have redistributed power between professionals – between political professionals at Westminster, Edinburgh, Cardiff and Belfast, and between politicians and judges. One can put the point rather crudely and say that the reforms show how the officer class has decided to divide up the spoils. But the reforms have done little to increase popular satisfaction or engagement with politics. That was one of the aims of the reformers, and they have failed to achieve it. The evidence is all around us.

Fewer of us vote in general elections than in the 1950s, when turnout was well more than 80 per cent. In the general election of 2010, by contrast, it was just 65 per cent; and amongst 18–24-year-olds, it was just 44 per cent. In 2001, turnout was 58 per cent – the lowest since universal suffrage. Fewer of us now join political parties. Both Labour and the Conservatives now have fewer than 200,000 members. In contrast, sixty years ago, the Labour Party had a million individual members, and the Conservatives around 2.5 million. One can put the point another way: sixty years ago 1 in 11 of us belonged to a political party;

today just more than 1 in 100 of us do. The Royal Society for the Protection of Birds has a million members, and the National Trust almost 4 million. That is ten times the membership of all the political parties put together.

Part of the reason for disenchantment is that people no longer trust elected representatives as much as they once did. Citizens seek to exercise power between elections as well as during the election itself. Moreover, they no longer accept politicians as the sole source of power and authority. Many no longer believe the system enfranchises them. Gordon Brown put the point well in a Fabian pamphlet, written as long ago as 1992. 'In the past', he argued, 'people interested in change have joined the Labour Party largely to elect agents of change. Today, they want to be agents of change themselves.'

Some argue that the lack of engagement in politics in Britain is only part of a wider loss of community engagement, a decline in social capital. But survey evidence has found that popular interest in politics in Britain is as strong today as it has ever been and that there is a powerful sense of civic obligation in modern Britain. Some years ago, 81 per cent of British adults donated to the tsunami appeal, twice the rate in the United States and two to three times the rate of many European countries. Around 40 per cent of us belong to a voluntary organisation. Amongst 18–24-year-olds, the very generation that is least likely to vote, around 3 million, volunteer every year.

Popular interest in politics remains high, but electors are no longer content to confine participation to the traditional channels. The democratic spirit is healthy enough – it is the institutions that seem wanting. It is not so much that there is a generalised disengagement with politics, but 'rather that a vital link that connected citizens to the state and the formal democratic process has been broken'.[16] The question is whether constitutional reform can be extended so as to channel this civic spirit and desire for community engagement.

Past reforms have redistributed power amongst the political and judicial classes. They dispersed power sideways but not downwards. Perhaps there is scope for another instalment of constitutional reform, designed to open up the political system, to enable ordinary people to play a greater role. The death of Margaret Thatcher should have reminded us that she opened up the economic system, enabling many more people to own their own homes or to own shares. There are indeed now more shareholders than there are trade unionists. John Major opened up the public services to much greater scrutiny and consumer control. Can we not also open up our political system?

---

[16] Matthew Taylor, 'Can Funding Reform Stir the Party Animal?' *Parliamentary Affairs* (2005): 640. See more generally, Vernon Bogdanor, *The New British Constitution* (2009).

It may be that the era of pure representative democracy, as it was understood for much of the twentieth century, is now coming to an end. During this previous era, the people, though enfranchised, exercised power only on relatively infrequent occasions at general elections. Between general elections, they trusted their elected representatives to act on their behalf. There was some degree of deference towards elected politicians; and in any case, in an era when educational standards were lower than they are now, few voters believed that they had the political competence to make decisions for themselves. In the late 1940s, for example, the level of political knowledge was pitiable. Just 49 per cent could name a single British colony, while, in a sample survey in Greenwich during the 1950 general election, barely half could name the party of their local MP.[17] Voting tended to be tribal and instinctive, based largely on an inherited viewpoint derived from parental attitudes and social position. That, however, was bound to be a transitional stage. It would take time before universal adult suffrage came to be taken for granted, and its implications for popular enfranchisement fully understood. Universal suffrage is, after all, a relatively recent phenomenon.

The model of representative democracy – perhaps *guided democracy* would be a better term – that was acceptable during the first years of universal suffrage is no longer adequate. The exercise of a modicum of power at relatively infrequent general elections is seen as insufficient. Voters wish to exert influence upon events between elections as well as at election time. Deference has largely disappeared, and it is no longer accepted that political decisions should be made only by politicians. Elected politicians, therefore, are no longer accepted as the sole source of power and authority. Few citizens now believe that the system of pure representative democracy is sufficient to enfranchise them, and this feeling of disengagement seems most pronounced amongst the young. It is one of the main reasons that turnout has fallen so precipitously amongst this age group. In addition, many voters, better educated than those of their parents' generation, find themselves empowered in many other areas of their lives, while the collective organisations, which previously ruled their lives, and in particular the trade unions, have lost much of their authority. Yet, in politics, people are still expected to remain passive and deferential. The political system has not yet responded to the new individualism. Despite the wave of constitutional reforms since 1997, the political system itself has not been opened up. There is a striking contrast between the empowered consumer and the passive citizen. So, if there is to be a further phase of constitutional reform, it must address this problem. That

[17]   David Kynaston, *Austerity Britain, 1945–51* (Bloomsbury, 2007), 382.

may mean a greater degree of direct democracy – more referendums, primary elections for the selection of parliamentary candidates, and the chance for ordinary citizens to play a greater role in decision-making.

There is, it seems to me, a serious tension between our inherited political institutions – which reflect a paternalistic view of the public – and modern popular attitudes, between governmental *forms* and social *forces*. Resolving that tension, in my view, is one of the most important challenges we face. And perhaps a further stage of constitutional reform would be very much in the spirit of Magna Carta, which we celebrate in 2015.

3

Eight Centuries On: Who Are Britain's Barons Now?

Anthony King

One famous image of the signing of Magna Carta – there are many – depicts King John signing the Great Charter witnessed by a number of barons clad in armour. He is the loser. They are the winners. Symbolically, he is seated while most of them stand before him. King John and the barons were – or at first glance appear to have been – the sole wielders of political power in the England of that time: on the one hand, King John with his temporal power diminished; on the other, the rebellious barons boldly and successfully asserting their rights. That is the image of the signing of Magna Carta – verbal as well as pictorial – that most English schoolchildren have imprinted on their minds: the King being subdued by victorious barons.

But a closer look at the image reveals a more complex picture. Standing behind both the King and the barons are the shadowy figures of two bishops with their staffs and mitres. Although they remain in the background, they are shown as being, literally, powers behind the throne. And there is a good deal of truth in that way of depicting them. In 1215, the barons by no means subdued King John on their own. They had the Church's backing, and the Church was a powerful force in thirteenth-century England. A quarrel between the King of England and Innocent III, the Pope in Rome, had led to the suspension of all church services in England in 1207 and then to the excommunication of King John himself two years later. John was a Christian, as were his subjects, and no Christian king could reign for long in thirteenth-century Europe without the sanction of the Vicar of Christ. Even before John struck a deal with the barons in 1215, he had already compromised with the Church. Not only barons but also large numbers of abbots and bishops were parties to the Runnymede agreement. The agreement itself was in part brokered by Pandulf Masca, the Pope's personal legate in England.

Governing a country such as England was far more dangerous then than it is now: at least seven of the eighteen monarchs who reigned between the Norman Conquest and the end of the Wars of the Roses died a violent death. But at the same time it was a far less demanding occupation than it is now, with those in power seeking to achieve much less than they do today (unless they were bent, as some of them were, on conquering France or retaking the Holy Land). Governing was also much simpler in 1215 than it is now. The parallelogram of early mediaeval political forces was not even a parallelogram: it was more like a triangle, its three sides composed of the king, his barons and the senior clergy. To be sure, the king was often insecure on the throne, the baronage could be disputatious and faction-ridden, and the Church's hierarchy could be too. But a meeting such as that at Runnymede, involving a limited number of individual participants and with a broadly agreed-upon outcome, was at least conceivable. In its way, it was a triumph of corporatism, however anachronistic that may sound.

The barons of today are far more numerous than those of yesteryear, and they take a far wider variety of forms. Anyone who sought today to paint a contemporary picture akin to the many depictions of the signing or sealing of Magna Carta would need an enormous canvass and exceedingly fine brushes as well as a lot of time; and undoubtedly the final product would resemble a Jackson Pollock or a Rorschach test more than a Rubens or a Rembrandt, let alone a modest Runnymede-style group portrait.

II

Who are the barons today? Many influences are brought to bear on modern British governments – today's rough equivalents of King John – but in 2015 who has the power, as King John's barons had, to thwart the aims or significantly to curtail the actions of our governments? Who are today's 'veto-players' vis-à-vis modern-day ministers and their officials?

A large proportion of today's baronial power-wielders are fairly easy to identify. They are individual human beings or, if not that, at least organisations with corporate headquarters, addresses, websites and logos. Because they are corporeal and identifiable, they can be negotiated with either face to face or else via emails, faxes and text messages. If need be, one can praise them or blame them.

Given the passage of time, it is not surprising that today's barons in the sense of being wielders of real power do not in 2015 include the men and women we

still insist on calling barons (and baronesses): the members of the House of
Lords. It is true that these players can sometimes be a nuisance; they can delay
the passage of legislation. But they are hardly barons in the sense that the men
who confronted King John at Runnymede were. The same is true of the
Christian churches, powerful in thirteenth-century England, all but impotent
today. In 2013–2014, almost all the Christian denominations opposed the
introduction of same-sex marriage. They were overwhelmingly – and easily –
defeated by the government and Parliament.

The House of Lords lost its absolute legislative veto in 1911. The power of the
Christian churches atrophied gradually during the decades following the
Second World War. The ejection of the trade unions from the barony was
much more precipitous. Between roughly the end of the last war and the mid
1980s, Britain's trade unions were almost universally, and rightly, regarded as
an estate of the realm. Indeed, their leaders were often called 'trade union
barons', when not 'trade union bosses'. Governments of both political parties
deferred to them and were sometimes forced to bow down before them.
Successive governments either made no attempt to curb the trade unions'
power or else did try but failed (Harold Wilson's government in 1969, Edward
Heath's in 1971). Again and again, successive governments' attempts to hold
down public-sector pay or to impose across-the-board wage restraint were
rebuffed by the unions, by means of either strikes or the threat of strikes. It
was left to Margaret Thatcher's government during the 1980s, along with high
unemployment and the unions' own unpopularity, to deprive the unions of
almost all their power in the state. For generations, prime ministers and trade
union leaders used to have Runnymede-like meetings – replete with beer and
sandwiches – at 10 Downing Street. No longer.

The people at large counted for almost nothing in 1215, although of course
they could be tiresome if they were sufficiently discontented or restless. Today,
however, the people at large count for a great deal. They have the vote. In liberal
democracies, governments – the reigning monarchs of our time – live in constant
fear of them. Although governments can always function under a wide variety of
headings without having to pay too much attention to voters or public opinion,
there are usually issues on which public opinion, meaning the opinions of
voters, matters a great deal. In recent decades, successive British governments,
fearful of the electoral consequences, have baulked at dealing effectively and
in good time with such issues as housing, global warming, the problems posed
by an ageing population, the possession and sale of illegal drugs and the need
(or at least the generally recognised desirability) of creating additional airport
capacity in the vicinity of London. Ministers are often heard to say in private
that they would be delighted to act if only the voters would let them.

Owners of newspapers and television and radio stations are frequently described – the language is telling – as 'media barons'. In Britain at any rate, that is an exaggeration. The media in Britain are definitely plural: to be sure, national newspapers, many of them with would-be baronial proprietors, but also the multitudinous social media plus the BBC and tightly regulated, though privately owned, television and radio stations. The so-called media barons – notably, the owners of News UK (formerly News International) and DMG Media (formerly Associated Newspapers) – undoubtedly seek to influence the policies of governments, and not merely the policies that relate to the media themselves. And they do have some influence on occasion. For example, successive governments have almost certainly been inhibited from reviewing their policy towards the possession of cannabis by their fear of the press assault that would surely ensue. However, to the extent that some newspapers are sometimes influential, it is largely as a result of ministers' belief that the newspapers in question influence public opinion, thereby influencing the way in which people vote. But whether that belief is well founded is open to doubt, especially in this multimedia age and at a time when newspaper readership is in decline. If there are media barons, their aristocratic estates – the spheres within which they can wield effective influence over governments – are far smaller than is often supposed. The very phrase 'media baron' is something of an anachronism.

Money is probably more important. Electoral politics in Britain is cheaper than in some other democracies, largely because there are legal limits on the amounts parties and candidates can spend during election campaigns and also because paid-for political propaganda on the main broadcast media is effectively banned. That said, those who fund the parties are in a position, at least in principle, to affect those parties' policies, including when the party to which they happen to donate is in government. How far they succeed is unclear. Although in the past trade unions were capable of influencing Labour policy, especially as it affected the unions, that period would appear to have passed. The unions may pay the piper, but they no longer, if they ever did, call the tune. The Conservatives look like being more biddable. A large proportion of their funding comes from individuals and firms in the financial-services sector, in particular from hedge funds. It may be an accident – but then again it may not be – that the Conservative party collectively is so keen to promote the financial-services sector and so keen to defend its interests. Large-scale donors to the party may not be fully fledged barons, but from a distance they do look a little like baronets.

Academic political scientists seem to have lost interest in Britain's pressure groups and interest groups, although a generation ago they wrote extensively about them. That may be partly because Britain is no longer the quasi-corporatist state it was between the end of the Second World War and the Thatcher years. Governments since then have not seen it as part of their business to negotiate with, and ideally to reach agreements with, for example, 'the two sides of industry' (a phrase no longer in use). Most notably, the Trades Union Congress and the Confederation of British Industry are no longer barons in any sense. Politicians have written them out of the script. However, the same cannot be said of other, more sector-specific firms, organisations and lobby groups: banks and bankers, hedge funds, the tobacco industry, the construction industry, 'big pharma', the oil industry, the producers of alcoholic drinks and so forth. Inevitably, their power and influence depends on circumstances and on governments' calculations of electoral advantage; but, under Labour as well as Conservative governments, the balance of public power is tilted, as it always has been, in favour of wealth and the wealthy. The barons at Runnymede were none of them poor. Governments today also need to be wary of the power of a small number of NGOs – for example, the Royal Society for the Prevention of Cruelty to Animals – which enjoy high levels of popular support.

As recently as the late 1980s, no one would have dreamt of including Britain's judges in a list of this country's more formidable power-holders vis-à-vis government. Today, thanks to the judges' greater willingness than in the past to exercise judicial review and also to the passage into law of the Human Rights Act 1998, incorporating into United Kingdom domestic law the European Convention of Human Rights, the judges count for a good deal more than they did. The scope of their actions is limited, and they almost never initiate major changes of policy, but men and women in positions of power – especially in the Home Office – can no longer ignore them. The judgments of the courts have thwarted or challenged the will of the government of the day in relation to a wide range of matters, including immigration, deportation, the detention of terrorist suspects, the rights of asylum-seekers and the voting rights, if any, of convicted prisoners. The British judiciary, its jurisdiction having been substantially expanded, has become a kind of barony.

III

As we have seen, already in the thirteenth century the affairs of an English monarch were intimately bound up with institutions and individuals beyond England's shores – in King John's case with the Church and the Pope in Rome. The Roman pope's actions affected the king's actions in faraway England. England at that time was already part of an all-embracing

European religious community, the European union of its day. It goes without saying that in the twenty-first century an infinitely wider range of institutions and individuals outwith the United Kingdom constrain the capacity of British governments to act. The post-1998 legal requirement that, in their judgments, British courts must take into account the jurisprudence of the European Court of Human Rights is only one example, albeit an important one, of a wide-ranging set of similar phenomena.

Although often exaggerated, the depth of the UK's engagement with today's European Union – with 'Brussels' – is nevertheless profound. British governments can still tax and spend more or less as they wish, especially as this country has remained outside the Eurozone, and the powers that be in Britain are still effectively in charge of such important matters as defence, education, energy, health, local government, pensions, social services, transport, the civil law and most aspects of the criminal law. Against that, the United Kingdom has ceded to the European Union, in whole or in part, a large measure of authority in such important fields as agriculture and fisheries, competition policy, consumer affairs, human migration among the member countries of the European Union and pretty much everything to do with the functioning of the European single market. A large proportion of UK ministers, including the prime minister, spend a large part of their time negotiating with their opposite numbers elsewhere in Europe. Senior British officials do the same. The UK's bargaining hand in such negotiations is sometimes strong, sometimes weak; but this country and its governments obviously lack the degree of autonomy they once possessed. Even if the United Kingdom were to withdraw from the European Union, its desire to have a free-trade pact with the European Union would mean the UK's effectively ceding to other European countries a wide range of powers that its own governments once possessed. No single individual in the European Union is gifted with the powers that lay in the laps of thirteenth-century popes, but the institutions of the European Union, taken together, possess far more power, over a far wider range of fields, than Innocent III ever did.

The European Union is not the only international or supranational body with a near-baronial capacity to limit the freedom of action of British governments. Britain is deeply embedded in the institutions, no longer of the Roman Catholic Church, but – in no order – of the North Atlantic Treaty Organization, the Council of Europe (custodian of the European Convention on Human Rights), the United Nations, the World Trade Organization, the International Monetary Fund (the IMF), the World Bank, the World Health Organization, the Food and Agriculture Organization, the International Civil Aviation Organization, the International Maritime Organization, the Organization for Security and Cooperation in Europe, the Organization for Economic Cooperation and Development and the International Atomic Energy Agency, to name only the most important. Obviously, some of these bodies have a greater capacity than others to influence and inhibit the activities of British governments; but all of them have some such capacity in at least some fields. None of them can simply be ignored.

The list of organisations set out in the previous paragraph comprises only intergovernmental bodies; but of course in the twenty-first century there are private-sector organisations – giant multinational corporations – whose decisions and behaviour, and probable future decisions and behaviour, the governments of so-called sovereign states, including Britain, must take into account when developing and implementing their policies. Eight hundred years after Magna Carta, companies, such as BASF, BP, ExxonMobil, Ford, General Electric, General Motors, Honda, Kraft, Monsanto, Nestlé, Nissan, Pfizer, Procter & Gamble, Siemens, Toyota and Unilever, are in a position to make massive investment decisions – ones likely to affect the livelihoods of many thousands – irrespective of national boundaries. They will base their decisions, at least in part, on how 'business-friendly' individual national governments are and on their corporate tax regimes. Some multinational corporations, such as Amazon, Google and Starbucks, organise their affairs in such a way that the governments of the countries in which they do business cannot extract from them the substantial tax revenues that would appear, on the face of it, to be due to them. Unlike the barons at Runnymede, multinational corporations seldom seek to impose a wide range of political conditions on national governments; but, within their spheres of operation, their capacity to influence and inhibit the actions of governments may be, and often is, substantial. In particular, competitive bidding by national governments that seek inward investment from multinational corporations may, and often does, have the effect of limiting those governments' room for manoeuvre in fields such as taxation, labour law and land-use planning. In their dealings with UK governments, as well as many others, successful multinationals are clad in their own kind of armour.

IV

So far, our analytic task has been relatively straightforward: to identify and name those institutions and entities that are the rough equivalents of mediaeval barons in their relation to modern governments. Some of them, notably voters in liberal democracies such as Britain's, are permanent fixtures on the political scene. Others, such as the trade unions and individual corporations, come and go. Some are more restricted in their range of influence than others. The range of British voters' influence is far wider than that of, say, Kraft Foods or the International Maritime Organization. But all have to be factored from time to time into the thinking and decision-making of governments.

At this point, however, our analysis needs to become more subtle and to take into account factors that do not take the form of identifiable individuals, institutions and other similar entities. We need to take into account more systemic factors – ones that do not take a simple corporeal form, or even a complicated one, but that bear heavily on what a democratically elected government such as Britain's can and cannot reasonably be expected to do or attempt.

In the mid 1210s, King John, the English barons and the English clergy were themselves caught up in a social system, a complex set of interrelationships that was greater than themselves and outlasted them. King John was succeeded by Henry III, the barons at Runnymede gradually died off, and the clergy who attended the Runnymede meeting were also dead within a few years. But the system survived for generations after that. It was a system that, among other things, gave the pope in Rome the power to exercise authority over both the king and his barons, as well as his personal legate and the clergy permanently based in England. That system rested on two pillars. One was the beliefs – notably their hopes of heaven and their fears of hell – that all Christians shared. The other was their conviction that these beliefs were indeed almost universally shared, so that, even if one individual happened not to share them, that individual was acutely aware that almost everyone else did. The actions of individuals throughout Catholic Christendom were conditioned and con- strained by their own internalised beliefs and also, separately, by the knowl- edge that the actions of others were similarly conditioned and constrained by *their* beliefs. Each could predict how others would be likely to react to whatever it was that they did or proposed to do.

At Runnymede, King John feared being excommunicated for a second time, and his barons and the clergy knew that he did. In his fear lay their power. The momentous events at Runnymede were more complicated than that, of course, but they cannot be fully understood as simply a struggle for power between two doctrine-free, ideology-free opposing forces – between two bands of robbers. All those present took for granted the need to show a proper Christian obedience, just as they took for granted the idea that the King was not just another run-of-the-mill baron but instead was the Lord's anointed, someone whose position was undeniably superordinate. The barons acknowl- edged their fealty to the King even as they sought to circumscribe his power. History remembers what divided King John and the upstart barons. It is apt to forget what united them: the social system of their century and the system of common understandings in which all of them were conjointly lodged.

The world of 2015 could scarcely differ more from the world of 1215; but they have in common the fact that large parts of the modern world, including most of its more prosperous parts, are also lodged in a socio-economic system that both transcends and also profoundly affects the behaviour of individuals and organisations, not least the most baronial ones – a system that, although it will not last forever, will undoubtedly outlast almost all those currently caught up in it. In other words, although the question 'Who are the barons now?' is a good one and one well worth asking and answering, it is not today the only question worth asking and answering. Another desirable question is 'What is the socio-economic system in which the barons of today have their power and being?' Without feudalism, there would have been no barons. Without capitalism, there would be no capitalists.

Today's paramount socio-economic system, of which Britain is certainly a part, we can call 'global market capitalism'. The system is very familiar, at least in outline, and, although the labels people attach to it vary, the underlying reality remains much the same. Like the early mediaeval system, global market capitalism is a compound of behaviours and beliefs about the probable beliefs and behaviours of others. It amounts to a kind of secular theology, with hundreds of thousands of decision-makers sharing – and knowing that they share – common assumptions and a common creed. The supranational system that the creed and its accompanying institutions sustain comprises two features and one non-feature.

The one non-feature concerns ownership. The concept of global market capitalism is often associated with private – that is, non-governmental – ownership; but, although there certainly is an empirical connection between the two, there is no necessary connection. Although a majority of firms that operate in the global marketplace are private-sector firms, by no means all are. A significant minority of London's red buses display the letters RATP alongside that firm's familiar (to Parisians) logo. The letters stand for *Régie Autonome des Transports Parisiens*, a company owned by the French state, one that operates in Italy, Morocco, Algeria, South Africa, China, India, South Korea and Brazil as well as in London and the Paris region. Much of China's overseas trade is conducted by state-owned, state-controlled or heavily state-influenced companies, and the Russian state has a controlling interest in Gazprom, one of the world's largest companies (and proud sponsor of European Champions League football). It is also the case that the line between the private and public sectors is often blurred to the point of invisibility. Some large firms, such as BAE Systems, a leading firm in Britain's defence industry, are indeed owned by their shareholders and are therefore nominally private-sector firms, but they have interests that are so intimately intertwined with those of their host state that to call them 'private' firms, while true up to a point, is seriously misleading.

The 'market' element in the system of global market capitalism, however, is real beyond any question. In 2015, the belief is almost universally held, at least by those in positions of power, that economic productivity and efficiency, and therefore human welfare, are maximised if individual companies, whoever happens to own them, are left free to compete with one another in markets that are either entirely unregulated or are regulated only minimally. The economic policies of almost all governments in the developed world are derived from that simple proposition. Beliefs and behaviour are in broad alignment. In the case of Britain, governments of all political complexions for the better part of half a century have operated on the principle that almost all services, including those that were traditionally called public services, are best provided by a multiplicity of free-standing, competing organisations. The services in question range from the supply of water and energy to the operation of railways, airlines and bus services to the provision of cataract operations and MRI scans in the National Health Service. In the early twenty-first century, the idea of the superiority of competitive markets over any other form of economic organisation is all but hegemonic.

The 'global' element in the system of global market capitalism is also real – and powerfully reinforces the market element. Soviet communists in their day could at least dream of 'socialism in one country'. In 2015, no one – even in the United States, let alone China – can begin to dream of capitalism in one country. Free-trade treaties and organisations that are meant to sustain them blanket almost the whole of the developed world. Steps towards ever freer trade are embodied in the European Union, the European Free Trade Association, the North American Free Trade Agreement, the ASEAN Free Trade Area, the South Asia Free Trade Agreement, the Asia-Pacific Trade Agreement, the African Free Trade Zone, the Gulf Cooperation Council and, not least, the World Trade Organisation. Some of these agreements and institutions are more aspirational than effective, but the European Union, of which Britain in 2015 is still a member, is undoubtedly both.

Formalities apart, the simple truth is that the British economy is one of the world's most globalised and is therefore an economy over which British governments, compared with the governments of some other countries, have relatively little control. Britain's chronic trade deficit means that it is liable to suffer disproportionately from economic downturns in its principal export markets. Any appreciation of the pound is liable to have the same effect.

Britain is heavily dependent on direct foreign investment over which it has little control. Its heavy reliance on the worldwide provision of financial services means that banks and other financial institutions in the City of London and Edinburgh are highly vulnerable to perturbations in international financial markets. Britain's economy has, of course, for many decades been unusually open. The Great Crash of 1929 in the United States and the collapse of Vienna's Kreditanstalt Bank in 1931 both hit this country hard. The latter helped destroy Ramsay MacDonald's minority Labour government. But this country's historic openness has been compounded in recent decades by the fact that the world now is even more interconnected than it was then. Movements of people, money, goods, aircraft, ships, images, ideas and fashions – and the speed of those movements – are on an unprecedented scale. The U.S. administration's unilateral decision in 2008 to allow Lehman Brothers to go bankrupt helped precipitate Britain's worst financial crisis since the South Sea Bubble. The age-old distinction between 'domestic' and 'foreign', never rigid, is now all but meaningless. British governments, like other countries' governments, are left having to cope as best they can.

Thus, there are still undoubtedly barons of a sort out there, whether humble voters in a liberal democracy or huge multinational corporations, but there is also the socio-economic system – the system of ideas and the institutions that embody those ideas – within which today's barons have their being. Flights of capital are actuated by individuals and companies (and may well be actuated by what those individuals and companies believe about the probable future behaviour of governments as well as other individuals and companies); but it is the system of global market capitalism that enables capital to fly off. Governments are by and large incapable of preventing capital from flying (that is, fleeing) if that is what its owners want it to do. In other words, modern governments can still govern – but only within limits and up to a point.

The consequences for a liberal democracy such as Britain are profound, not least the political consequences. Quite simply, there is today a substantial misfit between what voters want and expect their governments to do and what their governments are actually capable of doing. In 1215, the majority of ordinary men and women in England undoubtedly knew where they stood. The barons and their agents exercised secular power over them. The clergy exercised spiritual power over them. They themselves were virtually powerless and assumed that they would remain so. Their expectations of both barons and clergy were low; most of them probably hoped, at best, to be left alone. By contrast, in 2015 the majority of ordinary men and women have a modicum of power via the ballot box, are capable of exercising it and expect the men and women in government to respond to their demands and to meet their expectations. Unfortunately, they are doomed to disappointment.

Part of the difficulty, but only part, lies in the fact that democracy itself is a form of institutionalised disappointment. In mediaeval England, the lower orders were always low and, never having had any illusions about their powerlessness, were never in any danger of being disillusioned or disappointed by their lack of power. But modern democratic elections, while they always produce winners, also invariably produce losers. The winners' joy is accompanied by the losers' tears – and those tears may be ones of deep disappointment and genuine anguish, as in the case of the Conservatives' loss of power in 1945 and the lamentations of the losing side in the 2014 Scottish independence referendum. In British elections, the stakes are seldom desperately high and the disappointed therefore seldom feel desperately disappointed. But those – now a minority – who feel closely attached to one or another political party may well become disaffected and alienated, as well as disappointed, if their party loses repeatedly.

However, a more fundamental problem almost certainly lies in the fact that millions of voters exaggerate the sheer capacity of British governments to act effectively – an exaggeration that British political leaders do much to foster. The leaders promise to curb inflation, reduce unemployment, promote investment, increase productivity and curb immigration. They have even been known to promise to create 'a new Britain'. But, vis-à-vis global barons whom British governments are powerless to control, and in the context of the global market capitalist economic system, those promises, while undoubtedly made in good faith, are usually impossible to fulfil. British governments can prod, nudge, exhort and promote, but their actions seldom determine what actually happens. A British government in the modern world resembles an old-fashioned county council, able to act in such fields as highways and education, but only within the bounds of the powers allotted to it. In 2015, those powers are a pale shadow of what they were.

It may be that the citizens of countries such as Finland, Sweden, Norway, Denmark and the Netherlands recognise, without having to be told, that the capacity of their governments to influence events is minimal. But Britain's political leaders seem bent on giving the voters of this country the impression, without quite saying so, that Britain is still an imperial power, not in the sense of continuing to possess a vast overseas empire, but in the sense that this country, as a sovereign state, can continue to determine its own fate. The very continuity of British institutions, and their imposing physical presence in the form of Big Ben, the House of Commons and Buckingham Palace, probably has some effect in tempting Britain's political leaders to conceal from the public, and perhaps even from themselves, the extent to which Britain – like other formerly dominant powers, including the United States – no longer controls its destiny to the extent that it once did. Britain's political leaders certainly seem reluctant to educate the public, to own up to the fact that they can only do so much. The barons at Runnymede forced King John to acknowledge publicly that he was no longer in sole control. No such dramatic, once-and-for-all ceremony could possibly be held today.

As a result, and in the face of political leaders who are apparently in denial, it would seem that most British voters have no very vivid understanding of the complex structure of power in the modern world and of British governments' limited ability to influence that world. Politicians campaign on much the same basis as they always have, publishing manifestos that, if anything, become more and more ambitious and detailed as time goes on. Voters, if they bother to vote, appear surprised as well as dismayed by the paucity of many of the results. Expecting to be disappointed, millions of eligible voters do not bother to turn out at all. Millions of others do turn out, but then vote for parties that have – and are known by the voters to have – no realistic chance of winning the election in question and taking office. It is easy to understand why in 2015 many voters are tempted to vote for a party called the United Kingdom Independence Party.

But of course genuine independence in the modern world is a chimera, and not just in the United Kingdom. In distant Mongolia, the few people who can afford to do so drive Jeeps. Jeeps are manufactured in a variety of countries by the Chrysler Group of America. The majority shareholder in Chrysler Group is the Italian carmaker Fiat S.p.A. Needless to say, most of the decisions relating to the future of the car industry in Britain are not taken in Britain. It is not even clear that British voters by themselves need necessarily any longer determine the outcomes of British general elections. On 6 May 2010, voters went to the polls in the usual way. They elected MPs from a variety of parties, with the Conservatives emerging as the largest single party but without an overall majority. On 12 May 2010, six days later, the leaders of the Conservative and Liberal Democrat parties announced that they were going to form a coalition government. But no one had voted for such a government. Left to their own devices, the Liberal Democrats would probably have preferred to sustain in power a Conservative minority administration, thereby retaining their freedom of action on non-economic issues such as health, education and civil liberties. However, in early 2010, the Eurozone was in crisis, with fears mounting of sovereign-debt defaults by Greece, Spain and possibly even Italy. Global financial markets were in turmoil. It looked as though market traders might turn on Britain, as they had in 1992. The markets demanded, and therefore the country appeared desperately to need, a stable government in Britain, one committed to remaining in power for a period of years. Against that background, the Liberal Democrats were constrained. They felt they had no option but to agree to participate in a Conservative-led coalition. The voters had spoken, but so had the markets – and on this occasion the markets' voice was at least as loud as the voters'.

In a sense, the scene played out at Runnymede eight centuries ago epitomised the principles of the traditional English constitution – in due course, the traditional British constitution. A single sovereign was held to account at Runnymede by a group of powerful subjects. Gradually over the centuries, that single sovereign of mediaeval times morphed into the corporate body that we call the government. At the same time, the group of powerful subjects at Runnymede morphed into the modern democratic electorate. But the idea of accountability – that the government of the day could and should be accountable to the people, whatever form 'the people' currently took – remained a constant. Governments could act across a broad range of responsibilities. They could therefore reasonably be held to account for their actions in relation to that broad range of responsibilities.

However, it is no longer reasonable to hold British governments to account for a substantial proportion of what happens in this country today, including for many aspects of life that governments once did control. Successive UK governments have given away massive amounts of power, and they have had massive amounts of power taken from them: on the one hand, privatisation, devolution and the decisions to join NATO and what subsequently became the European Union; on the other hand, the steady and seemingly irresistible encroachments of global market capitalism. Who now is to be held accountable for what? There is now no omnibus answer to that crucial question, whether in Britain or elsewhere. The government of the day, whichever country it is in, is sometimes the answer, but not nearly as often as it once was. That is why the practice of democracy within the bounds of existing nation-states often seems so unsatisfactory and leads so often to frustration and disappointment. The world of King John and his barons has exploded. The fallout from that explosion has still not come to earth.

4

What Magna Carta Means to the Modern British Public

Roger Mortimore

At most points in the twentieth century, Magna Carta would probably have been regarded as falling into the category of historical events about which 'every schoolboy knows', in the once-familiar phrase. Certainly, when Sellar and Yeatman produced their famous 1930 parody of traditional history teaching, *1066 and All That*, they not only included a chapter on Magna Carta and its provisions, but chose for the original cover illustration a cartoon conflating Magna Carta with the Order of the Garter.[1] Similarly, when Galton and Simpson had Tony Hancock appeal to his fellow jurors 'Does Magna Carta mean nothing to you? Did she die in vain?' in a 1959 episode of *Hancock's Half Hour*, the joke would have been pointless if they were not able to assume that the vast majority of BBC TV viewers knew at least a little more about Magna Carta than Hancock's character did. Today, perhaps we are not so sure. Indeed, in June 2014 the Prime Minister, David Cameron, felt justified in announcing as a significant policy initiative that in future all school pupils should be taught about Magna Carta, with the aim of promoting British values.[2]

How far are the British public aware of Magna Carta today? To explore this question, Ipsos MORI conducted two brief opinion polls,[3] one towards the end of 2012 and one in May 2014. These followed in the steps of a 1998 MORI survey,

[1] W. C. Sellar and R. J. Yeatman, *1066 and All That: A Memorable History of England, Comprising All the Parts You Can Remember, Including 103 Good Things, 5 Bad Kings and 2 Genuine Dates* (London: Methuen, 1930).

[2] David Cameron, 'British Values Aren't Optional, They're Vital', *Mail on Sunday*, 15 June 2014, http://www.dailymail.co.uk/debate/article-2658171/DAVID-CAMERON-British-values-arent-opt ional-theyre-vital-Thats-I-promote-EVERY-school-As-row-rages-Trojan-Horse-takeover-class rooms-Prime-Minister-delivers-uncompromising-pledge.html (accessed 22 August 2014).

[3] Ipsos MORI interviewed representative quota samples of 1,005 adults aged 18+ resident in Great Britain by telephone on 20–24 October 2012 and of 1,003 adults aged 18+ resident in Great Britain by telephone on 10–12 May 2014. When lists were read out in the course of the survey, the order in which items appeared was randomised for each respondent. Data were weighted to

which had confirmed that there was at that point widespread recognition of the name at the very least, with 75 per cent of British adults saying they had heard of Magna Carta, putting it on a par with documents receiving widespread contemporary news coverage such as the Human Rights Bill and the Maastricht Treaty.[4] But we went further than the 1998 survey, exploring also the public's knowledge of some basic historical facts about Magna Carta, their beliefs as to what it contained and their attitudes to some of the rights it embodied.

In this we were interested not only in overall levels of knowledge and attitudes, but also in how these vary between different groups of the population – particularly by age. Most children in England would once have been taught about Magna Carta at an early stage in their school career, but perhaps only at a level uncomfortably close to the *1066 and All That* caricature (with its repeated refrain of 'except the common people'). School history curriculums have changed in recent decades. Would the effect of that be evident in differing levels of knowledge by generation? And if so, would the younger groups prove to have higher or lower knowledge and understanding of Magna Carta? Would there also be differences in the value people of different ages or different backgrounds put on various aspects of human rights, and therefore perhaps differences in the perspective from which Magna Carta might be viewed?

To this end, across the two surveys we included four components. We asked whether people had heard of Magna Carta. For those who had, there was a brief 'quiz' on very basic historical facts about it. Finally, respondents were read a short list of human rights; some of them were asked to say which of these rights (if any) Magna Carta had guaranteed, while others were asked to choose which two or three they thought were most important for a civilised society.

It turns out that is still true that the vast majority of the public have at least heard of Magna Carta (or, at any rate, claim that they have done so). They are less clear what it was and when and where it came about. Most of those who had heard of Magna Carta felt able to attempt to pick from a list the rights it guaranteed, and on the whole their answers were more right than wrong. However, there were a good many wrong answers; and only just over a third of the public managed to give the correct answer to even one of our three factual questions. (Particularly surprising, perhaps, is that most of the public seem to make no association between Magna Carta and King John, who is surely a

---

match the profile of the population. Full details of question wording and computer tabulations of the results can be found on Ipsos MORI's website, http://www.ipsos-mori.com.

[4]   MORI interviewed a representative quota sample of 2,024 residents aged 15+ (including 1,925 aged 18+) across Great Britain. Interviews were conducted face to face, in home, on 14–17 August 1998. Data were weighted to the profile of the population. The survey was conducted on behalf of the United Nations Association. (MORI was incorporated into Ipsos MORI in 2005.)

familiar-enough historical figure in his own right, if only from the so-frequently-filmed legends of Robin Hood.) In all of these findings, there were recurring demographic patterns: awareness and knowledge were distinctly lower than average among the young and members of ethnic minorities, and slightly higher at the upper end of the social class scale than at the lower. Men were also a little better than women at answering the factual questions.

More dramatic, however, were the attitudinal findings. Rights guaranteed by Magna Carta were picked by far fewer people as being important for a civilised society than were rights that have only in recent centuries been effectively protected in England. Three-fifths of the public see freedom of speech as one of the most important rights, while only 1 in 5 prioritise freedom from arbitrary arrest. Probably this does not mean that the Magna Carta rights are not valued at all, only that most of the public so take them for granted in modern society that the human rights at the forefront of their minds are those they see as being more potentially under threat. Nevertheless, it may be that for this reason the importance of Magna Carta is not likely to be immediately obvious to many Britons today, and its name may not be a potent symbol that can be successfully exploited for political gain.

AWARENESS OF MAGNA CARTA

The 2012 and 2014 surveys both began by testing whether people had heard of Magna Carta, including it in a list of other historical documents to give comparative context to the results. (See Table 1.) There was no significant difference between the two surveys in the proportion of respondents claiming to have at least heard of Magna Carta – 85% in the first and 87% in the second, roughly 6 British adults in 7. This is similar to the number that have heard of Domesday Book (88% across the two surveys) but a little lower than the numbers who say they have heard of the U.S. Declaration of Independence (91%) or the Universal Declaration of Human Rights (89%). Other historical documents were less familiar: the King James Bible (despite recent 400th-anniversary celebrations) was known to only 71%, the Lindisfarne Gospels to 42% and the Codex Sinaiticus to 15%. One in twenty, 5%, said they had heard of the *Textus Roffensis*, the medieval manuscript including the laws of Anglo-Saxon Kent.[5]

---

[5]   In conducting surveys of this type, researchers sometimes include a non-existent item in the list as an indication of how many of the sample might be claiming to have heard of the other items when they have not. In this case, the real but obscure *Textus Roffensis* serves the same purpose. Even if none of those claiming to have heard of the *Textus Roffensis* had really done so, the scale of over-claiming would be modest enough to suggest that our findings about Magna Carta can be treated as reasonably reliable.

TABLE 1. *Public Awareness in Britain of Various Historic Documents, 2012 and 2014*

Q: I am going to read out a list of some historical documents. Which, if any, of these have you heard of before this interview?

	2012	2014
U.S. Declaration of Independence	90%	92%
Universal Declaration of Human Rights	89%	89%
Domesday Book	87%	89%
Magna Carta	85%	87%
King James Bible	70%	71%
Lindisfarne Gospels	39%	45%
Codex Sinaiticus	13%	17%
Textus Roffensis	5%	5%
None of these	2%	2%
Don't know	*	*

Base: 1,005 GB adults aged 18+, 20–24 October 2012; 1,003 GB adults aged 18+, 10–12 May 2014.
* Indicates a number less than 0.5% but greater than zero.

The 2012 survey then went on to probe the knowledge of those who said they had heard of Magna Carta by means of three simple quiz questions about it (when it was agreed, by which king, and where in England this happened), which they had to answer without being prompted with a list of possible answers. These facts are, admittedly, trivial: knowledge of the answers may add some historical context to an awareness of Magna Carta but contribute little if anything to understanding its nature or significance. Nevertheless, they are the sort of details that would certainly have been emphasised, along with Magna Carta's content, in a typical history lesson of the 'old-fashioned' type, and which might form part of any generally shared understanding of Magna Carta as a historical event. In particular, if there is any popular myth or accepted narrative around the circumstances in which Magna Carta was agreed, we would expect at the very least that King John would be recognised as its central figure.

Each of these three questions was answered correctly[6] by around 1 in 4 of those asked, representing slightly more than a fifth of all adults. However, many got some but not all of the three questions right, so that 36% (43% of those who had heard of Magna Carta at all) got at least one correct answer, while only 8% knew all three of these facts. Nevertheless, almost two-thirds of

[6] Being able to name the right century was taken as a correct answer on the date; only 13% of those asked (11% of the public as a whole allowing for those who have not even heard of Magna Carta) placed it specifically in 1215.

British adults must be taken as knowing none of these things; and, contrary to our expectations, King John did not prove a significantly easier answer to produce than Runnymede or the thirteenth century.

Breaking down the results in more detail, several significant differences in knowledge emerge, the same patterns applying broadly to recognition of the name and to the ability to answer each of the three quiz questions. In general terms, men know more about Magna Carta than women, older people and more middle-class people know more about it, and knowledge is significantly lower in Scotland and among members of ethnic minorities (see Table 2).

Among the youngest group, of respondents aged 18 to 24, ability to answer the factual questions is very low indeed. Just 4% could name Runnymede as the place where Magna Carta was agreed, and 7% knew King John was the relevant monarch. Another figure which jumps out is that only 7% of ethnic-minority Britons know the significance of Runnymede.

Also interesting, although more for its implications than for any explanatory value, is that claimed knowledge of Magna Carta is much lower than average among the politically disengaged. Only 70% of those who say they are absolutely certain they would not vote in an immediate general election have heard of Magna Carta, compared to 92% of those who are absolutely certain that they would vote. People were also significantly more likely to say they had heard of Magna Carta if they remembered voting for one of the three major parties (Conservative, Labour or Liberal Democrat) at the last election (91%) than if they had voted for a smaller party (86%), not voted at all or could not remember (72%).

Of course, many of these factors are interlinked. The young, the working class and members of ethnic minorities are all less politically engaged than average. Nevertheless, their effect is cumulative: multivariate analysis of the survey data shows that each of these differences is significant even if all the others are controlled for. In general terms, if one were to attempt to delineate the most under-privileged, poor and politically inactive group in British society, one would also identify those to whom 'Magna Carta' means least. Nevertheless, age is easily the strongest explanatory factor.

We also found some striking patterns by regular newspaper readership, although these must be treated with caution, as subsample sizes are small. Regular readers of the *Daily Telegraph* were by far the most knowledgeable group in the sample: 62% knew that King John had agreed Magna Carta and 49% that it happened at Runnymede, with 72% able to answer at least one of the three quiz questions correctly, double the national average. Scores were also high among readers of the other broadsheets (*The Times*, 56%; *Guardian*, 52%; *Independent*, 51%) and higher than average for *Daily Mail* readers (43%).

TABLE 2. *Levels of Knowledge about Magna Carta*

| | Awareness | Knowledge ('Quiz questions') | | | |
	Claim to have heard of Magna Carta	Correctly named thirteenth century or 1215	Correctly named King John	Correctly named Runnymede	At least one question right
All	86%	22%	23%	21%	36%
Men	89%	27%	28%	26%	43%
Women	83%	17%	18%	16%	30%
18–24	61%	9%	7%	4%	12%
25–34	78%	15%	10%	7%	20%
35–54	89%	19%	22%	18%	34%
55+	95%	32%	35%	37%	54%
ABC1 ('middle class')	91%	27%	29%	24%	42%
C2DE ('working class')	80%	16%	16%	18%	29%
England & Wales	87%	22%	24%	22%	38%
Scotland	80%	17%	14%	8%	20%
White	88%	22%	24%	23%	38%
Ethnic minority	68%	16%	10%	7%	21%

Base for awareness question: 2,008 GB adults aged 18+, 20–24 October 2012 and 10–12 May 2014.
Base for knowledge questions: 1,005 GB adults aged 18+, 20–24 October 2012 (assuming those who had not heard of Magna Carta would be unable to answer the quiz questions correctly).

Those who read no title regularly – who include those who vary their choice as well as those who eschew papers entirely – were in line with the national average of 35%. Scores for the other tabloids were lower (31% of *Express* readers, 30% for the *Mirror*, 28% for the *Daily Star* and 24% for the *Sun*), but least knowledgeable of all – admittedly on a very low sample size – were readers of the *Metro*, only 17% of whom could answer any of the questions, while 42% of them had never heard of Magna Carta at all.

What explains these patterns of knowledge? We should note that the differences discussed here are not peculiar to knowledge of Magna Carta. In fact, for all four of the better-known British documents in the recognition question – Magna Carta, Domesday Book, the Lindisfarne Gospels and the King James Bible – some elements of the demographic pattern of claimed knowledge were broadly similar. In terms of age, respondents 18–34, and especially those 18–24, were significantly less likely to say they had heard of any of these than were their older counterparts. Men were also more likely than women to be aware of all four documents, although for Domesday Book the difference was very small, and middle class (ABC1) respondents were more likely to say they had heard of each than were those from working class (C2DE) backgrounds.[7]

For the difference between Scotland and the rest of the country, however, the pattern is more complex. The difference is bigger for recognition of Magna Carta than for the other three documents: while 20% of Scots have not heard of Magna Carta, compared to 13% in England and Wales, 16% have not heard of Domesday Book (compared to 12%), and 61% have not heard of the Lindisfarne Gospels (compared to 57%). In the case of the King James Bible, knowledge is fractionally higher in Scotland, where 27% say they have not heard of it, than elsewhere in Britain, where the figure is 30%. These figures are perhaps readily understandable in that, strictly speaking, none of Magna Carta, Domesday Book or the Lindisfarne Gospels are part of Scottish history, since all date from centuries before the Union with England. The King James Bible, by contrast, was produced while James VI & I was King of both Scotland and England. Assuming that knowledge acquired at school is an important source of awareness of Magna Carta, lower levels of knowledge are

---

[7]   This coincidence in demographic patterns of knowledge is not simply because the same people are knowledgeable in each case. In fact, although the proportions of the population claiming to have heard of Domesday Book and of Magna Carta are very similar, the overlap between the two groups is surprisingly low: 80% of the public have heard of both and 6% of neither, but 8% have heard of Domesday Book and not Magna Carta, while 6% have heard of Magna Carta and not Domesday Book. In other words, almost half of those who have not heard of Domesday Book have, nevertheless, heard of Magna Carta, and more than half of those ignorant of Magna Carta have at least heard of Domesday Book.

to be expected in Scotland, where any medieval history taught would be Scottish rather than English.

It is undoubtedly tempting to put the differences in knowledge by age down to changing fashions in history teaching. However, there are other possibilities. A pattern of lower knowledge and engagement among the young is familiar from many surveys on other political and social topics where the question of differences in schooling do not arise. Indeed, the normal presumption in such cases would be that differences reflect increased attention and receptiveness to information as adults grow older. There are, in fact, some reasons to doubt the generational explanation in the case of Magna Carta.

As already mentioned, MORI asked the British public a very similar question on the recognition of historical documents, using a different list of documents but with several common items, in a poll for the United Nations Association in 1998. Unfortunately, the 1998 poll was part of a face-to-face survey and the differences in methodology[8] make it worthless as an indication of whether knowledge of Magna Carta has increased or decreased in the interim. In 1998, 74% said they had heard of Magna Carta compared with 85% and 87% in the more recent telephone surveys.[9] But the differences in the figures for the other documents common to both surveys, with no obvious reason to expect any significant change in public awareness over time, warn that the comparison is not valid: the U.S. Declaration of Independence was recognised by 65% in 1998 and 91% in 2012–2014, while for the Universal Declaration of Human Rights the figures were 45% and 89%, respectively.

Nevertheless, with the difference in the numbers claiming recognition of Magna Carta being comparatively small, we can draw some cautious lessons from comparing the age profile of claimed recognition in the earlier and later exercises. Allowing for the change in methodology that has increased claimed knowledge in all age groups, the pattern is rather similar across the two surveys (Table 3), and certainly shows no sign that differences in knowledge are generational rather than purely age-related.

---

[8]   The face-to-face survey used a showcard, so that respondents were shown the whole list at once and asked to pick out all answers which applied. In the telephone survey, the list was read out one item at a time and a 'yes' or 'no' answer elicited for each. The showcard method normally tends to produce lower scores, as respondents will often concentrate on picking those answers of which they are sure, omitting any borderline cases (and possibly others for which the answer should be 'yes' are simply missed through error).

[9]   The 1998 survey was presented to a sample including respondents 15–17 years of age. However, for comparability with the 2012–2014 surveys, figures given in this chapter for the 1998 survey, except in Table 4, refer only to those aged 18+. More information on the questionnaire and results can be found at http://www.ipsos-mori.com/researchpublications/researcharchive/2111/Human-Rights.aspx.

TABLE 3. *Percentages Claiming to Have Heard of Magna Carta by Age Band, 1998 and 2012/2014 Surveys*

	All	18–24	25–34	35–44	45–54	55+
2012/2014 surveys	86%	61%	78%	86%	93%	95%
1998 survey	76%	51%	69%	79%	90%	81%

TABLE 4. *Percentages Claiming to Have Heard of Magna Carta by Approximate Year of Birth, 1998 and 2012/2014 Surveys*

Year of birth	Heard of Magna Carta, 2012/14 surveys	Heard of Magna Carta, 1998 survey
1900–1920	100%	68%
1921–1925	100%	78%
1926–1930	94%	89%
1931–1935	90%	83%
1936–1940	86%	82%
1941–1945	96%	81%
1946–1950	96%	90%
1951–1955	99%	91%
1956–1960	97%	77%
1961–1965	91%	77%
1966–1970	91%	68%
1971–1975	91%	62%
1976–1980	77%	47%
1981–1985*	78%	42%
1986–1990	70%	
1991–1996	60%	

* Note that those in the 1981–1985 group in the 1998 survey were aged 15–17 when completing the survey, an age group not included in the 2012–2014 surveys.

The same point is perhaps made more clearly if we directly compare the responses of cohorts rather than of age groups. Table 4 shows the percentage of respondents born in each five-year period[10] claiming to have heard of Magna Carta in each of the two surveys.

---

[10] Strictly speaking, this is an approximation, since respondents were asked their age at last birthday but not their date of birth: year of birth was simply taken as being survey year minus current age.

This does not seem to show evidence of a persistent generational, as opposed to age, effect. It is true that in both surveys there is a definite step change between those born in 1971–1975 and those born in 1976–1980; but in the earlier survey there is also a clear distinction between the 1971–1975 cohort and their more knowledgeable older counterparts, whereas the same is not the case in the 2012/2014 surveys, and the very clear difference that was evident between those born in the early and late 1950s which that was apparent in the 1998 survey has completely disappeared in the more recent one.

Although not conclusive, these results do rather suggest that the changing curriculum argument may be something of a red herring, and that the differences in knowledge merely reflect a more permanent pattern of greater knowledge and greater interest by age.

The Content of Magna Carta

The next survey question to be considered asked respondents which of a list of nine rights they thought Magna Carta guaranteed. The list with which they were presented was a mixture of items, some of which are unambiguously either included or not included in Magna Carta but others which are less specific and perhaps more debateable.

The purpose of this question was not merely as a further test of factual knowledge. For some respondents, answers may owe more to a general impression of Magna Carta's historical significance and consequences than to any memories, accurate or inaccurate, of its precise provisions. We are less concerned with establishing whether answers are right or wrong than with a general impression of the subjects dealt with by Magna Carta, which will give us an indication of its influence, both direct and symbolic, today. For example, it plainly did not guarantee 'democracy' in any modern sense, but it is nevertheless widely held to be one of the foundations on which democracy came to be built in later centuries, and we are therefore interested to see the extent to which this is one of the advances Magna Carta symbolises to the British public.

This question was included in both of the recent surveys (for the whole sample in 2012 and for half the sample in 2014) but asked in each case only to those of the group who said they had heard of Magna Carta. In 2012, this followed the three quiz questions; in 2014, it came immediately after the 'Have you heard of . . . ?' question. Those taking part in the 2014 survey tended to pick more of the items from the list than those in 2012 (3.3 of the 9 on average, compared to 3.0 in 2012), with the result that all the items' scores were higher in 2014 than in 2012, but the pattern of positive answers was very similar across the two surveys (Table 5).

TABLE 5. *Rights Believed to Be Guaranteed by Magna Carta*

Q: Which, if any, of these rights do you think the Magna Carta guaranteed?

	Total	2012	2014	18–24	25–34	35–54	55+
The rule of law	64%	60%	70%	72%	56%	64%	64%
The right to trial by jury of your peers	51%	49%	55%	52%	50%	47%	55%
Democracy	40%	38%	44%	56%	35%	37%	40%
Basic human rights	38%	35%	44%	56%	34%	34%	39%
Freedom of speech	37%	36%	41%	45%	35%	32%	41%
Freedom from arbitrary arrest	32%	30%	36%	47%	33%	29%	31%
Freedom of religion	28%	25%	32%	29%	23%	27%	30%
The right to vote	25%	21%	31%	45%	26%	21%	23%
Equal rights for women	12%	9%	17%	13%	9%	10%	14%
Didn't guarantee any rights (volunteered)	2%	2%	2%	0%	3%	1%	3%
Don't know	11%	12%	8%	8%	15%	11%	9%

Base: 887 GB adults aged 18+ who had heard of Magna Carta, 20–24 October 2012; 454, 10–12 May 2014.

In general terms, the answers suggest a reasonable but by no means flawless public grasp of what Magna Carta contained and a general but vague impression of it as a document related to issues of law or justice. The rule of law and the right to trial by jury were comfortably the most frequently picked options on both occasions, each selected by half or more of those who had heard of Magna Carta. Similarly, the right to vote and equal rights for women were at the bottom of both lists. Nevertheless, even the most frequently selected (and correct) answer was chosen by only two-thirds, and quite substantial numbers picked historically wrong answers: accurate understanding of Magna Carta is far short of universal. It was also noticeable that far fewer are apparently aware that Magna Carta provided against arbitrary arrest – perhaps because not all respondents are sure of the meaning of 'arbitrary' – and indeed that more guessed that Magna Carta protected freedom of speech than that it prevented arbitrary arrest.

As with the name recognition and quiz questions, we found very substantial differences in answers by age, with younger people, especially respondents 18–24, much less able to distinguish accurately between those rights that were and those that were not guaranteed by Magna Carta. In particular, they were much more likely than their older counterparts to suppose that Magna Carta provided for a right to vote; in fact, there was little to choose between the 45% who said that this right and freedom of speech were guaranteed by Magna Carta and the 52% who more reasonably mentioned the right to trial by jury. On the other hand, even among the youngsters, the association with the rule of law was far and away the most frequent choice, and equal rights for women much the rarest one, so their answers were not entirely lacking in some correct historical perspective.

As might be expected, those who were more knowledgeable about how Magna Carta was agreed were also better informed about the rights it guaranteed. Therefore, the admittedly trivial quiz questions seem to have proved a relevant indicator of wider understanding. Matching up the answers of participants in the 2012 survey who were asked the quiz questions as well as this question on its content, we find that of those who got none of the three quiz questions correct, only 41% thought Magna Carta included a right to trial by jury and 25% freedom from arbitrary arrest. Of those scoring 3 out of 3 on the quiz, 71% picked trial by jury and 47% freedom from arbitrary arrest; conversely, 40% of those doing worst on the quiz guessed that Magna Carta guaranteed freedom of speech, while for the high scorers the number was only 15%. The low scorers were also much more likely to suggest than anybody else that Magna Carta included provisions on the right to vote and equal rights for women, but even for this group these were well down on the list, suggesting that at the very least most of them are able to identify such concepts as comparatively modern developments and recognise that Magna Carta dates from an earlier period. It is notable too that 'the rule of law' was picked even by 57% of those who knew none of the historical facts – almost half as many again as went for any of the other options – suggesting that among those whose ideas about Magna Carta are very hazy there is still some genuine association between its name and this most fundamental of constitutional principles.

Importance to the Public of the Magna Carta Rights

Finally, in the 2014 survey, half the respondents were asked to pick from a list of eight rights the 'two or three' they felt were most important for a civilised society.[11] (The list was the same one used in the previous question except that

---

[11] Because a split sample was used, respondents were asked *either* which rights they thought appeared in Magna Carta *or* which they thought were most important, but not both. Therefore nobody had been prompted in any particular direction by having Magna Carta drawn to their attention first. (They had been asked whether they had heard of Magna Carta but also whether they had heard of the Universal Declaration of Human Rights and the U.S. Declaration of

Roger Mortimore

TABLE 6. *Perceived Importance of Human Rights*

Q: I am going to read out a list of rights that might be considered basic human rights. Which two or three of these, if any, do you think are most important for a civilised society?

	All	Heard of Magna Carta	Not heard of Magna Carta
	%	%	%
Freedom of speech	62	61	72
Equal rights for women	59	74	56
Democracy	39	42	25
The right to vote	39	38	44
The rule of law	33	35	23
Freedom of religion	30	31	29
The right to trial by jury of your peers	28	30	17
Freedom from arbitrary arrest	19	22	4
None of these	*	*	*
Don't know	1	2	1

Base: 503 GB adults aged 18+, 10–12 May 2014

'basic human rights' was omitted, being too ambiguous and too leading to include in an attitudinal question.) The results (Table 6) were striking.

Two of the eight options, 'freedom of speech' and 'equal rights for women', emerged well ahead of the other six, each picked as important by around 3 in 5, while the next most popular options scored only 2 in 5. Neither of these rights, of course, appeared in Magna Carta or was effectively protected in any European society until centuries after it. But 'democracy' and 'the right to vote' are closely related, and only a minority of those who chose either one of these also chose the other. If we interpret those choosing either of these options as meaning roughly the same thing, we find that 'democracy/right to vote' was named by 63% of the sample, edging it just ahead of freedom of speech into first place. This puts into even starker contrast the low scores of the three core Magna Carta rights on the list. In fact, these three occupied three of the bottom four positions (with freedom of religion being the fourth). Apparently, just 1 Briton in 5 feels that freedom from arbitrary arrest is one of the most important rights in a civilised society.

Independence, so although the general topic of human rights had already been raised with them, it was not in any particular historical or national context.)

Tellingly, there were only minor variations between different demographic groups in the relative priorities they gave to different rights; answers to this question show much stronger signs of a consensus amounting to a common national culture than do those to any of the knowledge questions. Perhaps understandably, equal rights for women was judged of higher importance by women (66%) than by men (51%), but even men placed it second in the list by a very wide margin over democracy, which was in third place. Freedom of speech and equal rights for women were the two most frequently chosen options in all age groups, although democracy was not far behind women's rights among the oldest group. Freedom from arbitrary arrest was almost always in last place, even though it had a slightly higher priority than freedom of religion among respondents 45–54 years of age (which may be no more than sampling error given the small numbers in each age group). One notable difference was that freedom from arbitrary arrest was a higher priority for ethnic minority (29%) than white (17%) respondents.

However, there were more dramatic differences between those who had and those who had not heard of Magna Carta, though again we must be cautious, as the latter group was a small one. Those who had not heard of the document were much less likely to pick any of the three core Magna Carta rights than those who had: 23% compared to 35% on the importance of the rule of law, 17% as against 30% on the right to trial by a jury of one's peers and, extraordinarily, just 4% compared to 22% on freedom from arbitrary arrest. (Note, however, that even those who *had* heard of Magna Carta put these three items in the three of the four last places.)

There are several possible explanations for this difference. It may be that the phraseology of the options (chosen to ensure clarity in the corresponding question on recognising the elements included in Magna Carta) was simply over-complicated and that what was meant by 'arbitrary' arrest and a jury 'of your peers' was not always understood. If so, this might be because those who were aware of Magna Carta were also the groups who in general terms were probably more knowledgeable and better educated – certainly more politically engaged – and therefore better equipped to make sense of the questions. But it may also be that their understanding of the concepts arose directly from their knowledge of Magna Carta and that in learning about the historical event and document they also learned about the meaning of the issues it covered. Alternatively, having learned about Magna Carta may in itself have instilled some belief in the importance of the concepts involved as well as promoting understanding of them. Finally, the difference may be unrelated either to knowledge of Magna Carta as such or to comprehension of the terms used in the question, but simply indicate that those with greater political sophistication are more likely to have deliberated in the past over questions such as the importance of different human rights and in some cases have reached different conclusions from the top-of-the-mind reactions that are elicited from those considering the matter for the first time.

The point should be made, of course, that what is elicited by this question is not in any sense a comprehensive measurement of all the rights that the public think important; rather, it relates specifically to the list of options with which they were presented (which within the compass of a single poll was necessarily of limited length). Moreover, the wish to use the same list as in the corresponding question on the content of Magna Carta to some extent dictated what could be included. As a result, all the rights between which respondents were asked to choose were essentially institutional ones, political or judicial, and mostly concerned with process rather than socio-economic rights: thus we were able to compare ancient rights to modern rights and arguably those rights that establish a civilised society to those which are predicated on its existence, but not rights of process to socio-economic ones. Other research into public attitudes consistently shows that the public tend to be more concerned with outcome than with process and to put a high value on socio-economic rights as well as political ones. For example, a 1995 survey found that the public put the 'right to hospital treatment on the NHS within a reasonable time' ahead of the 'right to a fair trial before a jury' as priorities to be included in any British Bill of Rights.[12] Nor, indeed, does polling find anything more than latent interest in constitutional reform or a Bill of Rights, even when widespread discontent arises over specific issues: most of the public do not think in such terms, being concerned with the correction of specific grievances but rarely interested in details of the process by which this might be achieved. It would be valuable if further research were able to evaluate attitudes to a wider range of rights and to place the rights established by Magna Carta more completely into context, as well as to explore more fully how the concept of 'rights' as understood by the public coincides with that concept as understood by a lawyer or by a politician of whatever persuasion.

Nevertheless, within its own scope our poll enables us to make an interesting comparison, and the public's answers clearly favour the more modern rights over those which can be directly traced to Magna Carta. Should we conclude that the British public genuinely put a low priority on the rights which Magna Carta asserted? It must be remembered that answers in any opinion poll can only reflect the opinions that the respondent is able to

---

[12] MORI *State of the Nation* survey for the Joseph Rowntree Reform Trust, 21 April–8 May 1995, http://www.ipsos-mori.com/researchpublications/researcharchive/2753/State-of-the-Nation-Survey-1995.aspx (accessed 28 July 2014).

articulate at the time of interview. If the questions cover a complex question to which he or she has not previously given much consideration, they can only elicit the immediate responses that come to mind, which may not be the same as those that would have been reached by more lengthy deliberation; and these may well be influenced by context or situation. When a respondent has not discussed an issue with others in the recent past, the weight and tone of media coverage may have a powerful effect. Pollsters take care, of course, to avoid prompting respondents to interpret a question in a particular way by the content of questions they have already been asked, but even the very fact of a question being part of an opinion poll may influence respondents to interpret a question in terms of current events and political issues, or to assume that that is the context according to which they are expected to answer. We should not be surprised, therefore, to find answers about the relative importance of human rights reflecting respondents' most pressing concerns about their own society when not explicitly framed in a different context. This is well in line with the findings of past research on constitutional priorities in valuing the immediate more than the remote and the practical more than the theoretical.

The high priority given by respondents to 'freedom of speech' and 'equal rights for women', therefore, probably simply reflects that doubts about how well they are currently protected in Britain are much more widespread than fears of serious threats to the rule of law or trial by jury. Both are very much issues of modern controversy, questions of how well they are protected today – and even of how far they should be – being live issues. Freedom of speech is also, naturally, an issue of particular interest to the media and perhaps for that reason receives more coverage than would otherwise be the case. In most respects the other items, with the possible exception of 'freedom of religion', are perhaps much more likely to be taken for granted and are certainly rarely seen as being under serious threat in Britain, although anybody following foreign news from various turbulent parts of the globe should nevertheless have reason to consider their importance. This interpretation – that responses indicate the degree to which a right is seen as under threat rather than reflecting views of its true value – would probably explain why freedom from arbitrary arrest was a much higher priority for ethnic minority than for white respondents, reflecting personal or community perceptions of abuse of police powers. (The Home Secretary's announcement of an overhaul of stop-and-search powers in the light of concerns about unfair targeting of ethnic minorities had been in the news less than a fortnight before our poll was conducted.)[13]

---

[13] BBC News, 'Police Stop and Search Powers to Be Overhauled', 30 April 2014, http://www.bbc .co.uk/news/uk-27224887 (accessed 6 June 2014).

Nevertheless, the survey findings are revealing. If responses are unduly reflective of short-term political concerns, it is because the public devotes little energy to deeper consideration of such issues. On the whole, the fundamental rights on which a civilised society is built are taken for granted in modern Britain; but there is sufficient controversy or doubt over whether other rights are under threat even today to ensure that it is these that spring to mind as important. What is less clear is whether, if this were not the case, Britons would instead be exercised about the need for the rule of law in many parts of the globe where foreign news reports indicate that it is still lacking. But it certainly seems to be the case that there is no established culture that proclaims the importance of Magna Carta, emphasises the supreme significance of the rights that it asserted or stresses the historical significance of these provisions being guaranteed by law in England at such an early date.

CONCLUSION

It seems clear that while most people in Britain have heard of Magna Carta, their level of awareness falls very far short of evidence that it has a firm place in the national culture or national consciousness. Certainly, there is no sign of any widely accepted understanding on the level of shared myth, such as presumably exists around historical events and people to which popular film and television (or even Shakespeare) have turned their attention – for example, Richard III, the Battle of Hastings or the Six Wives of Henry VIII. That less than a quarter of the public identify Magna Carta with the reign of King John argues the lack of any commonly shared narrative even on the superficial and misleading basis that we might expect to find in such cases. Magna Carta's nearest claim to a place in popular culture is probably the *Hancock's Half Hour* reference; but if that resonated strongly today, we might expect a much clearer public association between Magna Carta and trial by jury than we actually found.

Nor do we find any particular view of Magna Carta's content standing out, although the public are more right than wrong when asked to venture an opinion. In the absence of any pervasive source of impressions of Magna Carta in popular culture, the public's knowledge and awareness is presumably dependent to a considerable degree on what is learned at school, although – unless we accept a purely generational explanation based upon changes in the school curriculum, which our evidence does not seem to support – the higher knowledge levels of older Britons suggest that other sources of information accessed in adulthood must also play an important part in increasing knowledge beyond the school-leaving level.

The apparent lack of any national myth around the existence and significance of Magna Carta also helps explain our findings on the human rights that the British public say they consider most important. When faced with such a question, the average Briton has no mental checklist on which to draw, as might, for example, an American who reveres the U.S. Constitution; Magna Carta is arguably the obvious candidate for a similar status in Britain, but has not achieved it. In such circumstances, it is easy to understand that the most obvious answers are those which provoke the most contemporary thought by gaining the most media coverage, and also that such coverage will reflect issues over which there is controversy or rights which are perceived to be under threat (which may in its turn depend on the media's framing of its stories, particularly of foreign news in which the same story might be addressed from any number of different angles of human rights denied or unprotected). This will naturally mean that the 'importance' accorded to any right, as measured by a poll, will depend more on how urgently that right seems to need protection than on how far it is valued or to what extent the respondent would be content to lose it. In our survey, the public accorded a low priority to some of the most fundamental rights established by Magna Carta, which may mean no more than that they are forgotten because it is felt that they can be safely taken for granted.

Our findings probably indicate an important distinction between the potential for symbolic importance of Magna Carta among, on the one hand, a governing elite who are fully conscious of its significance and, on the other, a voting public with only a hazy awareness of its existence. Modern political communications rely heavily on symbolism and other shorthand rather than on detailed exposition of substance, as these can be more effective in mobilising support and swaying opinions among a voting public whose reasoning is emotional as well as deliberative and often responsive to heuristic cues. It must be doubtful whether current public awareness of Magna Carta itself is high enough for it to be a powerful symbol already, and the low 'knee-jerk' priority given to the rights it embodies may prevent it from being immediately repositioned as such. David Cameron's recent attempt to build a political message around the significance of Magna Carta probably communicated effectively to other politicians, but may have gone over the heads of the wider audience. On the other hand, however, the lack of strong and widely shared preconceptions about Magna Carta may make it a basis upon which a new myth could be established, with effective political leverage, in comparatively short order; but, if so, there can be no guarantee how far any newly acquired political symbolism will correspond to the historical reality.

PART 2

INFLUENCE AROUND THE WORLD

5

The Troublesome Inheritance of Americans in Magna Carta and Trial by Jury

Renée Lettow Lerner

The United States is famously a nation founded on universal principles, not on blood. At least, that is the theory proclaimed today. Many American colonists and revolutionaries had a different view: they thought of their rights as an ancient inheritance based on their blood. Instead of declaring the universal rights of man, as French revolutionaries later did, Americans often insisted on their inheritance as Englishmen. At every opportunity in proclaiming their liberties, they harped on their ancestors and their descendants – fathers, children, posterity and so on. For the most part, they did not mean spiritual ancestors or descendants; they meant flesh and blood.[1] The transformation from blood descent to spiritual descent came later, expressed most eloquently by Abraham Lincoln drawing on the words of the Declaration of Independence.[2]

---

[1] John Jay in The Federalist No. 2 emphasised the common blood of Americans as a basis for forming the new nation: 'Providence has been pleased to give this one connected country to one united people – a people descended from the same ancestors, speaking the same language, professing the same religion, attached to the same principles of government, very similar in their manners and customs, and who, by their joint counsels, arms, and efforts, fighting side by side throughout a long and bloody war, have nobly established their general liberty and independence.' The Federalist No. 2 (John Jay) (1787), reprinted in Clinton Rossiter (ed.), *The Federalist Papers* (New York: Penguin, 1961), 38. The preamble to the U.S. Constitution also uses the language of descent: 'We the people of the United States, in order to . . . secure the blessings of liberty to ourselves and our posterity, do ordain and establish this Constitution for the United States of America.'

[2] Abraham Lincoln, Speech at Chicago, Illinois, 10 July 1858, in Roy P. Basler et al. (eds.), *The Collected Works of Abraham Lincoln*, 9 vols. (New Brunswick, NJ: Rutgers University Press, 1953), vol. II, 499–500.

'We find a race of men living in that day [1776] whom we claim as our fathers and grandfathers. . . . We have besides these men – descended by blood from our ancestors – among us perhaps half our people who are not descendants at all of these men, they are men who come from Europe – German, Irish, French and Scandinavian – men that have come from Europe themselves, or whose ancestors have come hither and settled here, finding themselves our equals in all things. If they look back through this history to trace their

77

At the time of independence, many Americans believed that this inheritance was unchanging from ancient times, from 'time immemorial'. No king or parliament could rightfully alter this birthright of the English people. The body of this inheritance was the fundamental laws of England, especially as expressed in Magna Carta. Magna Carta was pre-eminent as an embodiment of the fundamental law because its antiquity demonstrated the endurance of the inheritance. To early Americans, Magna Carta not only symbolised the general idea of a government constrained by a formal charter, but it described specific rights. The right Americans most often invoked in connection with the Great Charter was the right to trial by jury. The barons at Runnymede certainly did not intend to enshrine common law trial by jury, which hardly existed in 1215. In linking Magna Carta with jury trial, Americans were following a line of thought that had begun in the late Tudor period with antiquarians interested in tracing the ancient constitution of England, in many cases back to the Anglo-Saxons. Edward Coke and others in the seventeenth century celebrated this link between Magna Carta and jury trial in their battles against royal prerogative.

Over time, trial by jury proved to be a troublesome inheritance. Americans of the colonial and revolutionary era exalted the jury as a means of furthering self-governance and nullifying despised British laws. In their enthusiasm for the jury, Americans put the translated words of Article 29 of Magna Carta directly into many of their new constitutions.[3] After Americans had created representative republics, however, the self-governing and law-nullifying functions of the jury came to seem unnecessary at best and often harmful. Increasingly, judges and legislators criticised the jury for its expense, delay and unpredictability.

The tone and content of judicial opinions reflected this change in attitudes towards the jury. Judicial opinions in the early republic continued the colonial and revolutionary rhetoric of an ancient blood inheritance in Magna Carta

connection with those days by blood, they find they have none, they cannot carry themselves back into that glorious epoch and make themselves feel that they are part of us, but when they look through that old Declaration of Independence they find that those old men say that "We hold these truths to be self-evident, that all men are created equal," and then they feel that that moral sentiment taught in that day evidences their relation to those men, that it is the father of all moral principle in them, and that they have a right to claim it as though they were blood of the blood, and flesh of the flesh, of the men who wrote that Declaration, and so they are. That is the electric cord in that Declaration that links the hearts of Patriotic and liberty-loving men together, that will link those patriotic hearts as long as the love of freedom exists in the minds of men throughout the world.'

[3] I will refer to this passage as Article 29, following the reissuance of 1225 rather than the original version of 1215, in which the passage appears as Article 39. Blackstone and many American sources use the numbering of the reissuance of 1225.

and interpreted the language of the Great Charter as a source of specific rules concerning the jury. In the nineteenth century, judges still praised Magna Carta but dropped references to ancestors and inheritance. Magna Carta lost its specific import and became a vague symbol of limited government. Judges and legislators gradually curtailed the power of juries, but they were never able fully to replace them. The fate of trial by jury in America suggests the hazards of enshrining certain specific procedural rights in constitutions. England, with the flexibility of an unwritten constitution, was able effectively to abolish the civil jury and to substitute bench trial, a form of adjudication more suited to a commercial age.

THE ANCIENT RIGHTS OF ENGLISHMEN AND THE INHERITANCE OF AMERICANS IN MAGNA CARTA

Edward Coke, writing amid the constitutional controversies of the early seventeenth century, was the most influential exponent of the idea of an English inheritance based on descent and consisting of 'fundamental laws'.[4] In Coke's view, this inheritance was static and from time immemorial: it preceded the Norman Conquest and endured to Coke's day.[5] According to the fundamental laws, expressed in Magna Carta and other sources, the king could not take property from or imprison his subjects without due process of law. The law of the land specified what process was due, and its most important component was the common law of England.[6]

English speakers in the seventeenth and eighteenth centuries held different views about the extent to which these rights applied outside of England. Although Coke himself did not believe that the full panoply of rights extended beyond England, English settlers in overseas colonies made the argument that they did.[7] Colonial charters encouraged this belief. The first charter to the

---

[4] Edward Coke, *The Reports of Sir Edward Coke, Knt. In Thirteen Parts Reprinted in New Edition*, 13 vols. (London: Joseph Butterworth and Son, 1826), vol. V, v (Preface) (first published 1605); Edward Coke, *Commons Debates 1628* (19 March–April 1628), Robert C. Johnson and Maija Jansson Cole (eds.), 4 vols. (New Haven: Yale University Press, 1977), vol. II, 357–58; Daniel J. Hulsebosch, 'The Ancient Constitution and the Expanding Empire: Sir Edward Coke's British Jurisprudence', *Law and History Review* 21 (2003): 470.

[5] J. G. A. Pocock, *The Ancient Constitution and the Feudal Law: A Study of English Historical Thought in the Seventeenth Century* (Cambridge: Cambridge University Press, 1957, reissued 1987), 35–36, 42–53, 125–26; Herbert Butterfield, *Magna Carta in the Historiography of the Sixteenth and Seventeenth Centuries* (Reading: University of Reading, 1969), 11, 22.

[6] Edward Coke, *The Second Part of the Institutes of the Laws of England* (London: M. Fleffer and R. Young, 1642), 46.

[7] *Calvin v. Smith*, 7 Coke's Rep. 1a; 77 Eng. Rep. 377, 401 (K.B. 1608); Hulsebosch, 'Ancient Constitution', 456–57.

Virginia Company in 1606 declared that every subject of the king living in the British colonies, and 'every of their children' born there, 'shall have and enjoy all Liberties, Franchises, and Immunities . . . to all Intents and Purposes, as if they had been abiding and born, within this our Realm of England. . . .'[8] The earlier letters patent for the settlement of Virginia issued to Sir Humphrey Gilbert in 1578 and to Sir Walter Raleigh in 1584 contained similar language.[9] And many later charters for the American colonies repeated the language.[10] In their original context, the clauses probably required equal treatment of the king's natural subjects within England, and possibly within other dominions as well.[11] At the outer limit, following Coke's most generous writings concerning overseas dominions, the language may have meant that English settlers were entitled to some rights, such as common law tenures, in the colonies.[12] In the mid eighteenth century, William Blackstone agreed with many English jurists in stating that the common law of England had 'no allowance or authority' in the American colonies; as conquered lands, the American colonies were under the control of Parliament.[13] American colonists, however, argued that their lands were settled, not conquered, and that they had inherited all the rights of Englishmen.[14]

In this inheritance, Magna Carta had pride of place. As the English constitutional struggles of the seventeenth century continued, Americans added other sources of fundamental law: the Petition of Right of 1628, the Habeas

[8] William MacDonald, *Select Charters and Other Documents Illustrative of American History, 1606–1775* (New York: Macmillan Company, 1910), 2.

[9] Wilfred J. Ritz, Book Review, 'The Road from Runnymede, Magna Carta and Constitutionalism in America, A. E. Dick Howard', *Washington and Lee Law Review* 26 (1969): 413–14.

[10] See colonial charters collected in Francis N. Thorpe (ed.), *The Federal and State Constitutions, Colonial Charters, and Other Organic Laws of the United States of America* (Washington, DC: U.S. Government Printing Office, 1909).

[11] Hulsebosch, 'Ancient Constitution', 476.

[12] Ibid.

[13] William Blackstone, *Commentaries on the Laws of England*, 4 vols. (Oxford: Clarendon Press, 1765), vol. I, 105–06.

[14] The colonists officially declared these views in the Resolutions of the Stamp Act Congress of 1765 and the Declaration and Resolves of the First Continental Congress in 1774. William F. Swindler, '"Rights of Englishman" since 1776: Some Anglo-American Notes', *University of Pennsylvania Law Review* 124 (1976): 1089–90. State legislatures made similar declarations. See, e.g., 'Resolves of the Maryland House of Delegates', printed in the *Maryland Gazette* (3 October 1765), Resolve I: 'Resolved unanimously, That the first Adventurers and Settlers of this Province of Maryland, brought with them, and transmitted to their Posterity, and all other his Majesty's Subjects since inhabiting in this Province, all the Liberties, Privileges, Franchises, and Immunities, that at any Time have been held, enjoyed, and possessed, by the People of Great-Britain.' For a favourable legal analysis of the colonists' position, see Barbara A. Black, 'The Constitution of Empire: The Case for the Colonists', *University of Pennsylvania Law Review* 124 (1976): 1198–203.

Corpus Act of 1679, the Bill of Rights of 1689 and the Act of Settlement of 1701.[15] Magna Carta, however, retained its primary hold on the American imagination. To an astonishing extent, the American colonists printed, distributed, invoked and formally enacted passages from Magna Carta.[16]

Thomas Jefferson's views about the immemorial English constitution, which were widespread among educated colonists, help to explain American devotion to Magna Carta. Jefferson imbibed early – and promoted energetically – the idea that the ancient English constitution and common law were legacies of the Anglo-Saxons.[17] Central to this ancient English constitution and common law was a primitive democracy supposedly embodied in such 'free' institutions as the folk moot and trial by jury. The Normans imposed feudalism and temporarily deformed these rights, but the ancient rights were restored in Magna Carta.[18] The constitutional battles of the seventeenth century were further examples of the English asserting their rights against tyrants. American saw themselves in a continuation of this struggle to preserve the ancient rights of Englishmen against usurpers.

As tensions built between the North Atlantic colonies and Britain, American invocations of Magna Carta became more aggressive. On a four-dollar bill printed in Maryland in July 1775, a woodcut depicts the figure of 'Liberty' handing a petition to 'Britannia', who is restrained by King George III, shown trampling Magna Carta (and, for good measure, setting fire to the port of Annapolis).[19] William Drayton of South Carolina, who had been educated at Westminster School and Balliol College, Oxford, declared his allegiance to the revolutionary cause in a famous pamphlet in 1774:

> That the Americans being descended from the same Ancestors with the people of England, and owing fealty to the same Crown, are therefore equally with them, entitled to the common law of England formed by their common Ancestors; and to all and singular the benefits, rights, liberties and claims specified in Magna Charta, in the Petition of Rights, in the Bill of Rights, and

[15] Blackstone's list of the fundamental laws of England that comprise 'the absolute rights of every Englishman', in the first chapter of the first book of his Commentaries, includes these and several more. Blackstone, Commentaries, vol. I, 120–41.

[16] H. D. Hazeltine, 'Magna Carta and the U.S. Constitution', in Henry E. Malden (ed.), Magna Carta Commemoration Essays (London: Royal Historical Society, 1917); Ritz, Book Review, 409–12; A. E. Dick Howard, The Road to Runnymede: Magna Carta and Constitutionalism in America (Charlottesville: University of Virginia Press, 1968), 13.

[17] H. Trevor Colbourn, The Lamp of Experience: Whig History and the Intellectual Origins of the American Revolution (Chapel Hill: University of North Carolina Press, 1965), 158–84; Stanley R. Hauer, 'Thomas Jefferson and the Anglo-Saxon Language', PMLA 98 (1983): 880–81.

[18] Hauer, 'Thomas Jefferson', 880.

[19] Four-dollar-bill, Maryland Provincial Currency, issued 26 July 1775, Maryland State Archives, Annapolis, MD, Vosloh Collection, SC 1267.

in the Act of Settlement. They being no more, than principally *declaratory of the grounds* of the fundamental laws of England.[20]

Many Americans claimed they had an inheritance, and were not giving it up without a fight.

Why did Americans make such a fuss over their inheritance, their birthright, in Magna Carta? It meant more to them than the comfort of belonging to an ancient tradition. Magna Carta had come to mean certain general ideas of governance, but also specific rights.

There was, of course, the general idea of Magna Carta as a sort of constitution protecting liberties, a fundamental law that endured. This was the sense in which Governor John Winthrop of Massachusetts used the term when he described the decision to draft a Body of Liberties for the colony, 'in resemblance to a Magna Carta'.[21] The colonial charters often referred to the 'Great Charter' as their model. This idea helped lead to the written constitutions of the independent states and the federal government. Such a fixed law had the virtue of limiting the power of the executive, which could become arbitrary and tyrannical. As Winthrop put it, without such a law, there could be 'great danger to our State in regard that our magistrates for want of positive law in many cases might proceed according to their discretion'.[22] Magna Carta's origins as a set of concessions from the king and limitations on royal prerogative resonated with Americans even more in the 1760s and 1770s, because they viewed themselves as engaged in a similar struggle with the Crown. As the revolutionary woodcut described previously suggests – and as the long list of accusations specifically against the King in the Declaration of Independence makes clear – in many American minds, George III had become a proxy for everything wrong with the British government.

But Magna Carta was not only, in the view of Americans, the symbol of general principles of constitutional government and the rule of law. It was also a source of specific rights. Colonial interpretations, sometimes following English ones, could be far from the understanding of the barons at Runnymede. Americans found the principle of no taxation without representation in Magna Carta.[23] One of the most prominent rights Americans found

[20] William Henry Drayton, 'A letter from freeman of South-Carolina, to the deputies of North-America, assembled in the high court of Congress at Philadelphia' (Charleston: Peter Timothy, 10 August 1774), 11–12. This passage occurs in the section of the pamphlet titled 'The American Claim of Rights', which is sometimes cited as the title of the pamphlet.

[21] John Winthrop, *The Journal of John Winthrop, 1630–1649*, Richard S. Dunn et al. (eds.) (Cambridge, MA: Belknap Press, 1996), 146.

[22] Ibid.

[23] The reasoning of the Maryland House of Delegates in 1765, during the Stamp Act controversy, is illustrative. 'Resolves of the Maryland House of Delegates', printed in the *Maryland Gazette*

in Magna Carta was that of trial by jury. Article 29 of Magna Carta was printed, invoked and enacted more than any other passage.

> No freeman shall be taken and imprisoned or disseised of any free tenement or of his liberties or free customs, or outlawed, or exiled, or in any other way destroyed; nor will we go upon him nor send upon him, except by the lawful judgment of his peers or by the law of the land.
> To no one will we sell, to no one will we refuse or delay, right or justice.[24]

During and shortly after the American Revolution, many states put a version of this language into their new constitutions. These states included Virginia (1776),[25] North Carolina (1776),[26] Delaware (1776),[27] Maryland (1776),[28] New York (1777),[29] South Carolina (1778),[30] Massachusetts

(3 October 1765). First, the House resolved, 'it was granted by Magna Charta, and other the good Laws and Statutes of England', that the subject should not be compelled to contribute to any tax 'not set by common Consent of Parliament'. The charter granted to Lord Baltimore to encourage immigration to Maryland stated that the king would not lay taxes on the colony. Marylanders had always been governed by laws made by the colonial legislature concerning taxes and internal policy, and therefore they had consented to these laws. The freemen of Maryland were not represented in the British Parliament. The House concluded that only the legislature of Maryland had power to lay taxes on the colony and that any other attempt to do so was 'UNCONSTITUTIONAL, and a direct VIOLATION of the RIGHTS of the FREEMEN of this Province'.

[24] Translation in Faith Thompson, *Magna Carta: Its Role in the Making of the English Constitution 1300–1629* (Minneapolis: University of Minnesota Press, 1948), 68.

[25] Virginia Constitution of 1776, § 8 ('no man be deprived of his liberty, except by the law of the land or the judgment of his peers').

[26] North Carolina Constitution of 1776, § XII ('That no freeman ought to be taken, imprisoned, or disseized of his freehold liberties or privileges, or outlawed, or exiled, or in any manner destroyed, or deprived of his life, liberty, or property, but by the law of the land.').

[27] Delaware Bill of Rights of 1776 ('That every freeman for every injury done him in his goods, lands, or person, by any other person, ought to have remedy by the course of the law of the land, and ought to have justice and right for the injury done to him, freely without sale, fully without any denial, and speedily without delay, according to the law of the land.').

[28] Maryland Constitution of 1776, § XVII ('That every freeman, for any injury done him in his person or property, ought to have remedy, by the course of the law of the land, and ought to have justice and right freely without sale, fully without any denial, and speedily without delay, according to the law of the land.'); id. § XXI ('That no freeman ought to be taken, or imprisoned, or disseized of his freehold, liberties, or privileges, or outlawed, or exiled, or in any manner destroyed, or deprived of his life, liberty, or property, but by the judgment of his peers, or by the law of the land.').

[29] New York Constitution of 1777, § 8 ('And this convention doth further, in the name and by the authority of the good people of this State, ordain, determine, and declare, that no member of this State shall be disfranchised, or deprived of any the rights or privileges secured to the subjects of this State by this constitution, unless by the law of the land, or the judgment of his peers.').

[30] South Carolina Constitution of 1778, § XLI ('That no freeman of this State be taken or imprisoned, or disseized of his freehold, liberties, or privileges, or outlawed, exiled or in any

$(1780)^{31}$ and New Hampshire $(1784).^{32}$ The Northwest Ordinance of 1787, enacted by the Continental Congress as a basic law for the governance of the Northwest Territories, included the guarantee: 'No man shall be deprived of his liberty or property, but by the judgment of his peers, or the law of the land.'[33] By invoking Magna Carta, Americans made a then-radical idea – the complete independence of former colonies – look like the continuation of an ancient tradition of rights.

ORIGINS OF THE LINK BETWEEN MAGNA CARTA AND JURY TRIAL

Americans had English precedent to follow in linking Article 29 with jury trial. The link, however, took centuries to develop. The meaning of Article 29 in 1215 concerned feudal tenures and courts, not common law jury trial. In the conflict-ridden fourteenth century, the passage became associated with certain common law procedures. It was not until the growth of antiquarianism in the late sixteenth century that the passage was connected with jury trial. That connection proved useful to Coke in the constitutional battles of the seventeenth century against the king's prerogative. With Blackstone in the mid eighteenth century, Magna Carta became the triumphant guarantee of jury trial, in effect preserving the voice of the people in legal judgments.[34]

With the language of Article 29, the barons at Runnymede could hardly have intended to guarantee common law trial by jury. Jury trial did not exist for criminal cases in 1215, and only for certain types of civil cases.[35] 'Judgment of

　　manner destroyed or deprived of his life, liberty, or property, but by the judgment of his peers or by the law of the land.').

[31]　Massachusetts Constitution of 1780, Art. VII ('And no subject shall be arrested, imprisoned, despoiled, or deprived of his property, immunities, or privileges, put out of the protection of the law, exiled, or deprived of his life, liberty, or estate, but by the judgment of his peers, or the law of the land.').

[32]　New Hampshire Constitution of 1784, § 15 ('And no subject shall be arrested, imprisoned, despoiled, or deprived of his property, immunities, or privileges, put out of the protection of the law, exiled or deprived of his life, liberty, or estate, but by the judgment of his peers or the law of the land.').

[33]　Northwest Ordinance, Art. II (13 July 1787).

[34]　Natalie Riendeau's chapter in this volume (Ch. 11) discusses this sort of myth-making concerning Magna Carta, and Craig Lerner's chapter (Ch. 8) describes the U.S. Supreme Court creating a recent myth about Magna Carta.

[35]　Frederick Pollock and Frederic W. Maitland, *The History of English Law before the Time of Edward I*, 2nd ed., 2 vols. (Cambridge: Cambridge University Press, 1898), vol. I, 144–49, 173; William S. McKechnie, *Magna Carta: A Commentary on the Great Charter of King John*, 2nd ed. (Glasgow: James Maclehose and Sons, 1914), 134; John H. Langbein, Renée Lettow Lerner and Bruce P. Smith, *History of the Common Law: The Development of Anglo-American Legal Institutions* (New York: Aspen Publishers, 2009), 58–64, 97–104.

his peers,' *per judicium parium*, appears to have meant that no one could be tried by his inferiors. Rank was determined according to feudal tenures. As a commentator on Magna Carta explained, 'the "peers" of a Crown tenant [one who held land directly from the king, typically an earl or a baron] were his fellow Crown tenants, who would normally deliver judgment in the *Curia Regis*'.[36] The 'peers' of the tenant of a mesne lord – an 'intermediate' lord, who held land from another lord who was not the king – were the fellow tenants of the mesne lord, who gave their opinion in the mesne lord's Court Baron.[37] King John had often ignored this principle and deprived his enemies of their estates or exiled them by judgment of a tribunal composed of Crown nominees.[38] The barons did not consider royal judges to be their peers.[39]

In the fourteenth century, certain understandings of Article 29 continued, and some new ones arose, that encouraged a future link to common law trial by jury. During this time of conflict between the Crown and nobles, references to Article 29 were frequent in Parliamentary petitions and statutes. Parliament enacted a later much-celebrated series of statutes referring to Magna Carta and confirming that a trial observing lawful procedures should take place before judgment, which in turn was necessary before execution.[40] The term 'freeman' was expanded to 'anyone'.[41] The term 'law of the land' became interchangeable with the new phrase 'due process of law'.[42] Due process of law was understood to include an indicting jury and procedure by original writ, and to limit the jurisdiction of prerogative courts.[43]

Beginning in the sixteenth century, English writers explicitly linked the phrase 'judgment of his peers' to jury trial and described this right as an ancient inheritance. The first to do so in print appears to have been William Lambarde in his *Eirenarcha* of 1581.[44] Lambarde was a barrister-antiquarian and a collector of Anglo-Saxon laws. In *Eirenarcha*, an enduringly popular

[36] McKechnie, *Magna Carta*, 378.
[37] This principle seems to have extended to Jews, foreign merchants, Welshmen and possibly Lord Marchers (lords given special powers to govern troublesome areas such as Wales). Ibid., 378–79. In accord with this principle, in 1302 a knight accused of a felony objected to his trial by a jury because they were not his peers. The court agreed, and a jury of knights was substituted. Y.B. 30 & 31 Ed. I, 531 (R.S. 1302). A bishop made a similar complaint, and the judges are quoted as saying, 'this challenge is usual, when a peer of the Realm is a party. . . .' Y.B. 12 & 13 Ed. III, 290–91. Both these cases are discussed in Thompson, *Magna Carta*, 70.
[38] McKechnie, *Magna Carta*, 378.
[39] Pollock and Maitland, *History of English Law*, vol. I, 173.
[40] 5 Edw. III, c. 9 (1331); 25 Edw. III, st. 5, c. 4 (1352). On this series of statutes, see Thompson, *Magna Carta*, 90–94.
[41] 25 Edw. III, st. 5, c. 4 (1352); 28 Edw. III, c. 3 (1354).
[42] 28 Edw. III, c. 3 (1354); 42 Edw. III, c. 3 (1368).
[43] 42 Edw. III, c. 3 (1368).
[44] See Thompson, *Magna Carta*, 185–86.

manual for justices of the peace, Lambarde described jury trial in criminal
cases as 'according to the antient libertie of the Lande, whereunto everie
Free bourne man thinketh himself inheritable. And thereupon it is named
(Mag. Chart. cap. 29) *Legale iudicium parium suorum*, the lawfull iudgment of
a mans own *Peeres*, or *Equalles*. . . .'[45] *Eirenarcha* was familiar to Americans,
being found in the libraries of Thomas Jefferson and George Wythe, among
others.[46]

Coke and John Selden continued the identification of Article 29 of Magna
Carta with jury trial in the seventeenth century. This link aided Coke's quest,
in his later career, to strengthen the common law courts and to limit Chancery
and the other prerogative courts, which sat without juries and were more
directly subject to royal control.[47] As Coke envisioned it, 'Upon this [Article],
as out of a roote, many fruitfull branches of the Law of England have sprung.'[48]
Coke explained this passage as requiring before seizure of a person's property
'the lawfull judgement, that is, verdict of his equals (that is, of men of his own
condition) or by the Law of the Land (that is, to speak it once for all) by the due
course, and processe of Law'.[49] Selden, in his commentaries on Fortescue's
work on English law, described *judicium parium* as 'legal judgment of his
peers or men of his condition, that is by jury'.[50]

In the mid eighteenth century, Blackstone exalted the identification of
Article 29 with the jury. He explicitly praised the jury for tempering the class
biases of judges.[51] In invoking Magna Carta, Blackstone created for the jury a
title it retained through the centuries in America – and which continues in use
today. 'In magna carta it [the jury] is more than once insisted on as *the
principal bulwark of our liberties*; but especially by chap. 29.'[52] Blackstone
lavished praise on the jury,[53] and in this he has been eagerly followed ever
since by American politicians, lawyers and judges.

---

[45] William Lambarde, *Eirenarcha, or, The Office of Justices of Peace* (London: Ra. Newbery and
H. Bynneman, 1581), 436–37.

[46] See http://lawlibrary.wm.edu/wythepedia/index.php/Eirenarcha.

[47] Butterfield, *Magna Carta*, 11, 18–19; Pocock, *Ancient Constitution*, 44–46; Maurice Ashley,
Magna Carta in the Seventeenth Century (Charlottesville: University Press of Virginia 1965),
10–11.

[48] Coke, *Second Institutes*, 46.

[49] Ibid.

[50] John Fortescue, *De Laudibus Legum Angliae*, with notes by John Selden (London: 1672),
ch. xxvi, quoted in Thompson, *Magna Carta*, 242.

[51] Blackstone, *Commentaries*, vol. III, 379.

[52] Ibid., 350 (emphasis added).

[53] See, e.g., ibid. ('a privilege of the highest and most beneficial nature'); ibid., 355 ('how
admirably this constitution [trial by jury] is adapted and framed for the investigation of truth,
beyond any other method of trial in the world'); ibid., 379 ('the glory of English law'; 'the most
transcendent privilege which any subject can enjoy').

MAGNA CARTA AND JURIES IN COLONIAL AMERICA
AND THE NEW REPUBLIC

We need to see through the rhetoric surrounding the jury right in the eighteenth century and try to understand what this devotion to the jury meant concretely. As with devotion to Magna Carta, there were general principles but also specific issues. At the heart of American fervour about the jury was that institution's ability to nullify laws. The unpopular laws that juries nullified varied over time, from seditious libel and customs laws in the colonial period to private debts in the early republic. American independence and republicanism, however, resolved the imperial tensions that had given rise to expansive claims for jury law-finding in late colonial times. After the first few decades of independence, judges and legislators increasingly criticised the expense and unpredictability of civil juries.

Concerning the criminal jury, as Alexander Hamilton remarked in The Federalist No. 83, Americans universally agreed that the institution was necessary to prevent despotism.[54] Especially, many Americans prized the criminal jury for its ability to nullify unpopular laws. One of the most prominent examples was the acquittal of the printer John Peter Zenger in 1736 in his trial for seditious libel of the colonial governor of New York.[55] American juries either refused to indict or acquitted so often in cases of seditious libel that the law essentially became a dead letter in the colonies.[56]

At the time of the revolution, American colonists' experience with civil juries, as with criminal juries, led many to value the institution as a means of nullifying the law. In the case of *Erving v. Cradock* [1761], for example, a Massachusetts merchant sued a customs inspector for trespass and won a large verdict from a jury.[57] The royal governor of Massachusetts, Francis Bernard, complained to a former governor that a 'custom house officer has no chance with a jury, let his cause be what it will'.[58] Bernard warned his superiors in

---

[54] The Federalist No. 83 (Alexander Hamilton) (1788), reprinted in Rossiter (ed.), 499.

[55] James Alexander, 'A Brief Narrative of the Case and Trial of John Peter Zenger' (1736), in Stanley N. Katz (ed.), *The Case and Trial of John Peter Zenger* (Cambridge, MA: Harvard University Press, 1989), 78, 100–01.

[56] Langbein, Lerner and Smith, *History of the Common Law*, 478–79.

[57] Governor Francis Bernard to the Lords of Trade, 6 August 1761, 2 Bernard Papers 46, 47, reprinted in Josiah Quincy, Samuel Miller Quincy and Horace Gray (eds.), *Reports of Cases Argued and Adjudged in the Superior Court of Judicature of the Province of Massachusetts* (Boston: Little, Brown, and Company, 1865), 553–55.

[58] Governor Francis Bernard to Thomas Pownall, 28 August 1761, reprinted in Quincy, *Reports of Cases*, 555–56.

London that such verdicts effectively overturned judgments of the Court of Admiralty – which sat without juries – and nullified customs laws.[59] Another colonial governor of Massachusetts wrote that 'a trial by jury here is only trying one illicit trader by his fellows, or at least by his well-wishers'.[60] Colonists viewed the jurisdiction of the juryless admiralty courts, which prevented nullification of customs laws, as a major grievance. In response to the Stamp Act of 1765, delegates from nine of the thirteen colonies met in New York the same year, a meeting known as the Stamp Act Congress.[61] They adopted a Declaration of Rights and Grievances, including '[t]hat trial by jury is the inherent and invaluable right of every British subject in these colonies. . . . [The Stamp Act] and other acts, by extending the jurisdiction of the courts of admiralty beyond its ancient limits, have a manifest tendency to subvert the rights and liberties of the colonists.'[62] The Declaration of Independence listed as a reason for separation: 'For depriving us, in many cases, of the benefits of trial by jury.'[63] The British government, in the view of many Americans, was depriving them of their birthright to jury trial in Magna Carta and thus preventing them from nullifying the hated customs laws. This view accounts for the immediate insertion of the language of Article 29 of Magna Carta into the new state constitutions.

Once the republican governments took power, however, jury nullification became deeply problematic. The people now had a say in the making of laws; they had consented to them. Why should twelve citizens have the power to nullify laws enacted by a legislature elected by the entire people? Furthermore, legislatures followed a process for enacting laws carefully specified in a written constitution, itself ratified by the people.

The Federalists publicly began to express doubts about the civil jury. The federal Constitution, drafted in 1787, did not include a right to civil jury trial in federal courts. In explaining the reasons to the public, Alexander Hamilton questioned civil jurors' ability to decide complicated issues of law and fact

---

[59] Governor Francis Bernard to the Lords of Trade, 6 August 1761, reprinted in Quincy, *Reports of Cases*, 554 ('Your Lordships will perceive that these actions have an immediate tendency to destroy the Court of Admiralty and with it the custom house, which cannot subsist without that Court.').

[60] Governor William Shirley, quoted in Stephen Botein, *Early American Law and Society* (New York: Knopf, 1983), 57.

[61] 5 Geo. 3, c. 12 (1765); C. A. Weslager, *The Stamp Act Congress: With an Exact Copy of the Complete Journal* (Newark: University of Delaware Press, 1976), 6.

[62] Resolves of the Stamp Act Congress, October 1765, in Weslager, *Stamp Act Congress*, 126. See also Drayton, 'A letter from freeman of South-Carolina', 13 (complaining of the powers of the admiralty courts).

[63] Declaration of Independence (4 July 1776), reprinted in Thorpe, *Federal and State Constitutions*, vol. I, 5.

correctly.[64] The Anti-Federalists countered with a variety of arguments. The legislature might be captured by special interests and legislate against the good of the whole.[65] The executive might use its power to reward friends or to punish political enemies.[66] The civil jury, in both England and America, had proved useful in awarding damages in trespass suits against executive officials.[67] The judiciary might be corrupt or biased in favour of elites.[68] The jury could check all of these abuses.

The specific issue underlying these arguments was the civil jury's ability to nullify debts. Debtors were a powerful political force soon after the revolution. State legislatures passed various laws that made it easier for debtors to escape creditors' demands.[69] In addition, state juries were sympathetic to debtors.[70] In contrast, the new federal Constitution contained various provisions that favoured creditors.[71] (Federalists generally thought it imperative to repay debts, for the credit and prosperity of the new nation.)[72] Anti-Federalists such as Patrick Henry of Virginia avoided openly praising the civil jury for nullifying debts, but they made the connection clear in their speeches.[73] Anti-Federalist protest succeeded in persuading a reluctant James Madison to draft a federal Bill of Rights, including a right to civil jury trial in the Seventh Amendment. Madison had argued against the need for a federal right to civil jury trial in the Virginia ratifying convention.[74] In drafting what became the

---

[64] The Federalist No. 83 (Alexander Hamilton) (1788), reprinted in Rossiter (ed.), 469–71.

[65] Matthew P. Harrington, 'The Economic Origins of the Seventh Amendment', *Iowa Law Rev.* 87 (2001): 186.

[66] Ibid., 185–86.

[67] Bradford R. Clark, 'The Eleventh Amendment and the Nature of the Union', *Harvard Law Review* 123 (2010): 1905–06; Akhil Reed Amar, 'Fourth Amendment First Principles', *Harvard Law Review* 107 (1994): 757, 775–78; David E. Engdahl, 'Immunity and Accountability for Positive Government Wrongs', *University of Colorado Law Review* 44 (1972): 1, 14, 19.

[68] See Max Farrand, *The Records of the Federal Convention of 1787*, 3 vols. (New Haven: Yale University Press, 1911), vol. II, 587 (argument of Elbridge Gerry); Harrington, 'Economic Origins', 187 (quoting arguments of Anti-Federalists). Alexander Hamilton agreed that checking the possible corruption of judges was the strongest argument in favour of civil juries. The Federalist No. 83 (Alexander Hamilton) (1788), reprinted in Rossiter (ed.), 500. He observed, however, that jurors could be corrupted as well as judges. Ibid., 500–01. Blackstone's principal argument in favour of the jury was that judges might be biased towards elites. Blackstone, *Commentaries*, vol. III, 379–80.

[69] Charles W. Wolfram, 'The Constitutional History of the Seventh Amendment', *Minnesota Law Review* 57 (1973): 639, 674–75; Harrington, 'Economic Origins', 170–72.

[70] Harrington, 'Economic Origins', 173–74; Wolfram, 'Constitutional History', 675–76.

[71] These included the Contracts Clause, which forbids the states to enact laws impairing the obligation of contracts. U.S. Const. Art. I, § 10.

[72] Harrington, 'Economic Origins', 173–76.

[73] See, e.g., Jonathan Elliot (ed.), *The Debates in the Several State Conventions of the Adoption of the Federal Constitution*, 2nd ed., 5 vols. (1836), vol. III, 317–19.

[74] Elliot, *Debates*, vol. III, 534–38.

Seventh Amendment, he studiously avoided glorifying the civil jury and therefore made no direct reference to Magna Carta.

MAGNA CARTA AND JURIES IN AMERICAN JUDICIAL OPINIONS

The Federalist concerns about the jury presaged the attitudes of many later legislators and judges in the United States. Politicians and judges continued – and continue – to praise the jury in Blackstone's extravagant terms and to exalt Magna Carta as the guarantee of this liberty. Year by year, however, they whittled the jury away. This erosion was especially true of the civil jury. At the founding of the American republic, the jury had been a political institution, as Tocqueville famously described it.[75] In the nineteenth century, however, many Americans in all areas wanted predictable, uniform legal rules that would help promote commercial development.[76] Use of civil juries could lead to unlawful, unpredictable results that undermined the authority of legislatures and courts, and thwarted the ability to plan and carry out actions. Besides, the expense and inconvenience of jury trial was great.[77] The jury began to be regarded more as a judicial institution than as a political one, and as a judicial institution the jury fell short.

We see this shift in attitudes towards the jury in the opinions of state and federal courts. Because Article 29 of Magna Carta had been enshrined in many state constitutions, it was formally the law. Most courts could avoid having to interpret this thirteenth-century language, because almost all state

---

[75] Alexis de Tocqueville, *Democracy in America*, J. P. Mayer (ed.), George Lawrence (trans.) (New York: Harper Perennial, 1969), 270–76.

[76] In the North, judges such as James Kent, Joseph Story, Isaac Parker and Jeremiah Smith worked to create uniform national private law that furthered commercial development and constrained juries. Daniel J. Hulsebosch, *Constituting Empire: New York and the Transformation of Constitutionalism in the Atlantic World, 1664–1830* (Chapel Hill: University of North Carolina Press, 2005), 286–87; John P. Reid, *Controlling the Law: Legal Politics in Early National New Hampshire* (DeKalb: Northern Illinois University Press, 2004), 107, 115–30; John H. Langbein, 'Chancellor Kent and the History of Legal Literature', *Columbia Law Review* 93 (1993): 566–69; Renée B. Lettow, 'New Trial for Verdict against Law: Judge/Jury Relations in Early Nineteenth-Century America', *Notre Dame Law Review* 71 (1996): 519–21. In the South, judges such as Joseph Lumpkin of Georgia and Hamilton Gamble of Missouri wanted to encourage commercial and industrial development and predictable legal rules. See Paul D. Hicks, *Joseph Henry Lumpkin: Georgia's First Chief Justice* (Athens: University of Georgia Press, 2002), 63–72; Timothy S. Huebner, *The Southern Judicial Tradition: State Judges and Sectional Distinctiveness, 1790–1890* (Athens: University of Georgia Press, 1999), 73–74, 81–86; Dennis K. Boman, *Hamilton Gamble: Dred Scott Dissenter and Missouri's Civil War Governor* (Baton Rouge: Louisiana State University Press, 2006), 18–22.

[77] Renée Lettow Lerner, 'The Failure of Originalism in Preserving Constitutional Rights to Jury Trial', *William and Mary Bill of Rights Journal* 22 (2014): 846–50.

constitutions had explicit guarantees of jury trial in addition to the language from Article 29.[78] The state jury trial rights typically used the language of preservation: 'The right of trial by jury shall remain inviolate.'[79] Many courts paused to heap praise on Magna Carta when interpreting the jury clauses in their state constitutions, but there was seldom need to address Article 29 extensively. Maryland, however, did not have a separate jury right apart from the language of Magna Carta, so courts had to interpret it. A few courts from other states – particularly those rare courts that found violations of the jury right – also analysed the language of Magna Carta in their opinions.

I will focus on two opinions that discussed Magna Carta language extensively as part of their holdings. The first was the opinion of the Supreme Court of South Carolina in 1794 in *Zylstra v. Corporation of Charleston*, based on a criminal case.[80] The second was the opinion of the U.S. Supreme Court in 1819 in *Bank of Columbia v. Okely*, a case of debt to a bank.[81] The differences between the two opinions reflect changing attitudes towards the jury.

A CASE IN THE EARLY REPUBLIC

Zylstra illustrates the strong echoes of the immemorial English constitution, the birthright of Americans, in the early republic. In *Zylstra*, the wardens' court of the city of Charleston had convicted Zylstra of violating a city ordinance forbidding keeping a tallow-chandler's shop within the city.[82] The wardens' court, which sat without a jury, fined Zylstra £100. Zylstra then sued for a writ of prohibition in the Supreme Court of South Carolina, claiming violation of the right to jury trial. Zylstra's counsel argued the point vigorously, claiming that a power to levy such a substantial fine vested in judges alone 'had a tendency to deprive a citizen of the inestimable trial by jury, the birthright of every citizen, secured to him by *magna charta* and our excellent constitution'.[83] This was the traditional language of inheritance of rights, familiar from the colonial and revolutionary period, and now carried into the new republic.

The Supreme Court of South Carolina issued the prohibition. The most elaborate opinion, by Judge Thomas Waties, considered in detail the meaning

---

[78] Ibid., 819–21.
[79] Ibid., 821 n. 54.
[80] 1 Bay 382, 382 (S.C. 1794).
[81] 17 U.S. 235 (1819).
[82] 1 Bay 382, 382 (S.C. 1794).
[83] Ibid., 384 (arguments of Peace, counsel for the plaintiff).

of language from Magna Carta. South Carolina's Constitution of 1790 contained a clause based on Article 29.[84] The constitution also contained a separate guarantee of jury trial, similar to that of many other states: 'The trial by jury, as heretofore used in this state, shall be forever inviolably preserved.'[85] Later judicial opinions about the right to jury trial would rest mainly, if not exclusively, on the specific jury guarantee. There was a difficulty with this line of analysis in *Zylstra* for a judge determined to find a violation of the right to jury trial. The court of wardens had been created before the South Carolina Constitution of 1790, and therefore the constitution might be thought to confirm the court's powers.[86] Judge Waties agreed that this would be a reasonable argument, if the constitution was the first acquisition of the peoples' right of trial by jury. In his view, this was not so.

> But the trial by jury is a common law right; not the creature of the constitution, but originating in time immemorial; it is the inheritance of every individual citizen, the title to which commenced long before the political existence of this society; and which has been held and used inviolate by our ancestors, in succession, from that period to our own time.[87]

Here again we see the language of inheritance and ancestors, from Coke's time immemorial. Although the right to trial by jury was not described as a natural right in the universal sense of the French Enlightenment, it was a right of the English people and their descendants in America. Interestingly, Waties gave different reasons for the right in England and America. In England, he wrote, the jury was necessary to control 'the usurpations of the government';[88] he seemed to refer mainly to the control of the executive, and possibly the legislature. In the republics of the United States, in contrast, the jury's main purpose was to check the judiciary, which might be biased in favour of the rich and powerful.[89] Nevertheless, the source of the inheritance was the same.

The claim of an ancient inheritance left Judge Waties with the problem of defining the precise scope of this right originating in time immemorial. To elucidate the meaning of the language of Magna Carta, Waties turned to a British author, Francis Stoughton Sullivan. Sullivan's *Lectures on the Constitution and Laws of England*, with additions by Gilbert Stuart and

---

[84] South Carolina Constitution of 1790, Art. IX, § 2 ('No freeman of this state shall be in any manner deprived of his life, liberty, or property, but by the judgment of his peers, or by the law of the land.').

[85] Ibid., § 6.

[86] 1 Bay, 395.

[87] Ibid.

[88] Ibid.

[89] Ibid., 396.

published in London in 1776, contained a commentary on Magna Carta that Waties regarded as a helpful 'illustration' of Coke's authoritative interpretation of the Great Charter.[90] Waties seems to have relied on Sullivan rather than on Blackstone in part because Sullivan addressed the language of Magna Carta more specifically and in part because of Blackstone's overly 'high ideas of the omnipotence of parliament'.[91] (Most American judges were content to rely on Blackstone's similar discussion.) Based on Sullivan's account, Waties described the various cases and courts in which the 'law of the land' permitted judgment without jury trial.[92] He concluded that the jurisdiction of the juryless court of wardens could not stretch to this case.[93] Waties's colleague Judge Elihu Bay, who agreed with Waties's opinion and reported the case, added the comment that the city ordinance was repealed after the decision and that 'no attempt was ever after made to exercise so unwarrantable a jurisdiction'.[94]

AN EXAMPLE FROM THE MATURING UNITED STATES

Later courts did not find limitations on the use of juries to be so unwarrantable. As the republic matured, courts dropped the language of ancestors and rights from time immemorial and focused on efficiency in adjudication. The 1819 opinion of the U.S. Supreme Court in *Bank of Columbia v. Okely* was widely influential.[95] *Okely* concerned a summary proceeding; a Maryland statute of 1793 authorised the Bank of Columbia to use a summary proceeding to collect debts owed to it, provided that the notes were made expressly negotiable at the bank at their creation. After an affidavit by the president of the bank, alleging the indebtedness, was filed with the clerk of a court, the assets of the alleged debtor were subject to immediate execution. The alleged debtor could dispute the indebtedness and demand a jury trial on the return of the execution. The preamble to the statute explained, 'It is absolutely necessary that the debts due to the said bank should be punctually paid, to enable the directors to calculate with certainty and precision on meeting the demands that may be made upon them.'[96] The Maryland act became part of the law of the District of Columbia through an act of the U.S. Congress in 1801,

---

[90] Ibid., 391.
[91] Ibid., 392.
[92] Ibid., 391–93.
[93] Ibid., 394–95.
[94] Ibid., 398.
[95] 17 U.S. 235 (1819).
[96] Maryland Act of November Session, 1793, c. 30, § 14.

incorporating the laws of Maryland. Okely moved to quash an execution under this provision, because the act violated the rights to jury trial in the Seventh Amendment to the U.S. Constitution and Article 21 of the Maryland Constitution.

In *Okely*, the U.S. Supreme Court was in the rare position of needing to interpret the language of Magna Carta. Maryland had no specific guarantee of jury trial apart from the language drawn from Magna Carta, and as the U.S. Supreme Court observed, if the statute was void under the constitution of Maryland, its provisions were not incorporated as the law of the District of Columbia.[97] Justice William Johnson, a native of Charleston, took a different attitude towards Magna Carta than had his fellow South Carolinian Thomas Waties. In his opinion for the court, Justice Johnson wasted no time with the usual fulsome praise of the words of the Great Charter. His tone, indeed, suggested impatience with the 'volumes spoken and written with a view to their exposition'.[98] Instead of trying carefully to interpret the words in light of respected scholarly authorities, as Judge Waties had done, Justice Johnson peremptorily declared that 'the good sense of mankind' had arrived at last at the idea 'that they were intended to secure the individual from the arbitrary exercise of the powers of government, unrestrained by the established principles of private rights and distributive justice'.[99] After this vague announcement, Johnson explained that there was nothing left for the defendant to complain of. Because the note was expressly negotiable at the bank at its making, Okely had voluntarily consented to the summary method of proceeding. '[T]he debtor chose his own jurisdiction', as in an arbitration, and therefore neither the Seventh Amendment nor the Maryland Constitution was violated. In effect, the defendant had waived the right of jury trial before execution. Besides, the defendant could, if he chose, demand a jury trial after execution. The court was apparently not concerned that these summary proceedings created significant obstacles to jury trial. Efficiency in the furtherance of a robust credit system and economy was more important. The case occurred during the financial panic of 1819, when the credit system in the United States was strained. It seems likely that these practical exigencies encouraged Justice Johnson's dismissive attitude towards the jury right embodied in the Great Charter.

Many American judges continued to hail Magna Carta as 'the great charter of English liberty' in connection with the right to trial by jury, but, as in *Okely*,

[97] 17 U.S. 242.
[98] Ibid., 244.
[99] Ibid.

allusions to the Charter were vague and did not entail detailed analysis of its meaning.[100] References to common ancestors and inheritance disappeared. The English and American peoples were thought to be separate. But although they were regarded as separate by the nineteenth century, they were still viewed as traveling parallel paths in the limitation of the jury.

In an opinion in 1841, Judge Trotter of the Mississippi High Court of Errors and Appeals quoted the U.S. Supreme Court's opinion in *Okely*. Trotter explained, after the customary praise of Magna Carta, that 'it is not regarded as any infringement of [the English people's] rights thus solemnly pledged, that in the arrangement and distribution of the powers in the several courts which have grown up under the common law in that country, modes of trial in many cases are allowed which dispense with the verdict of a jury'.[101] Judge Trotter followed Blackstone in declaring that the right to trial by jury 'is justly regarded as one of the strongest bulwarks of human rights, and is held dear by the people of this country'.[102] Nevertheless, the court held that the right could be waived in civil cases.

Chief Justice Joseph Lumpkin of the Georgia Supreme Court, in an opinion in 1848, went even further.[103] His opinion included extensive excerpts from the U.S. Supreme Court's opinion in *Okely*. Lumpkin reported with approval Judge Trotter's praise of Magna Carta and the jury, but like him added that many types of civil cases were tried daily without a jury.[104] 'Indeed, it is notorious, that modern law reform, both in England, and in this country, seeks, amongst other objects, to dispense, as much as possible with juries.'[105] He cited as evidence of this trend the provisions for waiver of jury trial in New York's then new Field Code (1848)[106] and the recent County Courts Act (1846) in England.[107] Another example was the summary proceeding that was established in the statute whose constitutionality was at issue in the case before the Georgia Supreme Court. Lumpkin and his colleagues held that the proceedings did not violate constitutional rights to civil jury trial. The summary proceeding, Lumpkin explained, promoted 'the interests both of agriculture

---

[100] See, e.g., *Lewis v. Garrett's Adm'rs*, 6 Miss. (5 Howard), 434, 455 (1841).
[101] Ibid.
[102] Ibid., 457.
[103] *Flint River Steamboat Co v. Foster*, 5 Ga. 194 (1848).
[104] Ibid., 206–07.
[105] Ibid., 207.
[106] Ibid. ('[A]s a justification for this change, it is stated that in the city of New York, where the right of election existed as to the mode of trial, 1285 judgments were rendered by the Court in Marine causes *without*, against 67 upon the verdict of a jury.'). See N.Y. Sess. Laws c. 379, § 221 (1848).
[107] 5 Ga. 207. See 9 & 10 Vict., c. 95 (1846). On the provisions of the County Courts Act concerning jury trial, see Conor Hanly, "The Decline of Civil Jury Trial in Nineteenth-Century England', *Journal of Legal History* 26 (2005): 269–74.

and commerce"[108] and resulted in 'a vast saving of time, trouble, and expense, to suitors and the country'.[109] The rhetoric of judges extolling jury trial helped distract attention from the effect of their decisions, which was to limit it. Efficiency in adjudication in order to promote economic growth was more important.

THE FATE OF THE INHERITANCE IN ENGLAND

England was traveling a similar path, and indeed went further than the United States in limiting the jury. The jury, especially the civil jury, was increasingly viewed in the land of its birth as a wasteful nuisance. By the nineteenth century, English judges had full independence and were believed to be on the whole intelligent, learned and free from corruption.[110] Under those circumstances, a bench trial seemed preferable to the trouble and expense of collecting lay jurors, trying to explain the facts and law to them, and awaiting their verdict. Jurors almost always followed the judge's hints in his summing up anyway.[111]

In the 1840s, the English legal profession fired criticism at the jury.[112] Even Punch joined in, publishing Gilbert à Beckett's *The Comic Blackstone* in 1846. The most quoted passage, and one singled out for admiration in the United States, was a satire of Blackstone's chapter on the civil jury. Beckett opened his chapter with a warning: 'It is difficult to get the British bosom into a sufficiently tranquil state to discuss this great subject; for every Englishman's heart will begin bounding like a tremendous bonse, at the bare mention of trial by jury.'[113] Beckett continued with a reference to the ancient inheritance of Englishmen: 'The trial by jury is of course a subject that every true-born Briton with a quarter of a pint of Saxon blood in his veins is prepared to revel in.'[114] After observing that jurors were often befuddled by the arguments of counsel and that they sometimes tossed up to decide cases, Beckett built to his climax: 'Such is trial by jury! The bulwark in which John Bull can walk triumphantly, the buttress of our rights, the clothes-prop of our liberties, the cloak-pin of law, and the hat-peg of equity.'[115] In fewer than a hundred years, the jury had

---

[108] 5 Ga. 217.

[109] Ibid., 207.

[110] Hanly, 'Decline of Civil Jury Trial', 255–59.

[111] Ibid., 258–59.

[112] Ibid., 259–66.

[113] Gilbert à Beckett, *The Comic Blackstone*, new ed. (Chicago: Callaghan and Cockcroft, 1870), 274) (first published London 1846).

[114] Ibid.

[115] Ibid., 275–76.

changed from a 'sacred palladium' to a figure of fun. Unhampered by a written constitutional guarantee of jury trial, England ultimately effectively abolished the civil jury and limited the criminal jury with the growth of summary jurisdiction.[116] Constrained by their constitutions, American legislators and judges had to use more indirect ways to curtail the jury, including summary judgment and encouragement of settlement and plea bargaining.[117]

A TROUBLESOME INHERITANCE

The story of the jury moving from an ancient and prized right of the people to a nuisance suggests the difficulties of constitutionalizing specific procedural rights concerning the legal system. Legal systems, economies, and politics can change, changing in turn the need or desire for a particular procedure. The idea of the jury as a right of Englishmen from time immemorial was a fiction: The criminal jury was unknown in 1215, and the barons at Runnymede insisted that the common law jury did not apply to them in the most important civil cases. The notion of the jury as an ancient right suited Coke in his struggles against royal prerogative in the seventeenth century, and Americans in their struggles against British control in the eighteenth century. After these battles were over, the civil jury seemed to many legal professionals and legislators to be a liability. The legal systems needed new procedures that were more efficient for commercial societies.

Part of the difficulty with constitutionalizing a particular procedure such as the late eighteenth-century jury is that the procedure was embedded in other procedures and institutions that were not constitutionalised. These other procedures and institutions underwent changes that inevitably affected jury trial. Examples of these changing procedures include the abolition of property requirements for jury service, the curtailment of judicial comment on the evidence in the United States and the shift to lawyer-conducted voir dire in the United States. Unless a constitution contains complete codes of civil and criminal procedure, the problem of changing associated procedures is inescapable.

There may be certain procedural rights that could be safely constitutionalised, but these would have to be basic to allow for appropriate change over time. Such basic rights might include adequate notice of the charges or claims against a defendant, and the evidence supporting them; the ability to respond; and adjudication by a reasonably impartial decision-maker. Of necessity,

[116] Hanly, 'Decline of Civil Jury Trial', 274–78.
[117] Lerner, 'Failure of Originalism', 845–69; John H. Langbein, 'The Disappearance of Civil Jury Trial in the United States', *Yale Law Journal* 122 (2012): 522, 542–72.

many details of a legal system must be in the power of legislatures or courts to determine, to ensure that a legal system can adjust as needed to changes in technology, the economy and society.

Constitutionalizing a particular sort of decision-maker is especially problematic. The court of feudal tenants that the barons wanted to enshrine in Magna Carta was not suited to the later age of freeholds, nor is the civil jury suited to an age of commerce. England, without a written constitution specifying trial by jury, was able effectively to abolish the civil jury and to substitute a more efficient form of adjudication. The United States, hampered by jury rights in the federal and state constitutions, has had to resort to various inefficient manoeuvres to circumvent jury trial. Americans continue to pay for their invented inheritance.

6

Magna Carta, the 'Sugar Colonies' and 'Fantasies of Empire'

Derek O'Brien

When British public lawyers proclaim Magna Carta's influence in Britain's colonies around the world,[1] they generally do so, even if obliquely, as a way of reconciling Britain's colonial past with its liberal-democratic and multicultural present. A narrative is thus constructed in which Magna Carta is presented as a symbol of a tradition of 'English liberty', which Englishmen took with them when they went abroad to settle these colonies and which endures to this day.[2] English liberty, thus conceived, includes the right to personal liberty, the right to personal security, freedom from imprisonment without just cause, and the free use and enjoyment and disposal of all property. To this list could be added the right to representative government.

In this chapter, I wish to challenge the foregoing account of a tradition of English liberty, as symbolised by Magna Carta, which England bequeathed to its former colonies, insofar as it relates to the so-called 'sugar colonies' of the Commonwealth Caribbean. In particular, I wish to argue that the version of English liberty that was exported to the West Indies in the seventeenth and eighteenth centuries by the first English settlers is not adequate to the task of reconciling Britain's colonial past with modern conceptions of democracy or multiculturalism. More than this, I wish to argue that the legacy of English liberty in the Commonwealth Caribbean is no mere matter of historical interest, but continues to be deeply problematic because of its lingering influence on contemporary human rights jurisprudence in the region.

I will begin by linking the transmission of Magna Carta, and the other bundle of rights associated with the concept of English liberty, to the arrival of

---

[1] See, e.g., Lord Woolf, 'Magna Carta: A Precedent for Recent Constitutional Change', available at http://magnacarta800th.com/lectures/magna-carta-a-precedent-for-recent-constitutional-change/, and Lord Irvine, 'The Legacy of Magna Carta', *LQR* 119 [2003]: 227.
[2] See A. Rupprecht, 'Excessive Memories: Slavery, Insurance and Resistance', *History Workshop Journal* 64 (1) (2007): 6–28.

the first settlers in the region who were determined to claim English liberty as part of their 'colonial birthright' as Englishmen. I will proceed to examine how these settlers succeeded in claiming the rights and privileges associated with English liberty for themselves while at the same time denying these rights and privileges to the West Africans transported to the region to work as slaves on their sugar plantations, who were subject to a set of brutal and oppressive Slave Code laws. Finally, I will examine how the settlers subsequently exploited the rights that they claimed exclusively for themselves as Englishmen in order to resist the efforts of the British government, initially, to ameliorate the conditions of the slaves and, when this failed, to abolish slavery altogether.

In following sections, I will seek to demonstrate why the links between English liberty, colonialism and slavery remain deeply problematic for the region because judges continue to invoke an English conception of liberty, rooted in the English common law, when interpreting the fundamental rights guaranteed by the region's Independence Constitutions. I will argue that this is problematic for three reasons. Firstly, it presumes that the rights guaranteed by the Independence Constitutions are coextensive with the rights associated with English liberty. Secondly, it deprives the rights guarantees of the Independence Constitutions of their normative force by appealing to a source that lies outside the Independence Constitutions. Thirdly, it appeals to a source that was once used to underpin the enslavement of vast numbers of African men and women.

In conclusion, I will argue that it is necessary to construct a new narrative of imperial history which acknowledges the role of English liberty in preserving a system of slavery that endured for nearly three centuries and which acknowledges that in the post-colonial Commonwealth Caribbean, the English conception of liberty has been replaced by the system of rights and freedoms guaranteed by the region's Independence Constitutions.

ENGLISH LIBERTY AND AFRICAN SLAVERY

Britain's former colonies in the Caribbean did not begin as slave societies. Instead, they were colonised by English settlers who operated under the auspices, variously, of chartered companies, proprietary groups and the Crown.[3] In this way thirteen separate island colonies were established in what became known as the British West Indies. The first islands to be settled, during the first six decades of the seventeenth century, were: Bermuda; Barbados; the four Leeward Islands of Antigua, Montserrat, Nevis, St Kitts

---

[3] J. P. Greene, *Exclusionary Empire: English Liberty Overseas, 1600–1900* (Cambridge: Cambridge University Press 2010), 50.

and Jamaica. To this group were added the Bahamas in the early eighteenth century, the Virgin Islands in the 1750s and, following the Seven Years War, the four ceded islands of Dominica, Grenada, St Vincent and Tobago in 1763. Trinidad and St Lucia came into British ownership as a result of the Napoleonic Wars in 1802 and 1814, respectively, while British Guiana (now Guyana) and British Honduras (now Belize) were later additions.

The Reception of Magna Carta and Other English Laws

Much academic ink has been spilt in attempting to explain the reception of Magna Carta and other English laws – such as the Petition of Right 1628, Habeas Corpus Acts of 1640 and 1679, the Bill of Rights 1689, and the Act of Settlement of 1701 – in these and other former British colonies.[4] McPherson, for example, traces the reception of Magna Carta in Britain's colonies in the Caribbean, variously, to colonial charters issued by the Crown, to commissions and royal instructions issued to colonial governors and to local reception statutes.[5] However, from the perspective of the settlers themselves, it is clear that they regarded the liberties and privileges afforded by Magna Carta and by these later statutes as part of their colonial birthright as Englishmen. Like the settlers in the mainland colonies described by Renée Lettow Lerner in her chapter, 'The Troublesome Inheritance of Americans in Magna Carta and Trial by Jury' (Chapter 5), English settlers in the West Indies regarded these rights as an inheritance based on their blood ancestry. So far as the settlers were concerned, no charter or other instrument could grant English people a right that they already enjoyed as a result of their birth: instruments such as Magna Carta were, in essence, merely a way for the Crown to confirm that such rights inhered in the people themselves.[6]

The idea that English liberty was inextricably linked to English ancestry is particularly helpful in understanding why these settlers did not think twice about denying the freedoms guaranteed by English liberty to the slaves in their midst, who were being imported in increasingly large numbers from West Africa to work on the sugar plantations that sprang up across the region from the mid seventeenth century onwards. Instead, the slave population was governed by a set of laws known as Slave Code Acts. These laws were enacted

---

[4]   See, e.g., D. Clark 'The Icon of Liberty: The Status and Role of *Magna Carta* in Australian and New Zealand Law', *Melbourne University Law Review* 24 (2000): 866; B. H. McPherson, *The Reception of English Law Abroad* (Brisbane: Supreme Court of Queensland Library, 2007); and J. Dupont, *The Common Law Abroad: Constitutional and Legal Legacy of the British Empire* (Littleton, CO: Fred B. Rothman Publications, 2001).

[5]   McPherson, *The Reception of English Law Abroad*, 208–10.

[6]   Greene, *Exclusionary Empire*, 55.

by colonial assemblies, which were composed mainly of slave owners. Unsurprisingly, the laws that they enacted were designed to promote the collective interests of the slave owners and offered absolutely no protection or redress to the enslaved population. As we shall see in the next section, these laws were as far removed from Magna Carta and the tradition of English liberty as it is possible to conceive.

Slave Code Acts

Slave Code Laws were not unique to the English colonies in the Caribbean. The French, Spanish and even the Swedes all had their own versions of Slave Code laws.[7] Though there was some variation between these Slave Codes, what they had in common was a set of rules that a minority tried to impose on a majority.[8] There was not a single island in the West Indies where European colonisers made up the majority of the population. In the British West Indies, however, the disparity between the number of white English (later British) settlers and slaves was particularly pronounced. Between 1680 and 1786, the number of slaves imported into Britain's West Indian colonies is estimated to have been 2,130,000.[9] Though the ratio of slaves to free persons may have differed between colonies and from time to time,[10] it is reckoned that by 1770, out of a total population of 500,000 in the British West Indies, approximately 428,000 were slaves.[11] This huge disparity in numbers between free persons and slaves meant that the subjugation of the latter could only be achieved by the strict enforcement of Slave Code laws.

The first British colony to develop a Slave Code was Barbados. The Barbados Slave Code Act of 1661,[12] which was influenced in part by its French and Spanish predecessors,[13] provides illuminating insight into the cultural assumptions of these slave-owning societies and their reasons for seeking to regulate the system of slave ownership:

---

[7] C. Gibson, *Empire's Crossroads: A History of the Caribbean from Columbus to the Present Day* (Basingstoke and Oxford: Macmillan, 2014), 106.

[8] Ibid.

[9] C. H. Wesley, 'The Negro in the West Indies', *Journal of Negro History* 17(1) (Jan. 1932): 51, 54.

[10] In Jamaica, for example, in 1788 there were 1,314 whites and 226,432 slaves, while in Tobago in 1808 there were 439 whites and 17,009 slaves. See Wesley, 'The Negro in the West Indies, 55. See also G. Heuman, 'From Slavery to Freedom,' in P. D. Morgan and S. Hawkins (eds.), *Black Experience and the Empire* (Oxford: Oxford University Press, 2004), 141.

[11] R. Blackburn, *The Overthrow of Colonial Slavery: 1776–1848* (London: Verso, 1988), 5.

[12] Though there were a number of forerunners to the 1661 Slave Code Act, no copies of the older statutes exist.

[13] Gibson, *Empire's Crossroads*, 106.

Negroes [are] an heathenish and an uncertaine dangerous kinde of people . . .
yet wee well know by the right rule of reason and order wee are not to leave
them to the Arbitrary cruele and outrageous wills of every evill disposed
person but soo farr to protect them as we doo many other goods and
Chattles and alsoe somewhat farther as being created Men though without
the Knowledge of God in the world.[14]

The Barbados Slave Code Act served as a prototype for Slave Codes enacted
in the other British colonies across the region.[15] These Slave Code Acts
performed two essential functions. Firstly, they legitimised the subjugation
of slaves by their masters. Secondly, they reduced slaves to the status of
chattels, thereby allowing slaves to be conveyed by the same techniques of
management and control that governed other types of property. I will now
consider the operation of each of these functions in turn.

Slave Codes as Instruments of Subjugation

The sheer size of the slave population relative to the number of slave owners
meant that there was, everywhere, the ever-present possibility of insurrection
and resistance. This had to be checked and crushed at all costs if slave-owning
societies were to prosper. The Slave Code Acts, accordingly, contained a
number of provisions designed to prohibit and suppress unauthorised movement and the congregation of large numbers of slaves.[16] As Dina Paton notes,
in the course of the seventeenth and eighteenth centuries,

more and more actions by slaves were criminalised: from beating drums or
blowing horns (both of which were viewed as means of communication
which might be used to help runaways or concerting uprisings); to hunting
and to gathering after dark.[17]

The maintenance of slavery also demanded the suppression of all signs of
initiative or independence on the part of slaves.[18] The 1771 Jamaican Slave
Code, for example, forbade slaves from keeping livestock and prescribed
whipping for slaves who sold meat, fish or manufactured articles, or who

---

[14] Barbados 1661 Slave Code, Barbados MSS Laws, 1645–1682, Colonial Office Series, P.R.O.
30/2/16–26.
[15] The Barbados Slave Code Act served as the prototype for Slave Code Acts enacted elsewhere in
the region: in Jamaica in 1664, in Montserrat in 1693 and in Antigua in 1697.
[16] E. V. Goveia, *The West Indian Slave Laws of the Eighteenth Century* (Mona, Barbados:
Caribbean Universities Press, 1970), 84.
[17] D. Paton, 'Punishment, Crime and the Bodies of Slaves in Eighteenth-Century Jamaica',
Journal of Social History 34(4) (Summer 2001): 923–54.
[18] E. Williams, *From Columbus to Castro: The History of the Caribbean 1492–1969* (London:
Andre Deutsch, 1970), 186.

hired themselves out to work for another without the permission of their owners.[19]

The Slave Code Acts also explicitly authorised masters to punish their slaves privately by requiring that 'all small ... misdemeanours shall be heard and determined by [their] master.'[20] The punishments that could be inflicted by masters included whipping. For masters who, for whatever reason, were not inclined to punish their slaves personally, a 'common Whipman' was made available by local parishes whom slaveholders could hire to inflict punishments on their behalf.[21]

There were very few limits on a master's power to 'correct' his slaves, and if a slave should die in the course of a punishment for a misdemeanour, it was usually provided that 'noe person shall be accomptable to any law' for such a death.[22] The rationale for the immunity afforded to masters who caused the death of their slaves was explained thus in a resolution of the Assembly of Antigua in 1723:

> Several cruel persons, to gratify their own humours, against the laws of God and humanity, frequently kill, destroy, or dismember their own and other persons' slaves, and have hitherto gone unpunished, *because it is inconsistent with the constitution and government of this island and would be too great a countenance and encouragement to slaves to resist white person, to set slaves so far upon an equality with, the free inhabitants, as to try those that kill them* ...[23]

In other words, it was better that masters who killed or dismembered their own or another's slave should not be punished; for to punish a master might encourage the slave population to regard themselves as equal to the white population and thereby incite a rebellion. This possibility had to be avoided at all costs.

For more serious offences, slaves were tried before slave courts. These were quite separate to the courts which exercised jurisdiction over the free population and were unique to British slave colonies in the West Indies and America. Slave courts were composed of five persons: three freeholders and two magistrates who were drawn from local property holders and who were almost

---

[19] Ibid.
[20] 1664 Barbados Slave Code. This language was also used in the 1674 slave code, 'an Act for the Better Ordering and Government of Slaves', P.R.O. CO 139/3.
[21] Paton, 'Punishment, Crime and the Bodies of Slaves', 927.
[22] Paton, 'Punishment, Crime and the Bodies of Slaves', 926. Indeed, the Slave Code Act of Montserrat of 1693 expressly permitted any white man to kill a slave who was caught stealing provisions.
[23] Quoted by Williams, *From Columbus to Castro*, 191 (emphasis added).

without exception major planters.[24] There was no question of trial by jury for slaves. As the Barbadian Assembly explained when it introduced a 'solemn court' for slaves in capital cases which were to be tried by the Governor in Council alone,

> Being Brutish slaves, [they] deserve not, from the Baseness of their condition, to be tried by the legal trial of twelve men of their Peers, or Neighbourhood, which truly neither can be rightly done, as the Subjects of England are.[25]

The symbolic importance of the jury trial in the English legal tradition meant that it could not be extended to slaves without admitting that English liberty was not uniquely the preserve of Englishmen.

It is, of course, important to judge these courts by the standards of their time, and there was, certainly, some overlap between the punishments meted out by slave courts and those by courts of the same period in England and in its colonies when sentencing free people – such as death, transportation and flogging.[26] However, there are at least three ways in which the punishments handed down by slave courts can be distinguished from those ordered by courts exercising jurisdiction over the free population.

The first is the complete absence of any principle of proportionality, which, as Craig Lerner notes in his chapter, 'Magna Carta and Modern Myth-Making: Proportionality in the 'Cruel and Unusual Punishments' Clause' (Chapter 8), was widely, if mistakenly, believed to have been guaranteed by Magna Carta. The Barbados Slave Code of 1688, for example, made theft of property, even to the value of a shilling, a capital offence.[27] Flogging was also inflicted for threatening behaviour towards a free person short of actual violence.[28] In the Bahamas, slaves could be flogged for selling such things as sugar, eggs, fruit or vegetables or if found gambling.[29] The average number of lashes was 76, though in some cases up to 300 could be inflicted.[30] An amendment to the Slave Code Act in Jamaica in 1740 provided that a slave could be burnt to death just for striking a white person.[31] As Dina Paton explains, this conspicuous lack of proportionality was predicated on the assumption that 'a violent act by a slave against a white person, no matter

---

[24] Paton, 'Punishment, Crime and the Bodies of Slaves', 927.
[25] Barbados Slave Code Act, Clause 13.
[26] Paton, 'Punishment, Crime and the Bodies of Slaves', 936.
[27] Williams, *From Columbus to Castro*, 186.
[28] Paton, 'Punishment, Crime and the Bodies of Slaves', 937.
[29] Ibid.
[30] Ibid.
[31] Paton, 'Punishment, Crime and the Bodies of Slaves', 931.

how minor, always carried with it the implicit threat of slave rebellion and the overthrow of white power'. Such acts had, therefore, to be severely punished.[32]

The second way in which these punishments can be distinguished from those for the free population is the barbarity that accompanied their infliction. As white settlers became even more outnumbered, increasingly inhumane means had to be devised to maintain control of slave societies.[33] Convicted slaves were flogged to death while tied to a cartwheel or were hung up in an iron cage until they died from hunger or thirst.[34]

The third distinguishing feature of the punishments is the frequent use of mutilation. This could entail the loss of one or both ears, the splitting of the nostrils or even dismemberment.[35] While not unknown in early English criminal law, such punishments were not by this point in time being imposed either in England or upon free people in the colonies.[36]

For the purpose of subjugating the slave population, it was important that all of the punishments should involve 'the *public* infliction of pain on the body of the convict'.[37] This 'spectacle of suffering',[38] which was attended by other slaves as well as their owners, demonstrated in the most dramatic fashion possible the power of the state over the slave population. As Dina Paton observes, 'the subsequent gruesome display of severed limbs and ears in prominent and symbolic locations around the parish extended the spectacular effect of the punishment still further beyond the brief moment of its actual infliction'.[39] The bodies of the mutilated slaves themselves would also have served as highly visible and permanent reminders of the price to be paid for any violation of the Slave Codes. As Bryan Edwards, himself a planter and a slave owner explained,

> In countries where slavery is established, the leading principle on which the government is supported is fear; or a sense of that absolute coercive necessity which, leaving no choice of action, supercedes all question of rights. It is vain to deny that such actually is, and necessarily must be, the case in all countries where slavery is allowed.[40]

---

[32] Ibid.
[33] Gibson, *Empire's Crossroads*, 120
[34] Paton, 'Punishment, Crime and the Bodies of Slaves', 936.
[35] Ibid.
[36] Ibid.
[37] Paton, 'Punishment, Crime and the Bodies of Slaves', 937
[38] P. Spierenburg, *The Spectacle of Suffering: Executions and the Evolution of Repression* (Cambridge: Cambridge University Press, 1984).
[39] Paton, 'Punishment, Crime and the Bodies of Slaves', 937.
[40] *The History, Civil and Commercial of the British Colonies in the West Indies* (4th ed.) (London: John Stockdale, 1807), 13.

Slave Codes and the Commodification of Slaves

The Slave Code Acts made slavery a permanent condition, inherited through the mother. They also ensured that slaves were bound by a legal status similar to that of goods and chattels, and were the exclusive property of their master.[41] The reduction of slaves to a species of property meant that slave owners could convey their slaves in exactly the same way as they could any other chattel. It also meant that slave owners could claim compensation from the slave courts for executed slaves. The Barbadian Slave Code Act of 1661, for example, provided:

> And that noe master Mistress or commander of a family should bee frighted by fear of losse to search unto and discover their owne negroes soe evilly intended. . . . It is farther enacted and ordained that the losse of negroes so executed shalbe borne by the publique . . .[42]

Most importantly, the reduction of slaves to a species of property meant that slave owners could demand that slave ownership be accorded the same respect as English law accorded to other forms of property ownership.[43] As Blackstone noted in his *Commentaries*, first published between 1765 and 1769,

> So great moreover is the regard of the law for private property, that it will not authorize the least violation of it . . .[44]

As we will see, the dehumanisation of slaves and their reduction to a species of property was to become a crucial component of the argument relied on by slave owners to resist the British government's attempts to ameliorate the conditions for slaves in the British West Indies in the first quarter of the nineteenth century, as well as the slave owners' demand for the payment of compensation as a precondition to their agreement to the eventual emancipation of their slaves in 1833.

Magna Carta and the Case for and against Slavery

That slavery was wholly incommensurate with the English tradition of liberty was not an issue that was much discussed in early settler societies. As Greene notes, it was as if the relationship between slavery and the settlers' identity as free-born English people was a taboo subject, 'the implications of which were

---

[41] N. Draper, *The Price of Emancipation: Slave-Ownership, Compensation and British Society at the End of Slavery* (Cambridge: Cambridge University Press, 2010), 5.

[42] Barbados, 1661, Slave Code, Barbados MSS Laws, 1645–1682, Colonial Office Series, Public Record Office 30/2/16–26.

[43] Goveia, *The West Indian Slave Laws*, 83.

[44] *Commentaries on the Laws of England* (Oxford, 1765, facsimile reprint, 1979), 134–35.

too dangerous and disturbing for public discussion'.[45] Until the second half of the eighteenth century, there was also little public discussion of the issue in Britain, despite the spread of Enlightenment ideas across Europe.[46] One possible explanation for this is the huge economic benefit that Britain derived from its colonies in the Caribbean, which had become the 'hub of the Empire'. It is estimated that, by the end of the eighteenth century, four-fifths of the income derived from Britain's overseas colonies emanated from these so-called sugar colonies.[47] Failure to discuss the issue of colonial slavery, however, meant that over the course of the seventeenth and eighteenth centuries, England had landed itself in 'a hopelessly illogical position'.[48] While proud of the personal liberty which Englishmen enjoyed under the common law, England not only tolerated but also actively sanctioned and promoted a system of slavery in its colonies.[49]

This illogicality was reflected in the case law touching upon slavery. On the one hand, the Chief Justice, Lord Holt, had declared in 1706 that 'there was no property in a negro more than another man'.[50] There was also the celebrated dictum of Lord Northington, in *Shanley v. Harvey*,[51] to the effect that the air of England was 'too purre for a slave to breathe'. On the other hand, the West Indian lobby in England had, in 1729, obtained an unofficial opinion from the then Attorney General, Phillip Yorke, First Earl of Hardwicke, and the Solicitor General, known as the 'Yorke-Talbot Opinion', which declared that the conversion to Christianity did not emancipate slaves and that planters could bring slaves from the colonies to England and still hold them as slaves. This view was upheld by the Attorney General in the case of *Pearne v. Lisle* when he later became Lord Chancellor.[52]

Nevertheless, by the second half of the eighteenth century, the tide of public opinion in England was slowly beginning to turn against slavery. For example, Blackstone, in his *Commentaries*, had proclaimed that

> Pure and proper slavery does not, nay cannot subsist in England; such I mean, whereby an absolute and unlimited power is given to the master over the life and fortune of the slave.... England abhors, and will not endure the

---

[45] Greene, *Exclusionary Empire*, 60.

[46] Gibson, *Empire's Crossroads*, 122

[47] See Hilary McD. Beckles, 'The '"Hub of Empire": The Caribbean and Britain in the Seventeenth Century', in N. Canny (ed.), *The Origins of Empire* (Oxford: Oxford University Press, 1998), 218.

[48] E. Fiddes, 'Lord Mansfield and the Somersett Case', 50 *LQR* [1934] 499 at 500.

[49] Ibid.

[50] 2 Salkeld 666.

[51] (Chancery 1762), ER, vol. 28, 2:125.

[52] Amb 75, 27 ER 47.

existence of, slavery within this nation. .... And now it is laid down, that a slave or negro, the instant he lands in England, becomes a freeman; that is the law will protect him in the enjoyment of his person, and his property.[53]

At around the same time as the *Commentaries* were being published, a group of anti-slavery activists, led by Granville Sharp, sought to challenge the legal foundation of slavery by invoking English liberty, as symbolised by Magna Carta and the Habeas Corpus Act 1769, in a succession of cases which culminated in the case of an African slave, James Somerset.[54]

Somerset had been brought to London in 1769 by his master, Charles Stewart, but subsequently absconded. Having been recaptured in November 1771 and having refused to return to his master's service, he was put up for sale and confined to irons aboard a ship bound for Jamaica. With the assistance of Granville Sharp, Somerset lodged a petition for habeas corpus. It is no exaggeration to say that the subsequent proceedings were, at the time, a cause célèbre. Early abolitionist efforts were pitted against the interests of the West Indian merchants, who rallied behind Stewart, anxious to have a ruling on the legal status of slaves in England:

[S]ince, if the laws of England do not confirm the colony laws with respect to property in slaves, no man of common sense will, for the future, lay out his money in so precarious a commodity.[55]

Although Lord Mansfield urged a settlement of the case, this proved impossible since both sides were keen to have an unequivocal ruling on the question of whether slavery was legal in England. As a result, the case went on for several months before Lord Mansfield was persuaded, finally, to rule against Stewart, ending his judgment with the following, famous peroration:

The state of slavery is of such a nature, that it is incapable of being introduced on any reasons, moral or political; but only positive law, which preserves its force long after the reasons, occasion, and time itself from whence it was created, is erased from memory: it's so odious, that nothing can be suffered to support it, but positive law. Whatever inconveniences, therefore, may follow from a decision, I cannot say this case is allowed or approved by the law of England; and therefore the black must be discharged.[56]

---

[53] Blackstone, *Commentaries*, 411–13.
[54] P. Linebaugh, *The Magna Carta Manifesto* (Berkeley: University of California Press, 2008), 113–14.
[55] J. Oldham 'New Light on Mansfield and Slavery', *Journal of British Studies* 27(1) (Jan. 1988): 45 at 53.
[56] 98 Eng. Rep. 499, 1 Lofft 1 (KB 1772).

The precise meaning of Lord Mansfield's ruling in *Somerset* is much contested. Some commentators, such as James Oldham, argue that the decision left the institution of colonial slavery virtually untouched by acknowledging that *positive* laws could support it, even if Lord Mansfield personally regarded it as 'odious' and against natural law principles. Some support for this view can be found in the later case of *R v. Inhabitants of Thames Ditton*,[57] in which Lord Mansfield made it plain that it had not been his intention in *Somerset* to make slavery unlawful, but simply to deprive a master of his power to take his slave out of England against the latter's will. In all other respects, a slave remained his master's property.[58]

Nevertheless, the ruling in *Somerset* elicited a vigorous defence of slavery by leading settlers in the West Indies and resulted in the production of three substantial pamphlets exploring the legal, historical and cultural foundations of slavery.[59] In these pamphlets, the authors sought not only to reconcile English liberty with the enslavement of the vast majority of the colonies' inhabitants, but also to challenge the invocation of Magna Carta by the abolitionists in England. There were essentially two main strands to the argument advanced by the pamphlets. The first was the insistence that slavery had always been part of the constitution in 'the antient law of England'. Thus, it was argued, in medieval England there were a 'class of people called villeins' who were subject to a 'severe bondage' in which almost their only right was not to be imprisoned without due cause. Neither Magna Carta nor the several statutes affirming it applied to villeins; freemen alone were the beneficiaries of these statutes. Moreover, there were a number of other contemporary statutes which aided and enforced the power a master exercised over his villein. As the Lord Chancellor, Lord Hardwicke, had observed:

> The state or situation of Negroes towards their masters or owners arose out of, and was founded upon, the remains of the antient laws of villeinage in this country.[60]

According to this logic, the settlers stood in the same relation to Magna Carta as the medieval barons discussed by Anthony King in his chapter (Chapter 3), 'Eight Centuries On: Who Are Britain's Barons Now?'

The second strand of the argument advanced in these pamphlets rested on the premise that slaves were the property of their masters. The sanctity of property was one of the principal guarantees of English liberty to which the

---

[57] 4 Douglas 300, 301; 99 Eng. Rep. 891, 892 (1785).
[58] Fiddes, 'Lord Mansfield and the Somersett Case', 499
[59] Greene, *Exclusionary Empire*, 65–66.
[60] Ibid.

settlers were entitled by reason of their birth. Accordingly, 'the pretended magical touch of the English air' could not 'like the presto of a juggler' turn slave owners' 'gold into counters', as they believed Lord Mansfield had suggested in *Somerset*. For if this was to occur, the slave owners would be deprived of their liberties as Englishmen, including the liberty to own slaves.

In conclusion, it was argued that the West Indies, like medieval England at the time of Magna Carta, consisted of two quite distinct categories of persons, only one of which was legally free. The other, the slave population, was in a similar legal position to medieval English villeins and 'in no higher degree of franchise than was allowed to villeins under 'Magna Charta, and the subsequent statutes passed in confirmation of this Great Charter'.[61]

Reform of the Slave Code Acts

Notwithstanding this spirited defence of slavery by the settlers, the threat posed by abolitionists in England continued to grow as public awareness of the horrors of slavery increased. In 1781, for example, the public learned of the shocking facts of the *Zong* case, which concerned 133 slaves who had been thrown overboard, allegedly in order to preserve provisions for those remaining on board.[62] Then, in 1784, a former Royal Navy surgeon, James Ramsay, having witnessed the horror of life on a British slave ship, and having given up his naval career to return to the Caribbean to work as an Anglican minister and doctor on a sugar plantation in St Kitts, published *An Essay on the Treatment and Conversion of African Slaves in the British Sugar Colonies*, recounting the horrific treatment of slaves.[63] This publication was followed in 1791 by a first-hand account of the brutality of slavery from an African slave himself, Olaudah Equiano.[64]

This torrent of negative publicity persuaded colonial assemblies that it was time to introduce some modest amendments to their Slave Code laws. In Antigua, for example, the Slave Code Act was amended, in 1787, to allow slaves the right to trial by jury in serious criminal cases. In 1793, the Jamaican Consolidated Slave Act imposed a fine of £100 for anyone found guilty of mutilating or dismembering a slave. In 1796 and 1798, Slave Amelioration Acts in the Bahamas and the Leeward Islands, respectively, regulated the minimum amount of food and clothing to be allowed to a slave. These

---

[61] Ibid.

[62] *Gregson v. Gilbert* [1783], 3 Dougl. 233.

[63] (James Phillips: London, 1784).

[64] *The Interesting Narrative of the Life of Olaudah Equiano, Or Gustavus Vassus the African* was first published in 1789.

reforms were not, however, sufficient to satisfy the abolitionists, and at the beginning of the nineteenth century, the British government finally gave in to pressure from the anti-slave trade lobby by enacting a bill providing for the abolition of the slave trade in 1807. Subsequently, when it became apparent that the abolition of the slave trade was not leading to any obvious improvement of the lives of slaves in the region, the British government was persuaded to become even more directly involved in reform of the slave system.

The first attempt at reform was the introduction of a Slave Registration Bill. The bill was designed to prevent the illicit importation of slaves into the region by ensuring that the absence of a name from the slave register would be deemed to be conclusive evidence of that person's right to freedom. It was hoped that by this means slave owners would realise that they could not continually replenish their 'stock' of slaves and would thus be persuaded to take better care of their existing 'stock'. Registries of slaves were established in Trinidad and St Lucia in 1812 by means of an Order-in-Council. This was possible because, as conquered colonies, Trinidad and St Lucia possessed no representative legislature of their own. They were, therefore, subject to the legislative authority of the Crown.

Elsewhere in the region, however, opposition to the introduction of a Slave Registry Bill was immediate and intense. Local assemblies in both the settled and ceded colonies (which, unlike the conquered colonies, had been allowed to establish 'representative' legislatures) argued that the attempt by the British government to force them to enact a Registry Bill was an unconstitutional interference in their affairs and their rights as Englishmen.[65] As one of the resolutions adopted by the members of the Assembly of St Vincent declared:

> [T]hey consider the interference of the Imperial Parliament in the internal regulations of the colonies as *an infraction of those original rights under which British Subjects were induced to settle in them.*[66]

This was echoed in a resolution adopted by the Jamaican Assembly:

> [T]he most important of the rights, privileges, immunities, and franchises which are inherent in British subjects as their birthright, and have by them been brought to this island, is to consent to those laws by which they are to be governed . . .[67]

---

[65] See R. L. Schuyler 'The Constitutional Claims of the British West Indies', *Political Science Quarterly* 40(1) (Mar. 1925): 1–36.

[66] *Royal Gazette* (Jamaica), vol. XXXVIII, no.14, 18 (emphasis added).

[67] *Journals of the Assembly of Jamaica*, vol. XII, 782–83.

Quite apart from the violation of the principle of representative government, the Jamaican Assembly also sought to invoke the spirit of Magna Carta
by complaining that the establishment of a system for the registration of slaves
'exercised a power over the estates and property of the inhabitants' and
imposed 'the most grievous penalties and forfeitures, to be inflicted at the
will of a single officer, without trial by jury'.[68] In the face of such opposition,
the British government was persuaded to agree to the enactment of a Registry
Bill in the settled and ceded colonies which was but a pale imitation of the
Slave Registration Act introduced previously in Trinidad and St Lucia.

The second attempt at reform was the introduction of slave amelioration
laws in the 1820s and 1830s. These were intended to eliminate the more vicious
provisions of the Slave Code Acts. As with the Slave Registration Bill, the
British government proceeded, in the first instance, by means of Orders-in-
Council in the Crown colonies of Trinidad and St Lucia. These Orders-in-
Council provided, inter alia: for the creation of a Protector of Slaves to hear
complaints by slaves against their owners, for slave testimony to be admitted in
all civil and criminal actions, for slaves to be able to purchase their freedom at
rates to be fixed by impartial appraisers, for better provision to be made for the
moral and religious care of slaves, for slaves to be able to marry, for the power
of slave owners to punish their slaves to be supervised and for the use of the
whip on females or in the field as a stimulus to labour to be prohibited.

Again, it was intended that these Orders-in-Council would serve as the
template for legislation to be enacted by the self-governing colonies in the
region. However, while some local assemblies did enact reforms to their Slave
Code Acts, this was done on a piecemeal basis and in many cases fell short of
the measures contemplated by the British government. For example, a prohibition against the flogging of female slaves was adopted in only two of the self-
governing colonies – the Bahamas and Dominica – and the recommendation
to admit slave evidence in civil and criminal proceedings was adopted in only
five colonies.[69] In Barbados, the admission of slave evidence was hedged about
with so many restrictions that it was effectively impossible for a slave to give
evidence, while the flogging of female slaves and the use of the whip in the
field were still permitted, though slave courts were no longer permitted to
order the slitting of noses or the branding of slaves' faces.[70]

Significantly, such ameliorative measures as were enacted by local assemblies left the legal status of slaves virtually unchanged: slaves continued to
remain beyond the protection of the common law. Even in the final decades of

[68] *Journals of the Assembly of Jamaica*, vol. XII, 696.
[69] C. Levy, 'The Last Years of Slavery', *Journal of Negro History* 44(4) (1959): 308 at 318.
[70] Ibid.

slavery in the 1820s and 1830s, colonial legislators and judicial officials in the self-governing colonies continued to maintain that 'the common law of England [was] not applicable to slavery in the West Indies'.[71] Insofar as the common law touched upon slaves at all, it was solely to protect a master's proprietary rights over his slaves.

Emancipation

Until emancipation in 1833, the subjugation of slaves continued to be enforced by Slave Code Acts, which remained largely untouched despite the best efforts of successive British governments to reform them. Efforts to challenge the legality of slavery in England in the last quarter of the eighteenth century also had very little impact on the actual practice of slavery in the West Indies. Indeed, judgments such as Lord Mansfield's in *Somerset* and, later, *Zong*, in which he appeared to equate the jettisoned slaves with livestock,[72] only served to reinforce the settlers' claim that slaves were, ultimately, their property. Even the Slave Registry Act, which was ostensibly intended to improve the treatment of slaves by their masters, expressly affirmed 'the right of property in slaves'.[73]

This equiparation of the ownership of slaves with ownership of other forms of property was to become a crucial element in the 'representational strategy' of the slave owners in the debate that preceded the Emancipation Act,[74] with the slave owners demanding compensation for the loss of the property in their slaves that would result from emancipation. So successful was this strategy that even the abolitionists – though they may have questioned the possibility of there being such a thing as 'property in man' – were prepared to concede the legal principle of compensation for slave owners, 'however, defective in a moral point of view might be their title'.[75] As far as the slave owners were concerned, compensation for the loss of their slaves was only consistent with the respect accorded to property by English common law. This could be traced directly back to Magna Carta and was part of their colonial birthright as Englishmen.

---

[71] F. Dwarris, 'Substance of the Three Reports of the Commissioners of Enquiry into the Administration of Civil and Criminal Justice in the West Indies', extracted from the *Parliamentary Papers* (London 1827), 113, 431 (cited by Goveia, *The West Indian Slave Laws*, 90).

[72] See J. Krikler, 'The *Zong* and the Lord Chief Justice', *History Workshop Journal* 64(1) (2007): 29–47.

[73] Draper, *The Price of Emancipation*, 76.

[74] Ibid., 80.

[75] Ibid., 79.

It was in recognition of this right that the Abolition Act of 1833 provided for £20 million to be paid to slave owners in compensation for the loss of their 'slave property'. Thus the Act that was supposed to put an end to slavery, paradoxically, sanctioned the whole concept of 'property in men' at the same time as it was striking it down.[76]

Post-Emancipation

The fault lines in the relationship between the free, almost exclusively white, population and the slave population, which was exclusively African or of African descent, did not, however, end with emancipation in 1833. Following emancipation, the minority white population found it increasingly difficult, without the benefit of Slave Code laws, to govern effectively, as the restive ex-slave population withdrew their labour from the plantation owners and began to demand a public voice. The simmering tension between the ex-slaves and their white rulers came to a head in Jamaica in 1867 with the so-called Jamaica rebellion. This uprising, which involved a demonstration by a group of protesters at the courthouse in Morant Bay, resulted in 586 of those alleged to have been involved being put to death, some receiving sentences of courts martial and others shot without trial. In addition, 1,005 houses were burned and large numbers – including some women – were flogged.[77]

The Jamaica rebellion, and the controversy surrounding the brutal methods used by Governor Eyre to suppress it, spelled the end of representative government in Jamaica. As a result of this horrific event, the white population lost faith in its ability to govern effectively. Fearing an uprising of the majority black population and the expropriation of their property, the Jamaican Assembly agreed to abolish itself and permit the imposition of Crown colony rule by Britain, which dispensed with the need for a representative assembly by vesting executive and legislative authority in an appointed governor and council. As Greene notes, 'by this means the white population hoped to close off any political channels that might be used for the benefit of the majority black population'.[78] The example set by Jamaica was quickly followed in the other settled and ceded colonies – with the exception of Barbados and the Bahamas, which retained their 'representative' assemblies.[79]

[76] Ibid., 76.
[77] For a detailed account of the 'Jamaica Rebellion' and its aftermath, see *The Cambridge History of the British Empire: Volume II The Growth of the New Empire 1783–1870* (London: Cambridge University Press, 1940), 735–37.
[78] Greene, *Exclusionary Empire*, 76.
[79] Crown colony government was already in place in the conquered islands of Trinidad and St Lucia.

Ultimately, therefore, the majority of the settled and ceded colonies opted to give up their right to self-government – one of the most zealously guarded of their suite of English liberties – rather than share it with former slaves and their descendants.[80] In its place a system of Crown colony rule was imposed, which remained largely in place across the region until the end of the Second World War, when the Westminster system, based on an elected legislature and cabinet government, was gradually introduced in preparation for independence.

INDEPENDENCE AND ENGLISH LIBERTY

As was to be expected after centuries of colonial rule, the Independence Constitutions of the Commonwealth Caribbean incorporated the model of government with which their politicians were most familiar – the so-called Westminster model. However, they departed from the British version of the Westminster model in two important respects. Firstly, they included a codified Bill of Rights, modelled broadly on the European Convention of Human Rights (ECHR).[81] Secondly, they declared the constitution to be the supreme law.[82] Caribbean courts, which included for this purpose the Judicial Committee of the Privy Council (JCPC) as the final appellate court for all the independent countries in the region,[83] were thus empowered to strike down acts of the executive and of the legislature that were deemed to be inconsistent with the fundamental rights guaranteed by the constitution.

In theory at least, this meant that the citizens of these countries were no longer required to rely on the residue of English liberty that had been transplanted to the British West Indies by the early settlers. Instead, they had a new source of rights, a Chapter guaranteeing their fundamental rights and freedoms which was deeply entrenched in their Independence Constitutions. Unfortunately, however, the Chapter of Fundamental Rights and Freedoms enshrined in these constitutions has not always been viewed as the primary and most important source of rights for the region's citizens in the post-

---

[80] For a more detailed account of the imposition of Crown colony rule and its aftermath, see D. O'Brien, *Constitutional Law Systems of the Commonwealth Caribbean* (Oxford: Hart Publishing, 2014).

[81] With the exception of the Bill of Rights contained in the 1962 Constitution of Trinidad and Tobago, which was based on the Canadian Declaration of Rights.

[82] With the exception of the 1962 Constitution of Trinidad and Tobago, which did not include a clause declaring the Constitution to be the supreme law.

[83] Guyana abolished the right of appeal to the JCPC in 1970, when it became a republic. More recently, with the establishment of the Caribbean Court of Justice (CCJ) in 2005, two countries have replaced the right of appeal to the JCPC with a right of appeal to the CCJ: Barbados and Belize. Guyana also now subscribes to the appellate jurisdiction of the CCJ.

independence era. This is due to a combination of two factors which I explore in the following section. The first is the inclusion in the Independence Constitutions of certain saving laws clauses. The second is an approach to constitutional interpretation which remains deeply rooted in the English common law.

Saving Clauses and the 'Nasralla Presumption'

Two types of saving clauses are to be found in the Independence Constitutions. The first type are 'general saving clauses', which provide immunity from constitutional challenge for *all* laws in force at the time of independence.[84] These include laws enacted by colonial assemblies during the era of slavery, as well as laws enacted by legislative councils during the period of Crown colony rule. The second type are 'partial saving clauses', which immunise against constitutional challenge all forms of punishment that were lawful immediately prior to independence; this includes hanging and flogging.[85] The impact of these saving clauses can immediately be seen in the first case to be heard by the JCPC in the post-independence era – *DPP v. Nasralla*, on appeal from Jamaica.

In this case, the JCPC was required to decide whether a provision in the fundamental rights chapter of the Jamaican Constitution regarding the rule on *autrefois acquit* was simply declaratory of the common law or whether it expressed the rule on *autrefois acquit* differently from the common law. In affirming that the rule as expressed in the constitution was merely declaratory of the common law, Lord Devlin asserted that

> Whereas the general rule, as is to be expected in a Constitution and as is here embodied in section 2 [the supreme law clause], is that the provisions of the Constitution should prevail over other law, an exception is made in Chapter III [the Bill of Rights]. *This Chapter ... proceeds on the presumption that the fundamental rights which it covers are already secured to the people of Jamaica by existing law.* The laws in force are not to be subjected to scrutiny to see whether or not they conform to the precise terms of the protective provisions.

[84] Section 26(8) of the Constitution of Jamaica thus provides that: 'Nothing contained in any law in force immediately before the appointed day shall be held to be inconsistent with any of the provisions of this Chapter, and nothing done under the authority of any such law shall be held to be done in contravention of any of these provisions.'

[85] Thus, while section 17(1) of the Constitution of Jamaica offers a guarantee against inhuman or degrading treatment or punishment, section 17(2) provides that: 'Nothing ... done under the authority of any law shall be held to be ... in contravention of this section to the extent that the law in question authorises the infliction of any description of punishment which was lawful in Jamaica immediately before [the date of independence].'

The object of these provisions is to ensure that no future enactment shall in any matter which the Chapter covers derogate from the rights which at the coming into force of the Constitution, the individual enjoyed.[86]

In other words, the aim of the fundamental rights guarantees enshrined in the Independence Constitutions was not to protect the citizens of these newly independent countries from laws enacted in the colonial era. Rather, those guarantees were meant to protect them from laws enacted by their freely elected parliaments in the post-independence era. Furthermore, the rights guaranteed by the Independence Constitutions were no different from, and certainly no greater than, the residue of rights which were bequeathed to these countries during the colonial era.

The *Nasralla* presumption, which has been reiterated by the JCPC on a number of subsequent occasions,[87] had a profoundly inhibiting effect on human rights jurisprudence in the immediate post-independence era. Local judges, unconsciously echoing the first settlers, began to invoke the English common law as the source of their citizens' rights. Thus, in *Lassalle v. AG*, in which the Court of Appeal of Trinidad was asked to consider whether the composition of a military tribunal violated the right to due process guaranteed by the Independence Constitution, Justice Phillips, who delivered the leading judgment, declared that

> The fundamental rights and freedoms guaranteed by the Constitution do not owe their existence to it. They were previously existing rights, for the most part derived from the common law . . .[88]

Indeed, the enshrinement of a set of fundamental rights in the Independence Constitutions was adjudged to be of little or no consequence in terms of the protection afforded to these rights. For example, in the case of *King v. The Queen*,[89] which concerned the admissibility of evidence obtained in violation of the defendant's rights under the Jamaican Constitution, the JCPC declared that

> The constitutional right [not to be subject to an unlawful search] may or may not be enshrined in a written constitution, but it seems to their Lordships that *it matters not whether it depends on such enshrinement or simply upon the common law*, as it would do in this country. In either case the discretion of a court must be exercised and had not been taken away by the declaration of the right in written form.[90]

---

[86] *DPP v. Nasralla* [1967], 2 AC 238, 24G (emphasis added).
[87] See, e.g., *de Freitas v. Benny* [1976], AC 239 at 244.
[88] (1971) (WIR) 379 at 395.
[89] [1969] 1 AC 304.
[90] Ibid., 319 (emphasis added).

The most profound consequence of the *Nasralla* presumption has been, however, that the citizens of these independent counties could not rely on a right guaranteed by their Constitution unless the right could also be shown to have existed prior to independence. On occasion, this has proven to be, quite literally, fatal for appellants. Thus, in *Riley v. AG Jamaica*,[91] the JCPC was asked to consider whether a period of prolonged delay in carrying out the execution of a prisoner sentenced to death amounted to a 'cruel and unusual punishment' contrary to section 17(1) of the Jamaican Constitution. In answering this question, the majority concluded that the appellant could not invoke the protection of section 17(1) unless he could show that the legality of a delayed execution could have been challenged before independence: 'If the like description of punishment had been inflicted in like circumstances before independence, would this have been authorised by the law?'[92] Since the appellant was unable to demonstrate that there was any lawful remedy for a delayed execution prior to independence, his appeal failed.

In a strongly argued dissent, Lord Scarman and Lord Brightman rejected the presumption that the rights guaranteed by Jamaica's Independence Constitution were merely coextensive with existing common law rights. They argued instead that the protection of the 'law' afforded by the Jamaican Constitution 'means both the pre-existing law so far as it remains in force ... *and the new law arising from the Constitution itself...*'. In their view, the effect of the partial saving clause was confined to authorising the *description* of punishments which a court could impose; it did not prevent an applicant from arguing that the circumstances in which the executive intended to carry out the sentence, including prolonged delay, violated his constitutional right not to be subject to inhuman or degrading treatment or punishment.

Common Law Constitutionalism

In the years that followed *Riley v. AG Jamaica*, the JCPC has sought to modify the impact of the *Nasralla* presumption somewhat by adopting a 'purposive approach' to the interpretation of the fundamental rights guarantees of the Independence Constitutions.

The requirements of this purposive approach were first outlined by Lord Wilberforce in a seminal judgment in *Minister of Home Affairs (Bermuda) v. Fisher*.[93] According to Lord Wilberforce, 'the very broad and ample style' in

[91] *Riley v. AG Jamaica* [1983], AC 719.
[92] Ibid., 726F.
[93] [1980] AC 319.

which the Bills of Rights contained in post-colonial constitutions were drafted, 'laying down principles of width and generality,' coupled with the fact that they had been greatly influenced by the ECHR, called for

> A generous interpretation avoiding what has been called 'the austerity of tabulated legalism', suitable to give individuals the full measure of the fundamental rights and freedoms referred to.[94]

Notwithstanding the adoption of this purposive approach, the English common law has remained a constant reference point in constitutional interpretation for both the judges of the JCPC and local judges. Thus, in *Pratt and Morgan v. AG Jamaica*, which was heard just over a decade after *Riley* and which, like *Riley*, concerned prolonged delay in the execution of a death sentence, the JCPC was persuaded to accept that undue delay could render the execution of a death sentence unconstitutional, but only because the court was satisfied that

> Prior to independence, *applying the English common law*, judges in Jamaica would have had the like power to stay a long delayed execution . . .[95]

The continuing predominance of the English common law can also be seen in a quartet of appeals which arose out of the ruling in *Pratt and Morgan* that argued that in order to be presumed constitutional a death sentence must be carried out within five years of its pronouncement. Alarmed by this ruling, a number of governments in the Caribbean region began to fix deadlines for the completion of petitions by condemned prisoners to international human rights bodies, such as the Inter American Commission on Human Rights (IACHR) and the UN Human Rights Committee (HRC). Notwithstanding the failure of these bodies to deal with petitions within the deadline, warrants of execution were being read to ensure that the execution could take place within the five-year period fixed by the JCPC in *Pratt and Morgan*. As a result, the JCPC was asked to determine whether the execution of condemned prisoners in such circumstances violated their constitutional rights.

In two of the appeals, *Fisher v. Minister of Public Safety and Immigration (No. 2)* and *Higgs v. Minister of National Security*[96] (both on appeal from the Bahamas), the JCPC held that the right to the protection of the law, which was guaranteed by the constitution, did not include a right to petition an international human rights body. Nor could such a right be read into the constitution because such a right did not previously exist under the common law. By

---

[94] Ibid., at 328F-H.
[95] *Pratt and Morgan v. Attorney General of Jamaica* [1994], 2 AC 1, 19 (emphasis added).
[96] [2000] 2 AC 228.

contrast, in the other two appeals, *Thomas v. Baptiste*[97] and *Lewis v. AG (Jamaica)*,[98] the JCPC held that the right which the appellants were seeking to enforce – not to have the outcome of any pending appellate or other legal process pre-empted by executive action – was a general one that was '*accorded by the common law*' and could, therefore, be read into the constitution. Thus, in all four cases, it was the English common law and not the fundamental rights guarantees of the respective Independence Constitutions that was ultimately determinative of the issue to be decided.

This approach, which is sometimes categorised as 'common law constitutionalism', has been deprecated by a number of leading Caribbean constitutional scholars for its reliance on an English and colonial conception of liberty. Tracey Robinson, for example, has argued that

> Caribbean common law constitutionalism relie[s] heavily on existing laws and the common law as the source of constitutional fundamentals. Post-independence common law constitutionalism [has] gained a bad reputation for elevating ordinary existing or colonial laws to higher order norms, giving them normative force as the repository of constitutional and human rights principles. . . . Implied norms cannot ethically be made to rest on fantasies of empire.[99]

For these scholars, the source of the fundamental rights of Commonwealth Caribbean citizens must be located in the text of their Independence Constitutions and not in laws that were received as part of the region's colonial inheritance. To give foundational status to the English common law is wrong, because it privileges colonial-era law above the post-independence legal order. It could be added, moreover, that it privileges a source of law which was once used to oppress and enslave those from whom the majority of the region's citizens are descended.

CONCLUSION

When making claims about the influence of Magna Carta in Britain's former colonies, it is important to acknowledge the role that Magna Carta played in the maintenance of slavery within the Commonwealth Caribbean. The protection which the original settlers derived from Magna Carta and the other liberties and privileges which they claimed as their colonial birthright was

---

[97] [2000] AC 1.
[98] [2000] 3 WLR 1785.
[99] 'Our Inherent Constitution', in D. Berry and T. Robinson (eds.), *Transitions in Caribbean Law* (Kingston, Jamaica: Caribbean Law Publishing Company, 2013), 273.

invoked by them to enact laws that reduced hundreds of thousands of African men and women to the status of chattels and, for a number of decades, to resist the efforts of the British government to reform the system of slavery in place in the region for nearly three centuries.

It is true that, in England, Magna Carta was a source of inspiration for abolitionists such as Granville Sharp, who succeeded in persuading Lord Mansfield that slave owners could not force their slaves to return to the colonies against their will. But it is equally true that, even at the point when slavery was being abolished, the slave owners were still able to rely on the respect accorded to property rights by Magna Carta to secure a handsome compensation package for the loss of property in their slaves – an obscene, if at the time necessary, gesture which still rankles with many in the region today.[100]

In the post-independence era, the legacy of English liberty bequeathed by the original settlers has continued to define and shape the rights and freedoms of Commonwealth Caribbean citizens by restricting them to their pre-independence incarnation. Not only has this undermined the normative force of the Independence Constitutions, but in so doing, it has evoked a source of law that is inextricably associated with the colonial era and slavery.

A new narrative of imperial history and of the influence of Magna Carta in these former colonies is, accordingly, needed. Such a narrative would not only acknowledge the problematic nature of Magna Carta's influence in the region, but would also affirm the existence of a new and independent post-colonial legal order as the exclusive source of the rights of the region's citizens.

---

[100] The payment of compensation to slave owners is often remarked upon by Commonwealth Caribbean governments in support of their claim for reparations for the economic and social poverty that is slavery's legacy to the region. See further F. Brennan and J. Packer (eds.), *Colonialism, Slavery, Reparations and Trade* (London: Routledge, 2012).

7

Magna Carta Frustrated? Institutional Delay in the Pacific Island States of the Commonwealth

David Clark

The law's delay has been the subject of complaint at least since Magna Carta 1215 and of course was satirised by Charles Dickens in *Bleak House* in the famous case of *Jarndyce v. Jarndyce*.[1] It also remains a problem despite constitutional obligations to guarantee a trial within a reasonable time. The standard of a trial within a reasonable time is now found in most of the written constitutions of Commonwealth countries, including in the Pacific Island Commonwealth states covered by this chapter. The central difficulty with this or any other legal standard expressed in very general terms is how to implement it. This was, of course, a feature of Article 40 of Magna Carta 1215 and its statutory successors in Article 29 of the 1225 and 1297 reissues of Magna Carta, in which the promise not to delay justice did not explain what delay meant or indicate how this was to be measured or enforced. Magna Carta did not impose limitations on the king's power, but through the efforts of later generations, it led to limits on executive power and the development of a tradition of constitutional government.[2] It was left up to later generations to create new rights and to give content to old promises. As a Fijian court pointed out in 2008, the law should not stand still, and since Magna Carta, common law courts and parliaments have changed the law.[3]

This paper considers both the direct and indirect influence of Magna Carta. The delay issue was specifically mentioned in Article 40 of Magna Carta (1215), and that article has traditionally been referred to in modern cases as the origin of the view that justice should not be delayed. As we shall see, there are major problems with this medieval promise, and in practice, the influence

---

[1] Magna Carta 1215, Article 40, translated in J. C. Holt, Magna Carta, 2nd ed. (Cambridge University Press, 1992), Appendix 6, 55; Magna Carta 1297, c 9, 25 Edw 1, c 29. A point recognised in the Pacific: *Atkinson v. Namale West Inc* [2012], FJHC 1363[13].

[2] *Qarase v. Bainimarama* [2009], 3 LRC 614, 643[79[(Fiji HC).

[3] *Republic of Fiji Military Forces v. Qicatabua* [2008], FJCA 50[26].

of Magna Carta has proved to be indirect in that it was only in modern constitutions that the promise not to delay justice was given a contemporary juridical foundation. In addition, it was only the judicial interpretation of these constitutional rights to a trial without unreasonable delay that gave the promise a more detailed modern form. In large measure, these interpretations are a response to an issue that is both ancient and contemporary, but the solutions proposed and the responses to the problem are to be understood in a modern context.

In practice, British statutes generally do not apply in the South Pacific states, except in Pitcairn, which remains a British Overseas Territory.[4] Despite this, Magna Carta ideas have survived and have been transformed by being embodied in the bill of rights sections of modern constitutions, including in the constitutions of Pacific states. Resort has also been had to the common law doctrine of abuse of process and international jurisprudence, both of which are arguably the indirect offspring of ideas in Magna Carta. A general constitutional standard provides both an obligation on the courts and the executive to adhere to it as well as an opportunity for the judiciary, given the open-textured nature of these mandates, to determine the content of the requirement. As one Canadian judge put it, the promise not to delay justice is 'beguiling in its simplicity' but presents 'the Court with one of its most difficult challenges'.[5]

This chapter begins by considering unreasonable delay in criminal cases in Canada, where the prohibition on such delays originated in a constitutional form in section 11(b) of the Charter of Rights and Freedoms (in force 17 April 1982). The Canadian cases have had a life outside North America, in particular in the smaller Pacific Commonwealth states where the Canadian criteria for assessing delay have been accepted, but where the very different institutional circumstances have resulted in a different judicial attitude towards institutional delay. It will be argued that the circumstances of the particular jurisdiction require a measure of judicial realism about how institutional delay is to be regarded. The adoption of the same constitutional standard in quite different states at different levels of development poses the central question of the paper: is it right to apply a common standard to criminal trial delay irrespective of the underlying institutional differences between jurisdictions? Even where the same ideas are found in different constitutions in different societies, it does not follow that they will be implemented the same way. This chapter directs attention to this implementation

---

[4]   Jennifer Corrin and Don Paterson, *Introduction to South Pacific Law*, 3rd ed. (South Yarra, Vic: Palgrave MacMillan, 2011), 19–22.

[5]   *R v. Morin* [1992], 1 SCR 771, 779.

problem. Although it is a problem often ignored by advocates of universal human rights, students of comparative constitutions are only too aware of the difficulties of securing rights where the underlying political, social and economic conditions do not support them. Another issue is whether judicial doctrine has made any difference to court delay. There is evidence from Canada that shows, despite judicial decisions since 1980 criticizing delay, that the problem of delayed trials is as bad as ever.[6] There are no comparable data for the Pacific.

Delay may be broken down into the following periods:

1. The period prior to charges.
2. Delay between the laying of charges and the commencement of the trial.
3. Delay between conviction and sentencing.
4. Delay between sentencing and the hearing of an appeal.
5. Delay between appeals and the carrying out of the sentence in death penalty cases in the Caribbean Commonwealth states and India, which retain the death penalty.

In this chapter, only the second through fourth categories count in a legal sense for the purposes of the constitutional standard. This limited view of what counts as delay may be questioned, especially since many of the problems created by delay, such as the impact on the accused and on the victims of crime, often apply equally to pre-charge and post-charge delay. The problems experienced by the accused and the victims as the result of delay include the loss of privacy; stress and anxiety; possible disruption of family, social life and work; and legal costs.[7] Of course, delay also has other effects, including a reduction in public regard for the legal system and increased pressure inside the court system as case lists lengthen and workloads grow.

THE CANADIAN CRITERIA

While the Canadian criteria were articulated in cases decided prior to *R v. Morin*, that case provides the most authoritative explanation of the criteria, is the case most often cited in Canada on the issue and, for the purposes of this study, is the Canadian case most often cited in Commonwealth jurisdictions on unreasonable delay.[8] In *Morin* – a case in which the accused was charged

---

[6] Clayton Ruby and Angela Chaisson, 'Waiting for Justice', *Precedent*, 28 June 2013, at http://lawandstyle.ca/waiting-for-justice/ (accessed 14 April 2014).

[7] *R v. Rahey* [1987], 1 SCR 588, 605.

[8] *R v. Morin* [1992], 1 SCR 771; see citations to *Morin* in *Mills v. State* [2005], FJCA 6[95].

with a drunk driving offence and where fourteen-and-a-half months lapsed between the laying of charges and the commencement of the trial – Sopinka J. set out the following criteria:[9]

- Length of the delay.
- Waiver of time periods.
- The reasons for the delay.
- Inherent time requirements.
- Actions of the accused.
- Actions of the Crown.
- Limits on institutional resources.
- Other reasons for the delay.
- Prejudice to the accused.

It is worth stressing that delay may be caused by the defendant and is often resorted to as a defence tactic. This sort of delay cannot be used to found a constitutional claim, for obvious reasons, even if the period is quite long.[10]

The Attitude of the Canadian Courts to Institutional Delay

The cases support the view that the period for calculating unreasonable delay starts from the time when the person is charged.[11] Earlier periods normally do not count, though there is a dictum that suggests that if charges are brought then dropped, followed by new charges, the first period might be included in the period to be assessed by the court.[12] The period only becomes a delay for legal purposes when it fails to meet the constitutional right 'to be tried within a reasonable time'. Post-sentencing delay caused by the hearing of appeals against a not guilty verdict does not count for the purposes of section 11(b), because that only applies where a person is charged. A person who is acquitted is not facing a charge and therefore post-trial appellate delay in that case does not count.[13]

Morin and later cases denied that breaches of section 11(b) are to be decided by the application of a mathematical or an administrative formula,[14] but rather involve a balancing of the factors that the section was intended to

---

[9] [1992] 1 SCR 771, 787–88.
[10] *Sorovanalagi v. State* [2011], FJHC 460.
[11] *R v. Kalanj* [1989], 1 SCR 1594, 1600.
[12] *Carter v. R* [1986], 1 SCR 981, 985.
[13] *R v. Poitvin* [1993], 2 SCR 880, 899, 910.
[14] *R v. Morin* [1992], 1 SCR 771, 787. See also *R v. MacDougal* [1998], 3 SCR 45, 66[41], where McLachlin J. wrote that 'The analysis must not proceed in a mechanical manner.' See also *Public Prosecutor v. Emelee* [2006], 2 LRC 76, 83i, 88b(Vanuatu CA).

protect as well as the circumstances of the particular case.[15] This is in keeping with the view that the common law 'usually recoils from absolute rules of mechanical or inflexible application. It does so because its long experience illustrates too often the need to retain elements of flexibility to cover an exceptional case'.[16] The 8- to 10-months guideline laid down in *Morin* was explicitly stated to be neither a limitation period nor a fixed ceiling.[17] Deviations from the guideline may be accepted, as they were in the case in which a period of fourteen-and-a-half months was held not to breach the constitutional standard. On the other hand, where the actual delay exceeds the guideline, this triggers an inquiry into the reasonableness of the delay. The courts may use statistical data on comparable delays in other parts of the same jurisdiction or even data from other provinces as an aid in making determinations about unreasonable delay.[18] This approach has actually proved to be a problem for the Canadian Supreme Court, because the comparative data may be wrong or even totally inappropriate.[19] There is also a debate about whether there really are resource problems in Canada at all, with a Law Reform Commission Working Paper suggesting in 1994 that it was the inefficient use of existing resources that was causing problems.[20] Nevertheless, the courts have identified actual instances of delay in practice, whatever the ideal situation suggested by reformers.

Forms of Institutional Delay in Canada

In a decision in 2011, a judge of the Ontario Superior Court of Justice followed *Morin* where Sopinka J. had held that institutional delay 'starts to run when the parties are ready for trial, but the system cannot accommodate them'.[21] The term refers to delays caused by a scarcity of resources, such as:[22]

- The lack of available courtroom space.[23]
- The judge is ill or dies.[24]

[15] In *R v. Morin* [1992], 1 SCR 771, 786(SCC), Sopinka J. identified these as primarily the protection of the individual rights of the accused and a secondary interest of society as a whole.
[16] *Wishprun Pty Ltd v. Dixon* [2003], 77 ALJR 1598, 1616[100](HCA).
[17] *R v. Morin* [1992], 1 SCR 771, 807.
[18] *R v. Lee* [2010], ONCJ 163[31].
[19] Carl Baar, 'Court Delay Data as Social Science Evidence: The Supreme Court of Canada and "Trial within a Reasonable Time"', *Justice System Journal* 19 (1997): 123–44.
[20] Law Reform Commission of Canada, Working Paper No 67, *Trial within a Reasonable Time* (1994), 11–14.
[21] *R v. Lahiry* [2011], ONSC 6780; 109 OR (3d) 187[26].
[22] *R v. Collins* [1995], 2 SCR 1104, 1109.
[23] *R v. CIP Inc* [1992], 1 SCR 843, 860.
[24] *Collins v. R* [2008], NBPC 53(New Brunswick Prov Ct)[8]–[9].

- Lack of essential court staff.[25]
- Slow forensic results.[26]

One point to note in Morin is that the case was decided in the context of a major upsurge in cases in Ontario between 1985/86 and 1989/90 from 80,000 cases per year to more than 180,000. This increase could not be predicted, and some of the increase was attributable to the more frequent resort to the Canadian Charter of Rights and Freedoms 1982 and other reasons.[27] The appeal in Morin came from the district of Durham in Ontario, where case-loads had increased by 70 per cent for adult cases and 143 per cent for youth court cases during the same the period. Data cited in Morin showed that between 22 October 1990 and 6 September 1991, 47,000 charges were stayed or withdrawn in Ontario alone.[28] This evidence indicates that compliance with the constitutional standard occurs outside of court proceedings not by meeting the Morin test, but by simply dropping large numbers of cases at risk of a stay were they to go to court. The evidence discussed in the case also shows that rises in caseloads may be unpredictable and possibly temporary. One odd effect of the late withdrawal of cases (called the collapse rate), which may occur for various reasons including failure to comply with the constitutional standard, is to actually leave some courts empty day after day.[29]

The categories of institutional delay identified in Canada occur in a developed jurisdiction with considerable financial and institutional resources. In principle, the Canadian state should be able to deploy sufficient resources to overcome these problems. As we shall see, while the same categories apply to Pacific Island states, they are considerably magnified in severity there, given the different context; and, as the rest of the chapter shows, there are additional forms of institutional delay not found in a developed jurisdiction.

DELAY IN THE SMALLER PACIFIC JURISDICTIONS OF THE COMMONWEALTH

Each of the jurisdictions included in this chapter have small populations and limited judicial and other legal resources, and they often struggle to provide the kind of legal services found in larger, developed states. Yet, in most of them there is a constitutional requirement to provide a trial 'within a reasonable

[25] R v. Morin [1992], 1 SCR 771, 791.
[26] R v. Godin [2009], 2 SCR 3, 7[6].
[27] [1992] 1 SCR 771, 806. Such as rapid population growth, the complexity of forensic evidence and the opening of a new airport that was used by drug smugglers from the United States.
[28] R v. Morin [1992], 1 SCR 771, 779.
[29] R v. Lahiry [2011], 109 OR (3d) 187[42].

time'.[30] As in Canada, the courts have had to wrestle with the problem of determining how such a test is to be applied, given local circumstances. In dealing with the meaning of the phrase, *Morin* has been a key case used in these jurisdictions, though other legal influences are also at work.[31]

The Importance of Local Conditions

Any appraisal of the reasonableness or otherwise of a particular delay depends, as the Judicial Committee pointed out in *Bell v. Director of Public Prosecutions*,[32] '. . . on the prevailing system of legal administration and economic, social and cultural conditions . . .'[33] Thus judgments about delays in a particular jurisdiction are to be made, not in the light of conditions and the practices in England, but in the light of local circumstances.[34] The problems facing legal systems in the Caribbean, for example, have been commented on many times.[35] The Judicial Committee cited the Trinidad and Tobago Court of Appeal to the effect that the high murder rate, the inundation of the courts of an excessive caseload,[36] death penalty appeals and the lack of trained staff are major reasons for delays.[37] Not all of these factors exist elsewhere in the Commonwealth. In the Pacific jurisdictions, for example, the death penalty does not apply. Nevertheless, as the Chief Justice of Samoa remarked in a case of a five-month institutional delay, 'As a third world developing nation, Samoa also has limited resources which have to be shared around all sectors of the community'.[38] Although some leeway is granted on account of this factor, the Pacific courts have said, as courts have elsewhere, that while institutional limitations might have more impact than in 'more affluent countries such as

[30] Constitution of the Republic of Vanuatu, Art. 5(2)(a); Constitution of Kiribati, Art. 5(3)(a); Constitution of Solomon Islands, s 10(1); Constitution of Tuvalu, Art. 22(11)(b); Constitution of the Independent State of Samoa, Art. 9; Constitution of Papua New Guinea, s 37(3); Constitution of Nauru, Art. 10(2); Pitcairn Islands Constitution Order 2010, UK SI 2010 No 244, s 7(3), Constitution Of Fiji 2013 s 14(2)(g).

[31] *Morin* is cited in *Republic v. Kaiue* [2003], KIHC 94[3](Kiribati HC); *Police v. Ropati* [2006], 2 LRC 62, 66 (Samoa SC); *Rokoua v. The State* [2006], FJCA 5[21]; *Mailamua v. R* [2009], TVHC 4[2](Tuvalu HC); *Dawson v. Public Prosecutor* [2010], VUCA 10[3](Vanuatu CA). Other sources, such as those cited in *Seko v. R* [2005], SBHC 100[2]–[3], include European jurisprudence and the Amnesty International Fair Trial Manual, available at http://www.amnesty.org/en/fairtrials.

[32] [1985] AC 937.

[33] Ibid., 953B–D.

[34] *Charles v. R* [2000], 1 WLR 384, 390C(PC).

[35] *Gibson v. Attorney General* [2010], 5 LRC 486[51](Caribbean Ct of Justice).

[36] *Robinson v. R* [1984], UKPC 3 at page 12.

[37] *Charles v. R* [2000], 1 WLR 384, 390D(PC).

[38] *Police v. Ropati* [2006], 2 LRC 62. 75d-e(Samoa SC).

Australia and New Zealand and the USA, it cannot stand in the way of securing a right entrenched in the constitution'.[39] Citing cases from Mauritius, the courts in the Pacific have more than once pointed out that the correct approach to assessing delay is to carefully examine the circumstances of each case and to avoid a rigid approach. In *Republic v. Teoiaki*,[40] the High Court of Kiribati cited the Privy Council in *Mungroo v. R*, where Lord Templeman wrote, '. . . in determining whether the constitutional rights of an individual have been infringed, the courts must have regard to the constraints imposed by harsh economic reality and local conditions'.[41]

In an important statement of principle, the Fiji Court of Appeal observed in 2003 that while the right to be tried without unreasonable delay exists in several countries such as Canada, New Zealand and Fiji, and therefore the basic issue is the same, '. . . regard must be had to the background against which the particular case is set, that is the society in which the prosecution is proceeding. A highly sophisticated, wealthy country may reasonably demand higher standards of its public facilities, such as courts. This is not to disparage the public facilities available in Fiji, but plainly it would be impossible to think in terms of some absolute international standard for the case-flow of prosecutions'.[42]

The court went on to say that, given the constitutional requirement, it could not simply accept delay on account of the institutional limitations and that one advantage of successful applications may be to induce the authorities to allocate greater resources to the courts or to take energetic administrative steps to improve case-flow, to overcome delays and to focus on the disposal of trials outstanding for unduly long periods.[43] On the facts of *Seru*, which was a case of delay that lasted for more than four years in a simple matter, the court held that the conviction and sentence for attempting to obtain credit by fraud should be quashed and no other trial permitted.[44]

Forms of Institutional Delay in the Pacific

No Legal Institutions in Place: Pitcairn Island

The ultimate lack of institutional resources was exposed as a result of a decision to try seven defendants for rape and other sexual offences on

---

[39] *State v. Khanna* [2004], FJHC 451[5].
[40] [1993] 3 LRC 385, 388b-c(Kiribati HC).
[41] [1991] 1 WLR 1351, 1355(PC).
[42] *Seru v. State* [2003], FJCA 26[6].
[43] Ibid.
[44] Ibid., 10.

Pitcairn Island.[45] Though a British territory since 1838, the island lacked all of the machinery of justice. As Lord Hope put it in the Judicial Committee in 2007, 'They had no operative legal system for almost all of the island's habitation other than a local island magistrate assisted by two assessors, none of whom had any legal training'.[46] There were no police, judges, lawyers, registrar, local prison or even a court building. None of this is surprising given that the Pitcairn territory consists of four islands, only one of which, Pitcairn Island, had a population, at the time totalling 47 persons on an island of 3.6 square kilometres (2.2 square miles). The practical problems were enormous and were solved following an agreement between the British and New Zealand governments whereby some of the legal proceedings would be conducted in New Zealand,[47] which passed legislation to allow sittings in Auckland of the Pitcairn Supreme Court. It was also agreed that Britain would cover the full costs of the legal proceedings and that New Zealanders would be sworn in as Pitcairn judges and lawyers to conduct the proceedings both on the island and in New Zealand.[48] In addition to this groundwork, 49 pieces of legislation were passed between 1999 and 2005 to provide the relevant institutions.[49] The creation of appropriate institutional arrangements took two-and-a-half years from the first interviews of the suspects until the charges were laid. Of course, pre-charge delay does not count for the purposes of Article 5(1) of the European Convention for the Protection of Human Rights and Fundamental Freedoms, which guarantees a trial within a reasonable time and is scheduled in the *Human Rights Act 1998* (UK). The Act applies to British territories.[50]

The charges were laid in Pitcairn on 3 April 2003,[51] and the trial began on 29 September 2004,[52] finishing with the sentencing on 29 October 2004.[53] Thus, nearly seventeen months lapsed between the laying of charges and the end of

---

[45] Charges were also laid against Pitcairn men living in New Zealand: A. H. Angelo and Andrew Townend, 'Pitcairn: A Commentary' (2003) 1 *NZJPIL* 229, 230.

[46] *Christian v. R* [2007], 2 AC 400, 422[59](PC). See also at 427[74] for an extract of a letter by the Acting Governor, who wrote in May 2000 that 'There is no civil authority on the island.'

[47] Pitcairn Trials Act 2002 (NZ) Schedule.

[48] Kathy Marks, *Pitcairn Paradise Lost: Uncovering the Dark Secrets of a South Pacific Fantasy Island* (Sydney: Fourth Estate, 2008), 90–93. For a collection of essays on the trials generally, see Dawn Oliver (ed.), *Justice, Legality and the Rule of Law: Lessons from the Pitcairn Prosecutions* (Oxford University Press, 2009). The total cost amounted to NZ$14 million.

[49] *R v. Christian* (No 2) [2006], 1 LRC 745, 771–775[83](Pitcairn SC). For the texts, see http://www.government.pn/Laws/index.php (accessed 16 July 2014).

[50] *R v. Christian* (No 2) [2006], 1 LRC 745, 807[203](Pitcairn SC); *Pitcairn Islands Constitution Order 2010*, UK SI 2010 No 2544, s 7(3).

[51] *R v. Christian* (No 2) [2006], 1 LRC 745, 806[193].

[52] Kathy Marks, n. 48 above, 112.

[53] Kathy Marks, n. 48 above, 179–82.

the trial process. Given the circumstances, this compares favourably with the fourteen-and-a-half months accepted in *Morin*. The Strasbourg jurisprudence provides that the starting point for assessing delay is when the charges are laid,[54] and in this case, the end point occurred when the case for a delay argument came before the court.[55] When the delay argument went to the Pitcairn Supreme Court, the court took into account the logistical problems of conducting the case in which nineteen persons had to be sent from New Zealand in order to run the trials. The trial of the facts and sentencing took place on the Island, but the subsequent legal arguments and appeals all took place in New Zealand. In view of these circumstances – which were not those of a trial in a developed state, but a trial partly on the most remote island in the world – the court rejected the delay argument.[56] On appeal, the delay point focused on the period between the announcement that the accused were being investigated and the laying of charges. It was conceded by the appellants that the trial itself had been conducted with reasonable dispatch.[57] The Court of Appeal accepted the problems that were entailed in conducting the hearing on Pitcairn and concluded that there was no prejudice to the defendants arising from the delay.[58] The Judicial Committee agreed with this assessment and noted that the creation of the administrative arrangements, including the agreement with New Zealand, was 'carried through with remarkable speed', that there was no prejudice to the accused and thus there was no abuse of process ground in this case.[59] The Judicial Committee went out of its way to commend all those involved for making the considerable resources required available.[60] Despite British neglect, the fact that Pitcairn remained an overseas possession of a developed state made it possible to provide the required resources – an option not necessarily available to an independent territory.

Disruption to the Legal Order: Fiji

Fiji has had five constitutions since independence in 1970. In each of them, there was provision for a trial within a reasonable time.[61] But Fiji has been a

---

54   *Eckle v. Federal Republic of Germany* [1982], 5 EHRR 1[72] cited in *R v. Christian* (No 2) [2006] 1 LRC 745, 809[212].

55   [2006] 1 LRC 745, 811[220].

56   [2006] 1 LRC 745, 817[240g].

57   *R v. Christian* (No 2) [2006] 4 LRC 746, 782[120](Pitcairn CA).

58   [2006] 1 LRC 745, 784[125].

59   *Christian v. R* [2007], 2 AC 400, 413[25](PC).

60   *Christian v. R* [2007], 2 AC 400, 415[32].

61   The Constitution of Fiji 1970 as a Schedule to the Fiji Independence Order 1970 (UK), s 10(1); Constitution of Fiji 1988, s 29(3); Constitution of the Sovereign Democratic Republic of Fiji (Promulgation) Decree 1990, s 11(1); Constitution of Fiji 1997, s 29(3); Constitution of Fiji 2013, s 14(2)(g).

troubled state, with serious conflict leading to the abrogation of four of these constitutions and a pattern of unconstitutional acts by its own leaders. The troubled history of periodic coups d'état since 1987 makes the Fijian case distinctive.[62] More than one judge has noted that the coup of 2000, in which the Prime Minister and his cabinet were held hostage on the parliamentary precinct for fifty-six days,[63] disrupted the legal system and the police in particular.[64] One problem was that several judges resigned as a result of these disruptions to the legal order, and investigating officers had to be replaced, usually in a dilatory manner. Although the coup of 2000 did not technically abrogate the Constitution and thus section 29(3) of that document that provided for a fair trial within a reasonable time remained in place, disruptions nevertheless took place.[65] Following the coup d'état of May 2000, there was a military mutiny in December of that year, and the mutineers were eventually put on trial by court martial in February 2003, with the trial itself lasting seventeen months. The court took into account the political instability and noted the limited institutional and personnel resources in Fiji. Applying the criteria, the Court of Appeal concluded that the delay was actually largely due to frequent adjournments sought by the defendants and for that reason was not a breach of the constitutional standard.[66]

The abrogation of the Constitution after the latest coup in December 2006 also resulted in a major disruption to the legal system. The entire Court of Appeal resigned in September 2007 over interference with the court by the Chief Justice. All of the members of the court were either from New Zealand or Australia and were replaced by judges from Malaysia and Sri Lanka.[67] Nevertheless, despite a period in which there was no constitution, the Fijian courts relied upon common law abuse-of-process arguments and on Article 14(3)(c) of the International Covenant of Civil and Political Rights 1966, which mandates a right to be tried 'without undue delay', and which

---

[62] There were two coups in 1987, and one each in 1988, 2000 and 2006. See Yash Ghai and Jill Cottrell, 'A Tale of Three Constitutions: Ethnicity and Politics in Fiji', *International Journal of Constitutional Law* 5 (2007): 639–69. Although Fiji's history is distinctive, it is not unique. The Solomon Islands experienced a period of anarchy in June 2000, when remand prisoners walked out of the prison and the Guadalcanal Liberation Front was responsible for numerous kidnappings and killings. On the Solomon Islands, see *Robu v. R* [2006], SBCA 14[23]; *Kelly v. R* [2006], SBCA 17.

[63] *Republic of Fiji Islands v. Prasad* [2001], 2 LRC 743, 748–51.

[64] *Tuimoala v. Public Service Commission* [2003], FJHC 297[4–5].

[65] Constitution of Fiji 1997, Art. 29(3).

[66] *Mills v. State* [2005], FJCA 6[96]–[100].

[67] 'Appeal Judges Resign over Gates' Actions', *Fiji Times Online*, http://www.fijitimes.com/story.aspx?id=69814 (accessed 7 February 2014).

is still part of Fijian law,[68] to assert a jurisdiction in matters of delay. The revised Fijian Constitution of 2013 reinstated the right to be tried 'without unreasonable delay', creating a constitutional right and with it the jurisdiction in the courts to adjudicate claims for breaches of this and other rights.[69] Unfortunately, section 170 of the Constitution preserved all of the limitations in the Administration of Justice Decree 2009, which created immunities for the coup leaders of 2006, while sections 152–155 entrench immunities for acts under various coups and decrees between 1990 and 2010. Given the overthrow of the Constitution and the sacking of judges in recent decades, it remains to be seen whether the new Constitution will prove enduring.

An Internal Crisis Leading to the Dismissal of the Judges

The instability caused by the coup of 2006 in Fiji had prolonged effects. In 2009, the Fiji Court of Appeal issued a declaration that the interim Prime Minister had acted unconstitutionally in dismissing the elected Prime Minister, in dissolving Parliament and in advising the President to ratify the illegal acts by the leaders of the 2006 coup.[70] The President responded by suspending the Constitution and sacking all of the judges.[71] These acts were part of a pattern since 1987 of indigenous Fijian elites ignoring the law whenever their power was threatened. They play by the constitutional rules when they get what they want but break or ignore the rules when the rules get in their way.

The most recent example of an internal crisis causing major delays and disruptions to an already-weak legal system occurred in January 2014, when the Nauru government effectively excluded both the sole Magistrate and the Chief Justice from the country by revoking their visas (both were Australians) when they were out of the country, thereby eliminating all judicial officers from the legal system.[72]

Lack of Courts and Judges

One of the problems faced by Pacific courts is that some have no resident judges at all, while others have only a single judge. Most do not have a resident

---

[68] Criminal Procedure Decree 2009 (Fiji) s 290(1)(f).

[69] Constitution of Fiji 2013, section 14(2)(g). See also sections 7 and 96(1). Section 96(5) provides that 'Parliament must ensure that the Judiciary has adequate financial and other resources to perform its functions and exercise its powers properly.'

[70] *Qarase v. Bainimarama* [2009], 3 LRC 614(Fiji CA).

[71] Fiji Constitution Amendment Act 1997 Revocation Decree 2009 in *Republic of Fiji Islands Government Gazette*, 10 April 2009, No 1.

[72] International Commission of Jurists, 'Nauru: Removal of Judges Violates Independence of Judiciary', 21 January 2014, press release available at http://www.icj.org/nauru-removal-of-judges-violates-independence-of-judiciary/ (last accessed 7 February 2014).

appellate court, and the personnel are largely supplied by Australia and New Zealand. This means that appeal courts often only sit once or twice a year, and this accounts for delays in hearing appeals.[73] The courts have often referred to the lack of resources in these jurisdictions as a constraint on the delivery of the constitutional requirement to provide a fair trial.[74] Samoa, for example, has only two resident judges, who also hear appeals from lower courts. One consequence of these limitations is a far greater tolerance for long delays that would be considered unreasonable in Canada, for instance. Thus, a six-year delay in Fiji between the charge and the present was held to be unreasonable but not stayed, as the court held that a fair trial was still possible.[75] There is also evidence that delays of up to two-and-a-half years – and even longer – have been accepted in Fiji,[76] though a stricter view is taken elsewhere.[77] This is obviously far greater than the 8–10 months accepted as the guideline in *Morin*, and it seems clear that while in Canada a long delay is presumptively prejudicial, in Fiji, for example, it is not. The applicants for relief, as these cases indicate, have to discharge the onus of establishing prejudice and show that a fair trial is not possible.[78]

In one instance from Fiji, court buildings were in such a bad state that occupational health and safety inspectors closed two courts in Lautoka, Fiji's second-largest city, thereby aborting all criminal trials there. No suitable alternative venues were available, and it was unclear when the situation would improve. Five applicants facing murder charges and scheduled to be tried in Lautoka argued that they had been denied a trial within a reasonable time. The delay had been compounded by the fact that they had been denied bail. In total, they had been in custody since December 1999 although they

---

[73] *Samoa Party v. Attorney General* [2010], WSCA 4[54](Samoa CA): 'The reason this Court sits only twice a year (until recently it was only once) is that Magna Carta's prohibition of judicial delay can receive only a reasonable response, not an immediate one.'

[74] *State v. Stevens* [1999], FJHC 143[3], seven-year delay partly caused by a lack of judges; *Seru v. State* [2003], FJCA 26[3], delay between November 1994 when charges were laid and the trial that commenced in July 1999; *Sahim v. State* [2007], FJHC 119[40] delay of six years held unreasonable, and court ordered a trial within the next 40 days.

[75] *In re Application by Nand* [2008], FJHC 191[12.1].

[76] *State v. Ledua* [2011], FJMC 20. See also *Bhika v. State* [2008], FJHC 179[10], where one year four months was held not unreasonable.

[77] *Mailemua v. R* [2009], TVHC 4(Tuvalu HC), where a delay of more than five years was criticised, but the matter was sent back to the trial court because the causes of the delay were not explained.

[78] *Nur v. State* [2009], FJHC 211, where a four-year delay was held unreasonable but no stay was granted because the applicants could not establish prejudice. The court ordered the trial in the magistrates' court to proceed; *Bavoro v. State* [2011], FJHC 235[5], where a stay was refused despite a six-year delay because the applicant could not establish that the delay had caused prejudice.

had made their application in May 2001. The court noted the eighteen-month delay in the case and held that this was excessive,[79] and, given the appalling conditions in the prison – which were also in breach of the prisoners' constitutional rights – decided in view of the serious charges to grant bail rather than a stay.[80] In another case in Lautoka, four years elapsed between the bringing of charges and the commencement of the trial, partly due to the lack of magistrates to hear cases. There were forty-five adjournments, most of which were caused by the applicant, and thus the delay argument failed for that reason.[81]

Lack of Lawyers

The availability of lawyers, especially prosecutors, is another chronic problem in small jurisdictions. In one complex matter from Vanuatu, the case could not be carried forward because the Public Prosecutor had left and only junior officers were available.[82] The lower court concluded that the eighteen-month delay in this case was a violation of the constitutional duty to provide a fair hearing within a reasonable time, and the application to strike out the case for want of prosecution was granted.[83] The Court of Appeal allowed the appeal against this decision, noting that nine months of the delay was caused by decisions by the respondents and therefore amounted to a waiver. This left nine months delay, which the court thought was not unreasonable.[84] In the result, the Court of Appeal re-instated the charges and ordered that they be heard 'as soon as possible'. The court did not discuss the lack of legal manpower, though it noted the problem of the public prosecutor's absence. Nevertheless, the shortage of 'skilled manpower', as one court put it, is a matter of complaint extending to a shortage of judges as well as lawyers.[85]

The establishment in 1994 of a School of Law at Port Vila, Vanuatu, with a branch in Suva, which has approximately 900 students drawn from twelve countries, in theory will go a long way to overcome the lack of locally educated lawyers. The reality, however, may be different. Five Solomon Islands law students about to graduate may not do so because their government is in arrears in the payment of student fees to the law school. One student had to resort to a public appeal to the government in the main newspaper in Honiara

---

[79] *Naba v. The State* [2001], FJHC 127[6].
[80] Ibid., [14]–[15]. There was no judge at Labasa for more than four years: *Ali v. State* [2008], FJCA 96[28].
[81] *Nalawa v. State* [2010], FJSC 2[30]–[33].
[82] *Public Prosecutor v. Benard* [2006], 1 LRC 418, 426(Vanuatu SC).
[83] Art 5(2)(a) Vanuatu Constitution in ibid. 424i.
[84] *Public Prosecutor v. Emelee* [2006], 3 LRC 76, 88a(Vanuatu CA).
[85] *Republic of Kiribati v. Teoiaki* [1993], 3 LRC 385, 377g–h.

to ask for the situation to be remedied. The situation deteriorated further, for in March 2014, twenty-three Solomon Islands law students had not been paid their allowance by their government five weeks into the semester, though the government promised to remedy the situation.

Lack of Expert Witnesses

A modern criminal trial requires more than lawyers and judges to operate properly. In an age of the expert witness where scientific evidence is routinely used in criminal cases, the conduct of a trial often draws upon expert evidence. All of this assumes that such experts are available. In a case from Kiribati, there was no doctor to give medical evidence in a manslaughter trial. The judge noted that as a young country with very limited resources, 'There is a shortage of trained professionals in every discipline, including medicine.'[86] Since the defence wanted to cross-examine the doctor, who by now was out of the jurisdiction, the trial was delayed, awaiting his return. Despite this, the court had little sympathy with the applicant for a stay because the applicant was mostly responsible for the delays that occurred in the case, which lasted three years and eight months. Similarly, delay occurred in the first Samoan case involving methamphetamine because the police were unfamiliar with the substance and there was doubt about the scientific analysis in the case. Initially it had been agreed to secure an opinion from a scientist in New Zealand, where the drug had been sent for analysis, without bringing him to Samoa, but defence counsel withdrew their consent to this arrangement. This circumstance, of course, caused a delay, because the chemist had to be brought from Auckland to give evidence.[87] To give an idea of some of the distances involved, Auckland to Apia, Samoa, is approximately the same distance as between London and Ankara, or Portland, Maine, and Puerto Rico. Auckland to Pitcairn Island is approximately the same distance as New York to London.

Basic Logistical Problems

Several of the jurisdictions are comprised of widely dispersed islands, and at the best of times transport between them can be haphazard.[88] This is especially true during the tropical cyclone season in the Southern

---

[86] *Teetea v. Republic* [1996], KIHC 101[3].

[87] *Police v. Falkner* [2005], WSSC 4[7]. The Court dismissed the motion for leave to appeal, and the delay point was rejected.

[88] *In re Buo* [2007], PGNC 235[5](Papua New Guinea National Court); *Kyio v. R* [2004], SBHC 90[5]. The Solomon Islands, for example, consists of more than 1,000 islands spread over 28,400 square kilometres, in which there are 63 distinct language groups.

Hemisphere, when transport between islands becomes impossible; and in some cases, the destruction caused by a cyclone may destroy the infrastructure, even in the capital.[89] Other islands are so remote that even with the limited transport available by air, complex trials simply cannot be held in the jurisdiction. In a civil case in Niue in 2010, the judge referred to this problem and the delays that it had caused, given that counsel at the time were located in both Australia and New Zealand and that the hearing was by telephone. The only solution in a complex matter was to ask counsel to agree on as much of the case as possible.[90]

General Incompetence and Slackness

The author spent time in Fiji in 2000 and discovered that half of all prosecutions did not proceed because the public prosecutors were too drunk to get out of bed. Cases routinely commenced many hours late and, in civil cases, delays became grotesque. In one adoption case that commenced when the child was a baby, the case remained unresolved twelve years later. Citizens of first world states are used to certain standards that do not always apply elsewhere: that the power is on, public officials are paid on time, law libraries have not been looted or illegally sold, records are properly kept and maintained, the phones work, people go to work on time, computer systems exist and are operational and the photocopier has paper that day, etc. The list of deficiencies is practically endless.

The good news is that both Australia and New Zealand are making considerable efforts to improve matters. Since the proposal in 1944 to create a South Pacific Commission, since renamed the Pacific Community, both countries have been major aid donors to the region. Currently, the region receives more than A$1 billion in aid from Australia and NZ$ 200 million from New Zealand each year.[91] Part of this aid is for legal development. There are now, for example, associations of Pacific lawyers and legal officers as well as judicial conferences held annually to provide technical assistance.[92] The Pacific Judicial Development Aid program (2010–2015) is funded by New Zealand and implemented by the Federal Court of Australia, in a joint effort

---

[89] *Republic of Kiribati v. Teoiaki* [1993], 3 LRC 385, 387g–h.
[90] *Flemming v. Talagi* [2010], NUHC 1(Niue HC)[1], [8].
[91] For aid data from Australia, see http://aid.dfat.gov.au/countries/pacific/Pages/home.aspx (accessed 7 February 2014). For aid data from New Zealand, see http://www.aid.govt.nz/about -aid-programme/aid-statistics/aid-allocations-201213-201415 (accessed 2 February 2015). This aid includes, for example, 60 scholarships awarded to Solomon Islands students to study in Australian and regional universities.
[92] Such as the Pacific Islands Legal Officer's Network: http://www.pilonsec.org/ (accessed 7 February 2014).

by those countries to improve the institutional performance of twelve Pacific legal systems.[93] There is also a program of legal assistance to eight Pacific states run by the Commonwealth Attorney-General's Department.[94]

Attitudes towards Delay

While the courts have at their disposal a number of remedies for unreasonable institutional delay, they have also commented on the responsibilities of the state 'to so organise their legal systems as to ensure that the reasonable time requirement is honored'.[95] Since the reasonable time standard is located in the constitutional context of a right to a fair trial, the courts have often over-looked long delays on the ground that, despite the delay, a fair trial is still possible.

There is a marked reluctance however to specify what should be done to overcome institutional delay, for the courts can neither prescribe budgetary or other solutions, nor are they equipped to do so. Occasionally they have urged the government to allocate sufficient funds to overcome institutional delay in order to meet the constitutional standard, but they cannot do more than this.[96] As the High Court of Australia pointed out in 1989: 'The courts do not have command of all of the resources which are necessary to secure prompt justice, and, if they were to assume a responsibility beyond their capacity, they would offer a hope of protection which they are unfitted to fulfill.'[97] Of course, these matters often go to the root causes of underdevelopment in states and econo-mies that are poor but which have, in essence, first world constitutional obligations. It is unlikely that the adoption of the unreasonable delay or related standards were ever initially understood as requiring facilities and resources to match this promise, or as requiring conditions far removed from the economic realities of small states.

There is evidence in Pacific courts that, apart from the inherent value of adherence to the constitutional standard, prompt trials are regarded as necessary for the suppression of crime and to protect the interests of victims of crime. In one Australian case, where abuse-of-process arguments were raised, a justice of the High Court of Australia expressed the concern that

---

[93] https://www.aid.govt.nz/media-and-publications/development-stories/october-2013/strengt hening-justice-across-pacific (accessed 7 February 2014). The program is described at http://www.fedcourt.gov.au/pjdp (accessed 7 February 2014).
[94] 'Pacific crime and policing assistance', http://www.ag.gov.au/Internationalrelations/International LegalAssistance/Pages/PacificCrimeAndPolicingAssistance.aspx (accessed 23 March 2014).
[95] *Kyio v. R* [2004], SBHC 90[5].
[96] *R v. MacDougall* [1998], 3 SCR 45, 71[54](SCC).
[97] *Jago v. District Court of New South Wales* [1989], 168 CLR 23, 45(HCA).

'the court must not forget those, who, though not represented, have a legitimate interest in the court's exercise of its jurisdiction. In broadening the notion of abuse of process, however, the interest of the community and the victims of crime in the enforcement of the criminal law seem to have been neglected, if not overlooked'.[98] In a case of sexual defilement of a seven-year-old victim by a thirteen-year-old defendant that took more than six years to get to court, the High Court of Tuvalu accepted that the delay was wholly the fault of the police.[99] But, after considering the Hague Convention on the Rights of the Child, which in Article 40(1)(b)(iii) guarantees every child a trial 'without delay' – a convention that had been ratified by Tuvalu in 1995 – the court held that the interest of the child defendant overrode those of the child victim. The court ordered a stay on the grounds that a fair trial could not be held because it would be impossible to ascertain the state of mind of the defendant at age thirteen – an essential element of the offence – now that he was eighteen years old.[100]

Unlike the Supreme Court of Canada, the courts in the Pacific have been reluctant to lay down a guideline for measuring the period of unreasonable delay. While *Morin* has been cited on the factors to determine the categories of delay, the courts in Fiji, for instance, have not laid down a 'general time limit'.[101] The view in Fiji, relying on New Zealand cases, is that, while appellate courts might lay down a guideline, they are reluctant to do so given the need to have sufficient information to arrive at a *Morin*-type standard. A second concern is that guidelines might be an improper interference with the executive function and therefore a breach of the separation between the judicial and executive powers of government.[102]

Remedies for Delay

The main remedy is a stay of the proceedings[103] or an equivalent, such as a writ of prohibition to a lower court to prevent a trial from proceeding.[104] The effect of a stay is tantamount to an acquittal.[105] This can have a devastating effect on the victim, for it means that the trial cannot proceed at all. In one recent rape

---

[98] *Jago v. District Court of New South Wales* [1989], 168 CLR 23, 50(HCA), cited in *R v. Setaga* [2009], 2 LRC 287, 291[3](Tuvalu HC).
[99] *R v. Setaga* [2009], 2 LRC 287, 294[6](Tuvalu HC).
[100] Ibid., [5].
[101] *State v. Rokotuiwai* [1998], FJHC 196[8].
[102] *Seru v. State* [2003], FJCA 26[4].
[103] *R v. Rahey* [1987], 1 SCR 588, 614–15(SCC).
[104] *Kimisi v. DPP* [1990], SBHC 32 [4].
[105] *R v. Jewitt* [1985], 2 SCR 128, 148(SC)(Dickson CJ).

case in Ontario, a stay was granted because of a four-year delay in bringing the case to trial. The victim, who had been gang raped, was told three weeks before the trial was due to commence that it had been stayed because of unreasonable delay.[106] She was predictably outraged and went to the media to protest against this situation. A stay may apply even in cases of murder and other serious crimes, which raises issues concerning the inefficiency of the prosecution when they are wholly responsible for the delay.[107] Certainly where the delay is for a very long period, the constitutional test for a stay will be met. In one Fijian case, the seven-year delay resulted in the loss of crucial witness statements gathered by the police, thus depriving the accused of the right to a fair trial.[108]

On the other hand, a stay is not inevitable, and the courts in the Pacific have said that a stay should only apply in exceptional circumstances.[109] One reason for this is that 'if the courts were always to stay proceedings, it would be seen as failing to protect the public from serious crime'.[110] A court may in an appropriate case make a peremptory order expediting the trial rather than grant a stay.[111] One other possibility is to shorten the sentence if the challenge is made after sentencing has been imposed,[112] or to substitute a fine for a sentence.[113] In cases where the person is remanded pending trial, the court may grant bail rather than dismiss or stay the case,[114] though they may not do so if the accused is facing murder charges and if there is evidence that, despite the delay, the commencement of the trial is imminent.[115] In *Ingivald*, the bringing of an application for a violation of the reasonable time standard may actually have motivated the authorities to fast-track the matter to avoid the risk that a person facing serious charges would not be tried at all. Where the delay arises after conviction but before sentencing, the courts will not grant a stay of the trial, for the trial phase has been completed; but they can order the trial court to impose a sentence

[106] *National Post* (Toronto), 27 September 2013: http://news.nationalpost.com/2013/09/27/ontario-mothers-gang-rape-case-thrown-out-because-of-ontarios-slow-and-inefficient-court-system/ (accessed 16 April 2014). For another case in Calgary of a 38-month delay where the case was stayed, see: http://www.cbc.ca/news/canada/calgary/crown-apologizes-for-rape-case-delay-1.822427 (accessed 16 April 2014).
[107] *R v. Tangisi* [2008], SBHC 108(Solomon Is HC).
[108] *Tawake v. State* [2009], FJHC 35[20].
[109] *Takiveikata v. State* [2008], FJHC 315[41]–[44].
[110] *R v. Hence* [2012], SBHC 54[21].
[111] *State v. Vunisa* [2000], 2 FLR 38, 39(Fiji HC).
[112] *R v. Maelisu'u* [2013], SBHC 181[43].
[113] *Boolell v. State of Mauritius* (2006)[2012], 1 WLR 3718, 3729[39].
[114] *R v. Mae* [2005], SBHC 115[3].
[115] *Ingivald v. The State* [1996], FJHC 196[5].

within a specific time limit if there has been a delay in imposing a sentence.[116]

CONCLUSIONS

A constitutional right to a trial within a reasonable time imposes obligations on both the courts and the other branches of government. While the courts must uphold the law, they cannot mandate measures to actually overcome institutional delay, other than to streamline their own processes. Ultimately, the capacity of a legal system to deliver on a constitutional requirement depends upon adequate resources being allocated by the legislature and the executive. As the Canadian cases show, even developed legal systems in wealthy countries struggle with the problem of delay.

The issue is even more acute in smaller, poorer jurisdictions. The causes of delay may range from disruptions to the legal order owing to internal unrest, the lack of judicial and legal personnel, the lack of specialist witnesses, logistical problems in states with poor communications, lack of money and even very low standards of administration.

The consequences of not meeting judicially mandated guidelines for a trial within a reasonable time are not very attractive. The emphasis on guaranteeing a fair trial to the accused is laudable, but there is another side to the problem. If a stay is entered, then persons facing serious charges escape justice and their victims are denied justice as their alleged perpetrators are let go. However, not sanctioning delays would mean that the accused, who are presumed to be innocent until judged to be guilty, may have a trial hanging over them for many years at a time. The solutions that the courts in the Pacific have crafted are based partly on principle and partly on an appreciation of local institutional realities. The evidence of the Pacific cases shows a greater tolerance for longer delays than would be acceptable in Canada, for example. Since the institutional problems vary from place to place, the courts have rightly recognised that flexibility has to guide any judgments they make about how a constitutional standard is applied both in particular cases and in particular places.

The commonly held view that the same standards should apply everywhere may be correct in principle – on the grounds that human rights standards are universal – and certainly international human rights instruments are expressed in universal terms. But the way in which the standards apply in practice does, as this chapter has shown, depend on local circumstances. The idealists who

---

[116] *Nacagi v. State* [2009], FJHC 171[42].

enunciated these standards in various national and international legal instruments probably never thought about the problems of actually applying common standards in radically different contexts. Nor did they think about the institutional assumptions that underlie the promise first made in Magna Carta not to delay justice. On the other hand, the development of the institutions and facilities now available in modern court systems has gone a long way to realizing the promise of 1215, and this development explains the remarkable survival of a very old ideal 800 years after it was stipulated in a meadow west of London and at a time when the authors of the Charter did not even know that the Pacific region existed.

PART 3

TWENTY-FIRST-CENTURY REFLECTIONS ON MAGNA CARTA

8

Magna Carta and Modern Myth-Making: Proportionality in the 'Cruel and Unusual Punishments' Clause[1]

Craig S. Lerner

> My object all sublime
> I shall achieve in time –
> To let the punishment fit the crime,
> The punishment fit the crime.
> – Gilbert and Sullivan, 'A More
> Humane Mikado', from *The
> Mikado* (1885)

American scholars now argue that Magna Carta embodies a 'proportionality principle' mandating that the punishment fit the crime.[2] This principle, according to a familiar narrative, found expression centuries later in the English Bill of Rights, which was reproduced another century later in the American Bill of Rights.[3] The Eighth Amendment's prohibition on cruel and

---

[1] A version of this essay appeared in *George Mason University Civil Rights Law Journal* 25(3) (2015).

[2] See, e.g., John F. Stinneford, 'Rethinking Proportionality under the Cruel and Unusual Punishments Clause', *Virginia Law Review* 97 (2011): 899, 912 (tracing a 'common law tradition requiring proportionality in punishment' to Magna Carta); Michael J. Wishnie, 'Proportionality: The Struggle for Balance in U.S. Immigration Policy', *University of Pittsburgh Law Review* 72 (2011): 431, 445 ('Proportionality is a concept with ancient roots in Anglo-American law, dating at least to Magna Carta.'); Erwin Chemerinsky, 'The Constitution and Punishment', *Stanford Law Review* 56 (2004): 1049, 1063–65 (2004) (tracing 'the principle of proportionality' to Magna Carta). The claim appears in perhaps the most influential American law review article on the Eighth Amendment in the past few decades. Anthony F. Granucci, '"Nor Cruel and Unusual Punishment Inflicted": The Original Meaning', *California Law Review* 57 (1969): 839, 844–47. A recent law review article, more attentive to the language of Magna Carta, produces a more nuanced interpretation. See Nicholas M. McLean, 'Livelihood, Ability to Pay, and the Original Meaning of the Excessive Fines Clause', *Hastings Constitutional Law Quarterly* 40 (2013): 833, 861 (referring to the 'Magna Carta's traditional dual principles of proportionality and salvo contenemento').

[3] See, e.g., Leonard W. Levy, *Origin of the Bill of Rights* (New Haven: Yale University Press, 1999), 231–32.

unusual punishments is thus said to originate in the dramatic encounter between the barons and King John on the fields of Runnymede. This story has proven to be of more than simply academic interest. Justices on the U.S. Supreme Court have claimed the authority of Magna Carta when infusing the prohibition against cruel and unusual punishments with a proportionality principle not immediately evident from the text of the Eighth Amendment. Thus emboldened, the Supreme Court has overturned supposedly disproportionate criminal sentences.[4]

This essay questions much of this narrative. My claim is that the articles in Magna Carta that are now cited to stand for the principle that the punishment must fit the crime do no such thing because, at bottom, those articles do not concern criminal activity. Natalie Riendeau's contribution to this volume explores Magna Carta's role in the 'legend and myth' of English life (Chapter 11). This chapter supplements hers by identifying and exploring how a myth surrounding Magna Carta has shaped the discourse on the meaning of the U.S. Constitution's cruel and unusual punishments clause. Scholars and jurists have anachronistically deployed Magna Carta to resolve a contested issue of constitutional law.

My plan is as follows: the first section traces the uses made of Magna Carta by American jurists in advancing the argument that the ancient document embodies a proportionality principle. The argument has lately focused on Articles 20 to 22, which restrict 'amercements' to those 'in accordance with the gravity of the offense'. *Amercement* is said to be a penalty meted out for criminal activity; hence, it is argued, the authors of Magna Carta thought that punishment ought to be proportionate to the gravity of the criminal offence.

The second section takes a closer look at Articles 20 to 22, along with other articles of Magna Carta, contemporaneous legal documents and historical events. Within the text of Magna Carta, there are clues that amercement was not regarded as a *criminal* punishment. Legal documents (Glanvill, Pipe Rolls, Bracton) confirm that this penalty was imposed on individuals or collective entities who had abused the litigation process or had failed to discharge one of the non-criminal duties that defined the medieval political order. Finally, given the prevalence of violent crime and the tolerance of cruel

---

[4] Seminal Eighth Amendment cases citing Magna Carta include: *Weems v. United States*, 217 U.S. 349, 376 (1910) (holding that Eighth Amendment incorporates proportionality principle); *Trop v. Dulles*, 356 U.S. 86, 100 (1958) (holding banishment unconstitutional); *Furman v. Georgia*, 408 U.S. 238, 242 (1972) (Opinion of Douglas, J.) (holding death penalty unconstitutional); *Solem v. Helm*, 463 U.S. 277, 284–85 (1983) (holding life without parole sentence unconstitutional).

criminal punishment, it is implausible to project humanitarian motives onto the authors of Articles 20 to 22.

The third section takes up the ambiguity of what is intended by the 'proportionality principle'. Although explored with notable subtlety by Aristotle, the principle is known to children and many animals. Virtually every legal document in recorded history embodies it, and at this banal level, Magna Carta does so as well. As jurists purport to extract more meaningful and specific lessons from Magna Carta, however, their arguments lapse into poor scholarship and hopeless anachronism.

MAGNA CARTA IN EIGHTH AMENDMENT JURISPRUDENCE

The Eighth Amendment of the U.S. Constitution provides: 'Excessive fines shall not be required, nor excessive bail imposed, nor cruel and unusual punishments inflicted.' On its face, the amendment imposes three limitations: (1) no excessive fines; (2) no excessive bail; and (3) no cruel and unusual punishments. Limitations (1) and (2), by prohibiting *excessive* fines and bail, evoke the idea of proportionality. The third limitation speaks more broadly – all 'punishments' – and an ordinary implication is that the 'not excessive' limitation in (1) and (2) applies only to the specified categories – that is, fines and bail. The third limitation, prohibiting cruel and unusual punishments, is broader in scope but does not embody a proportionality principle. The phrase simply prohibits punishments that are 'cruel and unusual' – that is, barbaric and bizarre. This was the view of the United States Supreme Court and noted constitutional scholars through the nineteenth century.[5]

Perhaps the first American case to hold that the cruel and unusual punishments clause embodied a proportionality principle was the 1878 North Carolina case *State v. Driver*.[6] Because that case has proved to be foundational, it is worth lingering on in some detail. *Driver* involved a defendant who had severely beaten his wife, was convicted of assault and was sentenced to five years in the county jail. Here is the defendant's testimony: 'He states that while in a passion and under the influence of drink, he whipped his wife with a switch with such severity as to leave the marks for two or three weeks, and that he kicked her once, and that he had whipped her before, but not with the same severity.'[7] The defendant challenged the sentence – which hardly shocks the modern conscience – as unconstitutional under the Eighth Amendment and state constitutional analogue. After conceding that there was 'very little

---

[5] See, e.g., *Wilkerson v. Utah*, 99 U.S. 130 (1878).
[6] 78 N.C. 423 (1878).
[7] Id. at 425.

authority' for defendant's argument, Justice Reade persevered, observing that the Eighth Amendment draws upon the English Bill of Rights of 1689.[8] And then, as an interpretative gloss on the English Bill of Rights, Justice Reade invoked the 1690 case against Lord Devonshire, in which the House of Lords overturned a £30,000 fine for simple assault as 'excessive and exorbitant, against Magna Carta, the common right of the subject, and the law of the land'.[9] Here may be the first suggestion in an American judicial opinion that the cruel and unusual punishments clause authorises judges to invalidate a disproportionate criminal sentence, and it is noteworthy that Magna Carta is summoned as nebulous support for the proposition. Which article of Magna Carta is relevant to the issue was left unclear. The *Driver* court's use of the phrase 'law of the land' may be an allusion to Article 39 of Magna Carta, but whatever the ambiguous phrase *lex terrae* in that article means, there is no plausible connection with a proportionality principle.[10]

Any hope that *Driver* would provoke an energetic cruel and unusual punishments jurisprudence was disappointed: it seems to have disappeared into history's dustbin.[11] But then, three decades later, the U.S. Supreme Court dusted off *Driver* and featured it in *Weems v. United States.*[12] In that case, a Philippine court, having convicted a customs official of falsifying a public document, imposed a sentence of fifteen years of what was called *cadena temporal*; this meant that the offender was required to carry a chain around his ankle for the entirety of the prison term. Unlike Driver's sentence, here was a punishment that cried out for correction. And little ingenuity would have been required. It was possible to craft a narrow opinion focusing on the unusual mode of punishment; or perhaps the constitutional issue could have been finessed altogether by invoking the hoary conflict of law rule foreclosing enforcement of foreign criminal law.[13] Six Supreme Court justices instead intimated that a proportionality principle existed somewhere within the Eighth Amendment. In so doing, the Court suggested that the question had divided the state courts, but the only case identified on the affirmative side of the issue was *Driver*. The *Weems* Court even quoted the language in *Driver*

---

[8] The English Bill of Rights provides, in relevant respect: 'excessive bail ought not to be required, nor excessive fines imposed, nor cruel and unusual punishments inflicted'.

[9] *Driver*, 78 N.C. at 427.

[10] The most careful and convincing treatment of the phrase 'law of the land' can be found in William McKechnie, *The Magna Carta: A Commentary on the Great Charter of King John* (Glasgow: James MacLehose and Sons, 1914), 379–81.

[11] In subsequent decades, a few North Carolina defendants cited *Driver*, but never to their advantage. See *State v. Pettie*, 80 N.C. 367 (1879); *State v. Reid*, 106 N.C. 704 (1890); *State v. Farrington*, 141 N.C. 844 (1906).

[12] 217 U.S. 349 (1910).

[13] See *The Antelope*, 23 U.S. (10 Wheat) 66, 123 (1825).

that had referenced Magna Carta.[14] Thus it was that a case invalidating a five-year prison term on a husband who had whipped his wife became foundational law in the U.S. Supreme Court.

As already observed, which article in Magna Carta embodied the proportionality principle was unspecified. The reasoning of *Driver* and *Weems* seems to have been this: Magna Carta is a noble legal document; the proportionality principle is a noble legal principle; Q.E.D., Magna Carta embodies the proportionality principle. The logical difficulties attending this syllogism prompted a search for more specific textual support. That was supplied in *Trop v. Dulles*.[15] Albert Trop was an Army private in 1944 when he escaped from a stockade in Casablanca. Picked up the next day, Trop was convicted of desertion, dishonourably discharged and sentenced to three years' imprisonment. In 1952, his application for a passport was denied on the basis of the Nationality Act of 1940, which stripped all deserters of citizenship. Trop challenged the denial of his citizenship under the U.S. Constitution's Eighth Amendment's prohibition of cruel and unusual punishments.

The claim was an odd one, for, as a dissenting Justice Frankfurter observed, the government could have simply executed Trop for desertion. For that matter, stripping someone of citizenship (also known as banishment) is the oldest of punishments,[16] so it is impossible to argue that the penalty imposed on Trop was 'unusual'. Surmounting these difficulties, the Supreme Court entered judgment in favour of Private Trop, educating the reader along the way on the historical backdrop for, and philosophical underpinnings of, the Eighth Amendment:

> The exact scope of the constitutional phrase 'cruel and unusual' has not been detailed by this Court. But the basic policy reflected in these words is firmly established in the Anglo-American tradition of criminal justice. The phrase in our Constitution was taken directly from the English Declaration of Rights of 1688, and the principle it represents can be traced back to the Magna Carta.[FN31] The basic concept underlying the Eighth Amendment is nothing less than the dignity of man. . . . [citing *Weems*] The Amendment must draw its meaning from the evolving standards of decency that mark the progress of a maturing society.[17]

Footnote 31, which the Court appends to its citation to Magna Carta, consists, in toto, of the following: 'See 34 Minn.L.Rev. 134; 4 Vand.L.Rev. 680.' The Minnesota Law Review citation is a three-and-a-half-page student

[14] *Solem*, 217 U.S. at 376.
[15] 356 U.S. 86 (1958).
[16] See Genesis 4:13 (God's banishment of Cain).
[17] *Trop*, 356 U.S. at 100.

note; nestled within is the assertion that the principle behind the 'prohibition against cruel and unusual punishments' is 'fundamental' and can be traced, inter alia, to Magna Carta. In a footnote, the unnamed student author indicates that the reference is to Article 20. The other citation, '4 Vand.L. Rev. 680', is another student note (albeit one weighing in at 7 pages), with a single reference to Article 20 of Magna Carta; the student author claims that the 'root' of the Eighth Amendment is to be found therein. The support for this claim is another student note, to wit, '34 Minn.L.Rev. 134'. In other words, *Trop v. Dulles* leads us into an excursion reminiscent of a Jorge Luis Borges story, but it turns out that the claim for the Eighth Amendment's origins in Magna Carta derives from a pair of student notes, one of which cites the other and neither of which engages in anything other than assertion.

That said, after *Trop*, claims that Magna Carta illuminates the meaning of the Eighth Amendment could at least be pegged to specific language in the text of that ancient document. The Article 20 mentioned by both student notes cited in *Trop* provides:

> (20) A freeman shall not be amerced for a slight offense, except in accordance with the degree of the offense; and for a grave offense he shall be amerced in accordance with the gravity of the offense, yet saving always his contentment; and a merchant in the same way, saving his merchandise; and a villein shall be amerced in the same way, saving his wainage if they have fallen into our mercy: and none of the aforesaid amercements shall be imposed except by the oath of honest men of the neighborhood.

In the next section, this essay will provide a close analysis of this article, but it is sufficient here to acknowledge the language ('in accordance with the degree of the offense') that is evocative of the proportionality principle. In identifying this article as relevant to the Eighth Amendment, the *Trop* court transformed Eighth Amendment jurisprudence.

This development is on display in Justice Douglas's concurring opinion in *Furman v. Georgia*, which imposed a temporary moratorium on the death penalty.[18] This opinion traced the influence of Magna Carta on the Eighth Amendment, the conduit said to be the English Bill of Rights of 1689. The opinion also identified textual support in the Great Charter for a modernised understanding of the cruel and unusual punishments clause. Justice Douglas wrote that '[Article 20][19] clearly stipulated as fundamental law a prohibition of

---

[18]   408 U.S. 238 (1972).

[19]   When Magna Carta was reissued in 1216, 1217 and 1225, certain articles were dropped and others were condensed. Article 20 in the 1215 version was eventually folded into what became Article 14. Because the 1225 Magna Carta was the version eventually adopted into English law, some

excessiveness in punishments.'[20] In the years that followed, four more justices argued that Magna Carta's embodiment of a proportionality principle in Article 20, traced through the English Bill of Rights, found expression in the Eighth Amendment.[21] This view emerged in 1983 as the triumphant majority position in *Solem v. Helm*,[22] which overturned a life sentence imposed on a non-violent offender:

> The principle that a punishment should be proportionate to the crime is deeply rooted and frequently repeated in common-law jurisprudence. In 1215 three [articles] of Magna Carta were devoted to the rule that 'amercements'[FN8] may not be excessive. And the principle was repeated and extended in the First Statute of Westminster, 3 Edw. I, ch. 6 (1275). These were not hollow guarantees, for the royal courts relied on them to invalidate disproportionate punishments. . . . When prison sentences became the normal criminal sanctions, the common law recognized that these, too, must be proportional. See, *e.g.*, *Hodges v. Humkin*, 2 Bulst. 139, 140, 80 Eng. Rep. 1015, 1016 (K.B. 1615) (Croke, J.) ("imprisonment ought always to be according to the quality of the offence").[23]

It is worth noting that the *Solem* Court found not one but three articles in Magna Carta embodying the proportionality principle. In addition to the

sources refer to what this chapter identifies as Article 20 as Article 14. This chapter uses the 1215 ordering of articles.

[20] *Furman*, 408 U.S. at 242.

[21] Dissenting from the denial of certiorari in *Carmona v. Ward*, 439 U.S. 1091, 1093–94 (1979), Justices Marshall and Powell wrote:

Few legal principles are more firmly rooted in the Bill of Rights and its common-law antecedents than the requirement of proportionality between a crime and its punishment. The precept that sanctions should be commensurate with the seriousness of a crime found expression in both the Magna Carta and the English Bill of Rights. [citing Article 20] And this Court has long recognised that the Eighth Amendment embodies a similar prohibition against disproportionate punishment.

Dissenting in *Rummel v. Estelle*, 445 U.S. 263, 288–89 (1980) (again involving a life sentence for a nonviolent offender), Justice Powell, joined by Justices Brennan, Marshall and Stevens, wrote:

The principle of disproportionality is rooted deeply in English constitutional law. The Magna Carta of 1215 insured that '[a] free man shall not be [fined] for a trivial offence, except in accordance with the degree of the offence; and for a serious offence he shall be [fined] according to its gravity'. By 1400, the English common law had embraced the principle, not always followed in practice, that punishment should not be excessive either in severity or length. One commentator's survey of English law demonstrates that the 'cruel and unusual punishments' clause of the English Bill of Rights of 1689 'was first, an objection to the imposition of punishments which were unauthorized by statute and outside the jurisdiction of the sentencing court, and second, a reiteration of the English policy against disproportionate penalties'.

[22] 463 U.S. 277 (1983).

[23] Id. at 284–85. A footnote states that '[a]n amercement was similar to a modern-day fine. It was the most common criminal sanction in 13th century England.'

aforementioned Article 20, there are also Articles 21 and 22 to cement the point:

> (21) Earls and barons shall not be amerced except through their peers, and only in accordance with the degree of the offense.
> (22) A clerk shall not be amerced in respect of his lay holding except after the manner of the others aforesaid; further, he shall not be amerced in accordance with the extent of his ecclesiastical benefice.

Article 21 explicitly and Article 22 implicitly repeat the language ('in accordance with the degree of the offense') that evokes the proportionality principle.

To sum up, the *Solem* opinion articulates the argument that Articles 20 to 22 embody a proportionality principle and that this principle illuminates the meaning of the Eighth Amendment. Although briefly extinguished as meaningful precedent,[24] *Solem* has been revived by a pair of recent cases that have invalidated life sentences imposed on juveniles. *Graham v. Florida*[25] and *Miller v. Alabama*[26] portend an ambitious Eighth Amendment jurisprudence by a Court increasingly willing to invalidate non-capital sentences.[27] *Graham* and *Miller* take for granted that the Eighth Amendment embodies a proportionality principle and do not bother to cite Magna Carta, the English Bill of Rights, miscellaneous student notes or any other source for the proposition. Apparently, this is now settled law.[28]

Yet what is now settled was not always so. For many years, the Eighth Amendment was not understood to authorise courts to invalidate disproportionate criminal sentences. That was once a contested claim, and in making the argument that the Eighth Amendment embodies a proportionality

---

[24] In *Harmelin v. Michigan*, 501 U.S. 957 (1991), the Supreme Court upheld a mandatory life sentence on a defendant who possessed 672 grams of cocaine and threw into doubt the continuing vitality of *Solem v. Helm*.

[25] 560 U.S. 48 (2010). Justice Kennedy's majority opinion cites *Solem* favourably many times, prompting a dissenting Justice Thomas to complain that 'the Court soon cabined *Solem's* rationale'. Id. at 104 (Thomas, J., dissenting).

[26] 132 S.Ct. 2455, 567 U.S. ___ (2012).

[27] For speculations on the trajectory of the U.S. Supreme Court's Eighth Amendment jurisprudence after *Miller*, see Craig S. Lerner, 'Sentenced to Confusion, *Miller v. Alabama* and the Coming Wave of Eighth Amendment Cases', *George Mason Law Review* 20 (2012): 25.

[28] Chief Justice Roberts and Justice Alito dissented in *Miller*, but their opinions accept that the Eighth Amendment embodies a proportionality principle. Only Justices Scalia and Thomas reject this proposition. See *Miller*, 132 S.Ct. at 2483 (Thomas, J., dissenting, joined by Justice Scalia) ('the Cruel and Unusual Punishments Clause was originally understood as prohibiting tortuous *methods* of punishment – specifically methods akin to those that had been considered cruel and unusual at the time the Bill of Rights was adopted') (emphasis in original; quotation omitted).

principle, Magna Carta was deployed. The next section considers whether Magna Carta really stands for this proposition.

A CLOSER LOOK AT ARTICLES 20 TO 22

This section begins with the text itself. Attention to the language of Articles 20 to 22, especially in tandem with other articles, undercuts the claim that these provisions contemplated criminal punishment. We then consider every reference to amercement in Glanvill's Treatise (written in the years 1187 to 1189); amercement appears as a non-criminal penalty for an administrative offence or an abuse of the litigation process. Nor is it likely, this section concludes, that thirteenth-century Englishmen, who were tolerant of cruelty and were faced with high rates of violent crime, would have been moved to codify the proportionality principle in any respect meaningful to the modern observer.

The Text

We begin with the text of the 1215 Magna Carta, paying close attention, as any lawyer should, to the words of Articles 20 to 22. The similar and often-identical language in the three articles, plus the language in Article 22 referencing the preceding two ('in the manner of the others aforesaid') reveals an intent to have the three articles considered together. Proof of this point is confirmed by the 1217 reissue of Magna Carta, which collapses these articles into one. The three articles of the 1215 version of Magna Carta broadly correspond to the three classes of men: commoners (Article 20), nobles (Article 21) and clergy (Article 22). Within Article 20 there is another tripartite division of commoners – into freemen, merchants and villeins. Significantly, all three articles concern 'amercement'.

This last point is obscured when modern editions of Magna Carta translate *amerciteur* as 'fine'.[29] But the authors of Magna Carta were attentive to the difference between fines and amercements. Article 55 provides for the remission of all unlawful amercements *and fines*. Lawyers are trained to pay attention not only to words but also to omissions. When the authors of Magna Carta intended to impose limits on fines, they knew how to do so, and the ordinary conclusion is that the restrictions of Articles 20 to 22 were not intended to apply

---

[29] Salisbury Cathedral is home to one of the four extant copies of the 1215 Magna Carta. Next to the document is a translation prepared by the British Library Board that perpetuates this misimpression. Article 20 is translated: 'For a trivial offence, a free man shall be *fined* only in proportion to the degree of the offense. . . .' Photographs taken on 22 June 2014 (on file with author).

to fines. When the three articles were condensed into one, the authors of Magna Carta, given the opportunity to correct a drafting error, persisted in limiting the scope of the renumbered article to amercement.

Further evidence that the authors of Magna Carta were attentive to the difference between amercements and fines can be discerned in Article 55. That article states that all 'fines' are 'facti sunt nobiscum', or 'made with us', while all 'amerciamenta' are simply 'facta', or 'made'. This reflects the primary distinguishing characteristic between the two penalties. Fines were negotiated with the royal judge, and hence were 'made with us'; amercements were imposed, and hence simply 'made'. That the authors of Magna Carta took the trouble to recognise this distinction belies any suggestion that their language was chosen carelessly.

Returning to Articles 20 to 22, we note that the text specifies one procedural restriction on amercements – that is, the penalty may be imposed only after having secured the consent of the offender's peers. Articles 20 to 22 also specify two substantive restrictions – that is, the amercement must be proportioned to the offence *and* leave the offender in possession of his livelihood. The principle of proportionality is said to inform these two substantive restrictions, but a moment's reflection suggests doubts. The two limiting principles can be harmonised in some cases, but they are neither identical nor are both coincident with the principle of proportionality. To be sure, with respect to minor offences, the proportionate penalty could be one that is both in accordance with the offence's gravity *and* leaves the offender with, at a minimum, his livelihood. But this is not the case with respect to serious offences. Then, the proportionate penalty could strip the offender of *all* his property, his liberty and even his life. It would sound bizarre to say that a murderer or rapist, although punished, must be left with his contentment intact.

This should be the first clue, from evidence internal to the text, that Articles 20 to 22 are not about criminal offences, or certainly not serious criminal offences. And upon reflection, it is noteworthy that Articles 20 to 22 do not refer to penalties for 'crimen' (crimes) or 'felonia' (felonies), but rather for 'delicto', a tame word generally translated as 'offenses'. Another article, however, unmistakably regulates the punishment of felonies. Article 32 provides: 'We will not retain beyond one year and one day, the lands of those who have been convicted of felony ['felonia'], and the lands shall thereafter be handed over to the lords of the fiefs.' The disturbing implications of this article of Magna Carta generally result in its being ignored, lest the pristine glory of the document be impaired. Article 32 seals the agreement of the King and the barons according to which those convicted of a felony faced the forfeiture of all their land. The issue separating the two sides was on the division of the spoils – how long the king was authorised to use the land before surrendering it to the convicted felon's lord. Magna Carta's compromise was 366 days. Article 32 bracingly suggests that Articles 20 to 22 have no application to penalties for felonies. It is, after all, impossible that a convicted felon could on the one hand be left with his contentment but on the other be forced to forfeit all his property.

Further proof that Articles 20 to 22 have no application to felonies can be found in Article 39, which, like Article 32, unmistakably deals with criminal punishment. It provides: 'No freemen shall be taken or imprisoned or disseised or exiled or in any way destroyed, nor will we go upon him nor send upon him, except by the lawful judgment of his peers or by the law of the land.' The final phrase of the sentence, by imposing a procedural requirement, adds lustre to Magna Carta and therefore figures prominently in the document's mythology. Interpretations of 'judgment of his peers' and 'law of the land' are often hopelessly anachronistic projections,[30] but that point aside, the article imposes limitations on the imposition of punishments ranging from dispossession of property, imprisonment, exile, and even torture and death (presumably what is meant by 'destroyed'). Amercement is unmentioned in Article 39, which suggests that the authors of Magna Carta regarded amercements as apart from criminal punishments. Article 39 reflects concerns about criminal punishments – imprisonment, outlawry, exile and destruction – but says nothing about a principle of proportionality restricting their usage. When the authors of Magna Carta wished to import a proportionality principle, they did so, as in Articles 20 to 22; but when speaking of criminal punishments in Article 39, they declined.

In sum, within the four corners of the document, there is substantial evidence that Articles 20 to 22 do not embody the principle that the punishment should be proportionate to the *crime*. As we move beyond the text of Magna Carta and consider contemporaneous legal texts, this suspicion is confirmed.

Contemporaneous Legal Texts

To simplify a story both complicated and shrouded in uncertainty, amercement seems to have been a Norman innovation.[31] Anglo-Saxon law provided for fines (wer, bot and wite), which were fixed according to the status of the offender and the victim, and to the gravity of the offence. The transition to

---

[30] See, e.g., McKechnie, *Magna Carta*, 381 (rejecting Coke's interpretation of Article 39; 'Anachronisms such as these must be avoided.').

[31] See John Fox, *The History of Contempt of Court* (Oxford: Clarendon Press, 1927), 120.

amercement is reflected in the Domesday Book of 1086, in which the phrase 'in misericordia regis', or 'in the mercy of the king', first appears.[32] Instead of a fixed tariff, amercement contemplates that all of one's property and even one's life is placed at the king's mercy. The distinguished Magna Carta commentator William McKechnie notes that '[n]one of our authorities contain an entirely satisfactory account of how the change' from fines to amercement occurred.[33] Henry I's Charter of Liberties, issued in 1100, perhaps reflects dissatisfaction with amercement, because the King promised to abandon the penalty and return to the ways of his grandfather. But the Charter seems never to have been seriously intended, and the practice of amercement not only persisted, but expanded in the twelfth century.

Indeed, Maitland asserts that '[v]ery likely there was no clause in Magna Carta more grateful to the mass of the people [than Article 20]'.[34] If amercement was so prevalent that the public was grateful for its regulation, this is another clue that it was not exclusively, or even predominantly, a *criminal* penalty. Most law-abiding people do not end up as criminal defendants or – at least in reasonably just political regimes – expend substantial mental energy fretting about this possibility. People are more likely to imagine themselves or their kin as victims of violent crime than as defendants in such cases. This would certainly have been true in thirteenth-century England, having as it did a highly undeveloped criminal justice system, a point to which this essay will return in the next part. Maitland's claim that the public was grateful for the regulation of amercement makes sense, however, if the penalty was widely imposed on private citizens and public officials to secure obedience on a range of non-criminal matters.

Among the guides to twelfth-century English legal practice is Glanvill's *Treatise on the Laws and Customs of the Realm of England*, written between 1187 and 1189. The work deals primarily with civil litigation in the king's court, but the final chapter, Book XIV, is entitled 'De placitis criminalibus', or 'Criminal pleas'.[35] The word *amercement* appears only once in Book XIV. Glanvill writes: 'If the appellor [the person who initiates the criminal process] is vanquished [at trial], he will be liable to amercement by the lord king', adding that '[t]he meaning of this has been sufficiently explain[ed] above'. By contrast 'if the accused is vanquished', then his life and limbs, as well as goods

---

[32] Id. at 121.
[33] See McKechnie, *Magna Carta*, 286.
[34] F. W. Maitland (ed.), Introduction to *Pleas of the Crown for the County of Gloucester* (London: Macmillan and Co, 1884), xxxiv.
[35] C. D. G. Hall (ed.), *The Treatises on the Laws and Customs of the Realm of England Commonly Called Glanvill* (Oxford: Clarendon Press, 1993), 171–73.

and chattels, are all in jeopardy.[36] In other words, amercement is not a potential penalty for those convicted of a crime; amercement is imposed on a person who erroneously initiates the criminal process.

It is unclear which of the earlier references to amercement Glanvill intended by the phrase 'the meaning has been sufficiently explain[ed] above'. A modern editor plausibly proposes a passage in Book IX about purpresture. Glanvill there writes:

> When anyone is convicted of encroachment by building upon royal land in a city, then those buildings which are proved to have been built on royal territory shall belong to the lord king and, notwithstanding this, he shall be liable to amercement by the lord king. Amercement by the lord king here means that he is to be amerced by oath of lawful men of the neighborhood, but so as not to lose property necessary to maintain his position.[37]

It is remarkable (although to my knowledge never remarked upon) how closely this passage in Glanvill tracks Article 20 of Magna Carta – a similarity so pronounced that one wonders whether the authors of Magna Carta drew from this passage, or whether Glanvill and the authors of Magna Carta drew from a common source. In both texts, amercement is limited procedurally (it can be imposed only by the 'oath of lawful men of the neighborhood') and substantively (the property taken must leave the offender with enough to 'maintain his position'). In Glanvill, the context has nothing to do with criminal law but specifies the penalty for building on royal lands, which might be likened to the civil offence of trespass.

Glanvill's text contains seven other references to amercement, none of which touch upon any issue remotely implicating the criminal law. Most of Glanvill's references to amercement involve penalties imposed on private parties who have abused the judicial process in some way. (This emphasis is understandable given that Glanvill's work is mostly about procedure.) Amercement is said to be imposed upon a litigant (or his sureties) who brings a false claim in court or against the church, who fails to pay a fine, who falsely alleges a seal is fraudulent or who fails to pursue an action he has initiated.[38] Contemporaneous documents are similar. For example, the Curia Regis Rolls note that Geoffrey de Say brought a bad pleading in 1214 and was amerced.[39] Several passages from Bracton's *The Laws and Customs of England*, written around 1235, also treat amercement as the forfeiture of a bond if litigation is not

---

[36] Id. at 173.
[37] Id. at 114.
[38] Id. at 43, 51, 98, 127 and 169–70.
[39] J. C. Holt, *Magna Carta* (Cambridge: Cambridge University Press, 1993), 148.

diligently pursued.[40] The litigation process can, moreover, be burdened not only by delinquent parties but also by incompetent judges; and to this end, another reference in Glanvill reports that a judge who rendered a false judgment was liable to amercement.[41] This is consistent with references to amercement in other documents that cast it as the penalty imposed upon public officials who failed to do their jobs properly.[42]

It was not only royal officials who had public duties in the medieval order. Law enforcement, in the absence of any official police force, was largely a matter of self-help and private monitoring. All men were joined together in collective entities, such as the frankpledge, and were jointly responsible for the misdeeds of others. Amercement was the crucial penalty in enforcing these arrangements. According to the *Oxford History of the Laws of England*, there are 'numerous plea roll entries record[ing] chief pledges and tithings being amerced' for the failure to produce an accused or a fugitive for whom a collective was accountable.[43] Apart from one's formal responsibilities as a member of a collective entity, the legal system in thirteenth-century England penalised failures to act in ways that may seem alien to a modern American or Englishman. For example, the penalty imposed on a private citizen who failed to inform the coroner of a dead body, or failed promptly to raise the hue and cry, was amercement.[44] One could multiply the examples, but the crucial idea is that amercement was not levied as a penalty for criminal conduct, but for the failure to discharge one's civic duties.

Modern codes distinguish between civil and criminal law and then, within the criminal law, between felonies and misdemeanours. The law in medieval England was more fluid. If we project modern legal categories, a review of thirteenth-century documents suggests that amercement was never the punishment imposed for serious crimes. In John Fox's *History of Contempt of Court* (1927), the author concludes that 'in Henry II reign, "to be in the King's

---

[40] See, e.g., *Bracton on the Laws and Customs of England*, 4 vols. (Harvard online library), vol. IV, 366, available online at http://bracton.law.harvard.edu/Unframed/English/v4/366.htm#TITL E.501 ('if one finds pledges for prosecuting and does not prosecute, all will be in mercy, both pledges and principals').

[41] Glanvill, *Treatises*, 101.

[42] For example, during litigation in 1207 between Eustace de Vescy and Richard de Umfraville over custody of Henry Batail, the justices allowed a concord between the barons without the King's consent. The Pipe Rolls record that King John amerced the judges. See Holt, *Magna Carta*, 186.

[43] John Baker (ed.), *Oxford History of the Laws of England: 871–1216* (Oxford: Oxford University Press, 2013), 717.

[44] Id. at 718. Another reference in Glanvill provides that the remedy for a writ of constraining a tenant (i.e. for failing to discharge one's duties to one's landlord) included amercement. Glanvill, *Treatises*, 113.

mercy" was applicable to offenses less than felony. Such offenses [were] then known as trespasses and later as misdemeanors'.[45] In his history of English criminal law, James Fitzjames Stephen comes to the same conclusion. Focusing on the precise words used in Article 20, Stephen concludes that what the authors of that article intended would 'subsequently develop into the law relating to misdemeanours'.[46] Stephen makes clear that these 'misdemeanours' were generally not offences of a truly criminal nature. Drawing upon, and quoting from, primary documents, Stephen writes:

> Under the head of amercements for misdemeanours occur a great variety of matters, some of which we should regard as indictable offences, as, for instance, harbouring a robber, and interfering with jurors; *but others are, according to our notions, far remote from criminal offences*, e.g. 'Fossard was fined for a mortgage unjustly taken.' 'The hundred of Stanberg was amerced for denying before the justices what they had acknowledged in the County Court.'[47]

In sum, much of what amercement involved was 'far remote from criminal offenses'. Articles 20 to 22 certainly reflected dissatisfaction with aspects of the legal system, but there is no evidence that this dissatisfaction was directed towards criminal punishment, or at the very least towards punishment for felonies. It would be more accurate to regard Articles 20 to 22, given their focus on amercement, as directed towards the unconstrained and sometimes exorbitant penalties imposed for any manner of regulatory offences.

Medieval Attitudes towards Violence and Cruelty

In modern England and the United States, police forces are lavishly funded and equipped, and prosecutors wield probing powers to ferret out criminal wrongdoing. By contrast, the thirteenth-century 'criminal justice system' – if one is even entitled to use that expression – was the work of amateurs. There were no police and no prosecutors; and for most criminals, there was a vanishingly small chance of being charged and convicted.[48]

In the absence of any meaningful justice system, violent crime was rampant. Cities were as rife with crime as rural areas. One historian writes: 'This was a knife-carrying society, in which potentially fatal fights could easily

---

[45] Fox, *History of Contempt*, 124–25.
[46] James Fitzjames Stephen, *A History of the Criminal Law of England*, 3 vols. (London: Macmillan, 1883), vol. II, 197–98 (1883) (emphasis added).
[47] Id. at 199.
[48] See H. R. T. Summerson, 'The Structure of Law Enforcement in Thirteenth Century England', *American Journal of Legal History* 23 (1979): 313, 315.

arise.'[49] Estimates of homicide rates in London from 1200 to 1400 range from 10 to 50 per 100,000 inhabitants. In 1340, Oxford attained a homicide rate of 110 per 100,000 inhabitants, more than one hundred times that of twenty-first-century England.[50] Graphical depictions of the decline in English homicide rates from the thirteenth century to the present are obliged to employ a logarithmic scale to compress the exponential decline. Pollock and Maitland conclude: 'We must not end this chapter without recording our belief that crimes of violence were common and that the criminal law was exceedingly inefficient.'[51]

For those rare defendants caught and convicted of a serious crime, the list of gruesome punishments was long, stretching from blinding to castration to drawing and quartering.[52] Nor were such punishments reserved for rapists and murderers. Although examples are legion, the case of Thomas of Eldersfield in 1217 – an almost exact contemporary of the signing of Magna Carta – is illustrative. Convicted after trial by battle of trumped-up charges of assault and burglary, Thomas was blinded (his eyes dislodged from their sockets) and castrated (his testicles playfully kicked around by some local lads).[53] From this case and others like it, the conclusion is inescapable that the typical thirteenth-century Englishman was not averse to punishments that shock the modern conscience. Nor should this be surprising, given that cruelty was not only commonplace, but treated as acceptable and even as a source of entertainment. After recounting several gruesome 'sports' involving the torture of animals, the historian Barbara Tuchman concludes, 'Accustomed in their lives to physical hardship and injury, medieval men and women were not necessarily repelled by the spectacle of pain, but rather enjoyed it.'[54]

It is often said that the past is another country. For a modern Englishmen or American to enter into the mind of a thirteenth-century Englishmen requires an act of the imagination. We need to imagine how human beings would think and feel in an age in which violent crime is rampant, few

---

49 John Hudson, *The Formation of the English Common Law: Law and Society in England from the Norman Conquest to the Magna Carta* (London: Longman, 1996), 57.
50 Steven Pinker, *The Better Angels of Our Nature: Why Violence Has Declined* (New York: Viking, 2011), 60.
51 Frederick Pollock and Frederic William Maitland, *History of English Law before the Time of Edward I*, 2 vols. (Cambridge: Cambridge University Press, 1898), vol. II, 557.
52 Larissa Tracy, *Castration and Culture in the Medieval Ages* (Cambridge: D. S. Brewer, 2013), 95.
53 The tale is colourfully told in an online article. See Paul Hyams, 'Tales from the Medieval Courtroom: The Fall and Rise of Thomas of Elderfield' (1985), available at http://authors.library.caltech.edu/18859/1/HumsWP-0107.pdf.
54 Barbara Tuchman, *A Distant Mirror: The Calamitous Fourteenth Century* (New York: Ballantine Books, 1978), 135.

criminals are caught and the prevailing attitude towards cruelty is one of acceptance and even flippancy. It is unlikely that in such circumstances people would obsess over whether a murderer, rapist or robber could be executed. The chronicler Orderic Vitalis (1075–1142) makes a notable observation in this regard about one such convicted criminal: 'The murderer was bound to the tails of four wild horses and torn to pieces by them, *as a terrible warning to evil doers.*'[55] Very public and very cruel punishments were, the chronicler teaches, intended as 'terrible warnings' to would-be criminals. Given low conviction rates, the general public apparently opted in favour of cruel punishment. Modern deterrence theory would regard this as a plausible solution, although contemporary moral attitudes towards cruelty foreclose such punishments. There is no evidence that medieval Englishmen possessed identical moral allergies.

WHAT DO WE MEAN BY THE 'PROPORTIONALITY PRINCIPLE'?

So does Magna Carta embody a 'proportionality principle'? At one level, of course it does. Excluding the hopelessly crude or corrupt, every legal system in recorded history reflects an embrace of proportionality. In some respects, ancient systems of justice may have entailed a less finely tuned calibration of culpability and punishment than is expected of twenty-first-century Western legal systems. Under the oldest common law, for example, all unlawful killing was murder, punishable by death; by contrast, Anglo-American jurisdictions today specify a dozen or more levels of homicide, with correspondingly graded sentences. But this does not prove Englishmen long ago were ignorant of proportionality; after all, even in the thirteenth century assault and larceny were seldom capital offences. For that matter, the laws of Alfred the Great bespeak an appreciation of the proportionality principle that at times puts modern codes to shame. Consider this passage:

> If the great toe be struck off let twenty shillings be paid him as bot. If it be the second toe, fifteen shillings. If the middle-most toe, nine shillings. If the fourth toe, six shillings. If the little toe be struck off let five shillings be paid him.[56]

To the best of my knowledge, no modern American legal code distinguishes aggravated assaults according to the size of the severed toe.[57]

---

[55] Hudson, *English Common Law*, 59.
[56] Stephen, *Criminal Law*, vol. II, 56.
[57] For example, in Virginia any assault that results in a severed toe would constitute aggravated malicious wounding and be punished as a Class 2 felony. See Va. Code 18.2–51.2.

As set forth in this discussion, Magna Carta distinguishes some crimes ('felonia') that merit the forfeiture of all one's lands from lesser offences ('delicto') that merit the modest penalty of amercement. With respect to serious crimes, Magna Carta contemplates a range of punishments (exile, outlawry, death), presumably pegged to the severity of the offence. With respect to misdemeanours and administrative offences, the amercement distinguishes among the greater or lesser, making clear that in neither case should the offender be deprived of all of his property or even so much of it that he is denied his livelihood. All of this is true, but at this level of generality, Magna Carta is no more distinguished in its appreciation of the proportionality principle than the Codes of Hammurabi or Alfred the Great.

Indeed, one need not be a great lawgiver to discern the truth of the proportionality principle. Two-year-olds in sandboxes draw distinctions based on the severity of the crime visited upon them (stolen shovel versus fist to the nose). This deflating observation calls into question the Supreme Court's claim in *Trop v. Dulles* that the proportionality principle is grounded in Magna Carta and more tendentiously 'the dignity of man'.[58] It is, after all, not just two-year-olds who appreciate and apply the proportionality principle; animals get it as well. A dog responds differently if it is intentionally kicked or inadvertently tripped. The law of contracts better testifies to the dignity of man – our capacity to visualise the future, express intentions and bind ourselves through voluntary agreements – than the criminal law principle of proportionality.

So Magna Carta generally embodies a proportionality principle, but at that level the principle is trivial and obvious. The question is whether Magna Carta has anything to say about the appropriate punishment for seventeen-year-old Terrance Graham, who committed several armed robberies.[59] Or Kuntrell Jackson, also aged seventeen, who participated in an armed robbery that resulted in the death of a store clerk.[60] Is a sentence of life without parole (a modern analogue to the ancient or medieval punishment of banishment[61]) disproportionate? Does Magna Carta have anything to say to these questions? The prosaic starting point is that the signers of Magna Carta regarded death or worse as just punishments for the crimes of robbery or murder. So the modern scholar and jurist are obliged to propose a more sophisticated argument – to

[58] *Trop*, 356 U.S. at 100.
[59] 560 U.S. 48 (2010). For example, the amicus brief filed by the Center for the Administration of Criminal Law on behalf of Graham claims support from Magna Carta. 2009 WL 2236773 at 8.
[60] 567 U.S. ___ (2012). For example, the amicus brief filed by Amnesty International on behalf of Miller claims support from Magna Carta. 2012 WL 174238 at 9.
[61] See Craig S. Lerner, 'Life without Parole as a Conflicted Punishment', *Wake Forest Law Review* 48 (2013): 1101, 1127–31.

wit, that Magna Carta encapsulates the principle that punishment should be calibrated to current attitudes towards the severity of a crime. The thin reed upon which this argument is piled is the phrase 'in accordance with the degree of the offense' in Articles 20 to 22.

An honest grappling with those articles reveals that the authors did not have serious crimes in mind. And it is noteworthy that American courts, litigants and academics who invoke the majesty of Magna Carta generally preserve a respectful distance from the text, contenting themselves with gestures in the direction of the Great Charter. Those courts that grapple with the text seldom produce analyses that merit passing marks. Consider again *Solem v. Helm*, the catalyst for what has become an increasingly active Eighth American jurisprudence. The passage quoted earlier claims support for '[t]he principle that a punishment ... be proportionate to the crime' from the 'three [articles] of Magna Carta ... devoted to amercements', adding that this principle was 'repeated and extended in the First Statute of Westminster, 3 Edw. I, ch. 6 (1275)', and evidenced by a later case, which is cited as '*Hodges v. Humkin*, 2 Bulst. 139, 140, 80 Eng.Rep. 1015, 1016 (K.B. 1615) (Croke, J.)'.[62]

Let us grade this foray into legal history. Half credit to Justice Powell for acknowledging that the articles are limited to amercement. But deductions are in order for failing to address what amercement was and how Articles 20 to 22 have no application to serious crimes, which were addressed in other articles of Magna Carta. The citation to the First Statute of Westminster supplies an aura of pedantry to the Court's argument, but it is doubtful that Justice Powell consulted the ancient statute. Article 6 of the 1275 statute is entitled 'Amercements shall be reasonable, and according to the Offense', but the text of the article provides a sense of what is intended:

> And that no City, Borough, nor Town, not any Man amerced without reasonable Cause, and according to the Quantity of his Trespass; that is to say, every Freeman having his Freehold, a Merchant having his Merchandise, a Villain having his Gainage, and that his or their Peers.[63]

The language is similar to Articles 20 to 22 of Magna Carta, suggesting a similar purpose. But Article 6 of the Statute of Westminster is obviously not addressed to *criminal* offences: cities, boroughs and towns do not commit crimes. They do, however, like individual men, fail in the discharge of their duties to the Crown and are therefore liable to amercement. The penalty is, furthermore, not assessed for crimes or felonies, but 'trespass[es]'. Felonies are explicitly addressed in other articles of the Statute of Westminster. For

---

[62] *Solem*, 463 U.S. at 284–85.
[63] 3 Edw. 1 (1275).

example, Article 12 speaks of the 'Punishment of Felons Refusing lawful Trial'; of course, the punishment is not amercement, but 'strong and hard Imprisonment'. And 'strong and hard Imprisonment' was a term of art: 'Custom settled it that the defendant who was put to [strong and hard imprisonment] was laid over with weights that would crush him to death unless he relented.'[64]

The *Solem* court's citation to *Hodges v. Humkin* is also noteworthy. Justice Powell apparently thought the case impressive, but it is possible he confused its author, Justice Croke, with a more distinguished jurist with one fewer letter. (Or, more mischievously, perhaps he hoped his readers would confuse Croke and Coke.) Apart from the fact that *Hodges* was decided nearly four centuries after the sealing of Magna Carta and therefore dubiously casts light on the Great Charter's original meaning, one must be struck by the case's obscurity: is this really the best precedent the Supreme Court could summon? References to *Hodges v. Humkin* are few and far between and are generally not flattering. In *Queen v. Rea* [Court of Queens Bench] (1865), for example, Justice Held was unimpressed when one of the litigants cited *Hodges*. Judge Held wrote that '[i]t is not easy to make the case intelligible' and goes on: 'It may be observed that though Croke, J., took such a part in the decision, it is not reported in Croke's own reports, nor is it in any of the contemporaneous reports, ... which detracts from [its] authority.'[65] So to sum up, the *Solem* court invoked Magna Carta, but it failed to grapple with the text, inaptly cited a relevant statute and dredged up an obscure and irrelevant case four centuries after the signing of Magna Carta. Low marks indeed.

CONCLUSION

In Gilbert and Sullivan's *The Mikado*, a Japanese emperor announces that his sublime object is to let the punishment fit the crime. The 'dull and prosy sinner' will be sentenced to listen to 'mystical Germans/Who preach from ten to four'.[66] The pool shark will suffer a possibly worse fate:

> He's made to dwell
> In a dungeon cell
> On a spot that's always barred.
> And there he plays extravagant matches
> In fitless finger-stalls

[64] John H. Langbein, Renée Lettow Lerner and Bruce P. Smith (eds.), *History of the Common Law: The Development of Anglo-American Institutions* (New York: Aspen Publishers, 2009), 61.

[65] *Queen v. Rea* [1865], 17 Ir. Jur Rep. 219, 225.

[66] *The Complete Plays of Gilbert and Sullivan* (New York: W.W. Norton, 1997), 331.

> On a cloth untrue
> With a twisted cue
> And elliptical billiard balls![67]

Several American judicial opinions have invoked Gilbert and Sullivan in overturning or affirming criminal sentences challenged as disproportionate.[68] No one would suggest that these judges regarded *The Mikado* as binding precedent, but the clever lyrics gave a panache to the opinions that would otherwise be lacking. The same could be said of the use of *The Mikado* in this essay.

Perhaps judicial citations to Magna Carta are of a similar nature. It is doubtful that Justice Powell (author of *Solem v. Helm*) regarded Magna Carta as binding authority. It is even more doubtful that he was uncertain as to the correct result in that case until he consulted Magna Carta. More likely, of course, is that having reached the desired result, Justice Powell hunted for a citation to supply a gauzy magnificence to his opinion. And nothing fits that bill better – at least for modern Anglo-American lawyers – than Magna Carta. Why this should be so is a long story, but it is sufficient here to point out that for centuries, during the Tudor period, the Great Charter was largely ignored – and Shakespeare's *King John* makes no mention of it.[69] Edward Coke dusted off Magna Carta and created a mythology that proved useful in parliamentary attacks on royal authority, but much of Coke's account has been dismissed by disinterested observers as 'a skyscraper built on anachronisms'.[70]

Many scholars have dissected anachronistic readings of other articles of Magna Carta, manufactured to create a jury trial right and other rights nowhere present in the Great Charter. This essay's contribution has been to expose the anachronistic readings of Articles 20 to 22. The claim that these articles, and Magna Carta more broadly, embody a proportionality principle is true in a trivial sense that could be ascribed to every legal code in recorded

---

[67] Id. at 332.

[68] Opinions citing *The Mikado* include *State v. Bowser*, 926 S.E.2d 714 (Ohio App. 3rd 2010); *Watson v. United States*, 979 A.2d 1254 (D.C. 2009) (Schwelb, J., dissenting); *State v. Brooks*, 739 So.2d 1223 (Fla. App. 5th 1999).

[69] See McKechnie, *Magna Carta*, 120.

[70] Bill Shuter, 'Tradition as Rereading', in David Galef (ed.), *Second Thoughts: A Focus on Rereading* (Detroit: Wayne State University Press, 1998), 79. Coke has not been the only figure in English history to make use of Magna Carta; on the uses made by some of the Levellers, see Vernon Bogdanor's contribution to this volume (Ch. 2). For an imaginative, contemporary effort to deploy Magna Carta to further a legal/political agenda, consider Geraldine Van Bueren's contribution (Ch. 10). In addition, as noted in this chapter's introduction, Natalie Riendeau's contribution (Ch. 11) explores Magna Carta's place in the 'legend of English life'.

human history. As one tries to extract more meaningful lessons, however, Articles 20 to 22 are of little or no *legal* relevance to us, most notably because they are not addressed to the question of criminal punishment. Magna Carta's significance today is not in explicating the law, but in mythologizing it, and in surrounding human-made law with the transcendence it perhaps requires, at some level, to enjoy legitimacy.

9

Judicial Supremacy: Explaining False Starts and Surprising Successes

Victor Menaldo and Nora Webb Williams

In many of the world's democracies, the judicial branch is supreme. Judicial review allows it to have the final say over the laws of the land, as well as decisions made by the other branches of government. In other words, the judiciary, alone, resolves controversies about the legitimacy and scope of legislation or executive action. Usually what this means is that a higher court exercises the authority to nullify legislative and executive actions on the basis of the constitution.[1]

In the United States in particular, a supreme, federal court accomplishes this task by strategically selecting case law that bears constitutionally on other cases and legislative statutes. The upshot is that it frequently restrains the other branches, if not rebukes them. The seminal *Marbury v. Madison* [1803] decision inspired a series of subsequent decisions in which the court either struck down or affirmed national and state laws, even though they could not punish executives if they were to ignore their judgments. The Supreme Court's 2012 decision in *National Federation of Independent Business v. Sebelius,* which declared the Affordable Care Act constitutional, is perhaps the most notable recent example.

This is a very puzzling development. The judicial branch lacks any obvious way in which it can enforce its decisions; it lacks a militia or any other organised coercive force that can sanction the other government branches if they disobey its decisions. Moreover, the judicial branch lacks the power of the purse – it is at the mercy of the legislative branch for financial support. And furthermore, in the U.S. system and several other democracies characterised by judicial supremacy, judges are appointed by executives and vetted by legislatures. Even though unelected justices have the final say over the con-stitutionality – and thus legitimacy – of a country's laws in these contexts, they

---

[1] This definition is adapted from A. V. Dicey, *Introduction to the Study of the Law of the Constitution,* 10th ed. (London: Macmillan & Co Ltd, 1959), 137–80.

seem, in the most basic sense, beholden to the other branches of government. Why would judicial supremacy ever arise if the judiciary lacks the means to finance itself and even select its own personnel, let alone enforce its will through the threat of force?

This chapter explores several questions raised by this fundamental puzzle that are at the intersection of comparative politics, judicial politics and the political history of the United States, England and several European democracies. How and why does judicial supremacy come about instead of its alternatives – parliamentary supremacy or presidentialism by decree? Why does judicial supremacy survive if, over time, judiciaries are inevitably called upon to make an ever greater number of decisions that challenge the interests – if not the authority – of other government branches? Why did some democracies that had the potential to develop judicial supremacy instead settle on parliamentary supremacy? Do executives have to hold a normative commitment to the court's judicial review of its decisions, or is there some outside force that makes its adherence self-enforcing? If it's the latter, then what could this source possibly be, considering that the executive branch commands authority over the armed forces and police?

This chapter addresses these questions and their implications. It does so by looking at a hitherto neglected laboratory in which there were many opportunities for judicial supremacy to arise and perhaps gain hold, but where it failed to emerge. In Europe, there were several constitutional experiments during the thirteenth century. First among these was England's Magna Carta, through which there was the potential for judicial supremacy to arise, though ultimately parliamentary supremacy prevailed.

This chapter outlines why England never developed judicial supremacy, even though Magna Carta contained the seeds needed to bring this possibility to fruition in 1215, while the United States went the other way. The answer has important implications for the rule of law, democratic consolidation and the ability of the popular will to express itself. On the one hand, judicial supremacy appears to be one way to make democratic consolidation possible; it allows for arbitration of higher-order disputes and disallows the executive branch from breaking the rules when it is convenient. On the other hand, in the English and other European cases – some of which we will take up in this chapter as well – parliamentary supremacy was the culmination of a gradual transition away from absolute monarchy to what has become, in the eyes of many, the paragon of representative government.[2]

---

[2] Explaining the rise of parliamentary supremacy is outside the scope of this paper. For the canonical view of this development, see Douglass C. North and Barry R. Weingast,

Consistent with one of the key themes of this volume, this chapter touches upon a hitherto neglected aspect of Magna Carta, one which has implications for both the study of constitutions, more generally, and judicial politics, more specifically. First, we firmly identify Magna Carta as a fundamental precursor to the U.S. Constitution. Second, we demonstrate that Magna Carta possessed the potential for judicial supremacy. Third, we are able to place the Charter in a comparative perspective, in that we adduce evidence for the claim that the pusillanimity and the organisational dysfunction of the disparate actors involved in crafting Magna Carta explain its inability to live up to that potential, whilst the power and coherence of their American counterparts enabled judicial supremacy to emerge from the Philadelphia Constitution.

There is considerable agreement on the obvious fact that Magna Carta is a touchstone in legal and constitutional development, in both England and the rest of the world.[3] Thus, Magna Carta held the seeds that future entrepreneurs would grow into recognisable branches of democratic government. This includes the United States of America. Consensus is weaker around the ideas that (1) the Charter contained ingredients that would eventually help give rise to judicial supremacy in the U.S. case, and that (2) it could just as easily have done so in England.

Scholars do agree that the seventeenth-century English jurist and parliamentarian Sir Edward Coke used Magna Carta to argue that the nation's monarchs should be subject to the law. We argue that his line of reasoning was not some radical confabulation and could have conceivably been advanced earlier, during Magna Carta or shortly after its aftermath. Coke's assertions, of course, were ultimately for naught – but no one has yet offered a satisfactory explanation why judicial supremacy remained stillborn in the English case.

This chapter puts forth an answer to the puzzle of judicial supremacy by comparing the American experiment in self-government to precocious European attempts to circumscribe the power of the sovereign. We attempt to explain why judicial supremacy took hold in the American case but failed to do so across England and other European cases, despite the fact that several constitutional principles and practices adumbrated the possibility for judicial supremacy. Unlike the American case, where thirteen colonies, and eventually fifty states, coordinated to vest the judicial branch with the authority to represent their interests against the executive and legislative branches, in the

'Constitutions and Commitment: The Evolution of Institutions Governing Public Choice in Seventeenth-Century England', *Journal of Economic History* 49(4) (1989): 803–32.

[3] See Vernon Bogdanor's chapter in this volume (Ch. 2) on the impact of Magna Carta on British constitutional development and how it inspired constitution-makers in other parts of the world.

European cases the adoption of 'feudal constitutions' was a top-down affair.[4] Sovereigns attempted to strategically tie their own hands to gain a discrete, and short-run, benefit. Invariably, they limited their power in circumscribed, manageable ways, usually to foster stability or generate greater fiscal or financial resources. They never fully delegated authority to a co-equal, let alone constitutionally superior, partner.

Conversely, we argue that in the American case coercion stands behind judicial supremacy. It does so because it ultimately represents the pooling of military and financial resources by a disparate set of actors. On the eve of the Philadelphia Convention in 1787, thirteen states sent delegates appointed by their legislatures, and those delegates projected their principals' military and financial power. In turn, these political actors ultimately delegated political authority to a newly established federal judicial branch. It, alone, was deputised to adjudicate federal-level issues. The way in which these states subsequently protected their rights and interests is that they were in charge of enforcing these judicial decisions. Serious transgressions against judicial supremacy would trigger either military or financial retaliation against the central government. Therefore, another way to think about the U.S. Constitution is that it was a vehicle created by the states to make collective decisions with a greater scope than possible through the Articles of Confederation that preceded it, whilst ensuring that said scope was never large enough to considerably weaken its creators.

DEFINITIONS AND LITERATURE REVIEW

The literature on judicial supremacy is far from conclusive when it comes to defining key terms. Keith Whittington points out that some academic arguments about judicial supremacy are presented as discussions of judicial independence or judicial review.[5] For some authors, judicial independence seems to imply judicial review.[6] For others, judicial review and judicial supremacy are synonymous.[7] Interestingly, the concepts and patterns often

---

[4] Similar to Anthony King's chapter in this book (Ch. 3), we are concerned with the actors surrounding Magna Carta.

[5] Keith E. Whittington, 'Extrajudicial Constitutional Interpretation: Three Objections and Responses', *North Carolina Law Review* 80 (2002): 776.

[6] Gretchen Helmke and Frances Rosenbluth, 'Regimes and the Rule of Law: Judicial Independence in Comparative Perspective', *Annual Review of Political Science* 12(1) (June 2009): 345–66.

[7] Charles Grove Haines, *The American Doctrine of Judicial Supremacy* (New York: Macmillan Company, 1914); Jack Knight and Lee Epstein, 'On the Struggle for Judicial Supremacy', *Law and Society Review* 30(1) (1996): 90.

associated with judicial supremacy transcend democracy; many authors have considered how judicial independence and judicial review might come about in and be practiced by autocratic polities.[8]

Judicial independence implies that the judicial branch of government is protected, in great part, from the meddling of the other branches and of political actors.[9] De jure independence indicates that provisions protecting the independence of the judiciary are enshrined in constitutions or other forms of law. These formal rules might take the form of judicial institutions such as life-tenure appointments and relatively high official salaries, which exist to protect judges from the material influence of the other branches. For independence to exist in practice (de facto), judges must exercise this independence without influence or repercussions from the other branches. While influence includes bribes from other government branches for favourable decisions, repercussions include threats after judicial decisions which might diminish judges' ability or willingness to render sincere and effective judgments in the future.

Judicial review is, fundamentally, something that the judiciary *does* or *has*. This contrasts with judicial independence, which refers to what the judiciary *is*. Thus, while the judiciary can *be* independent by construction, or tradition, it *has* the option to exercise judicial review. The term overlaps significantly with constitutional review – the ability of a court to void laws or executive rules predicated on its interpretation of the constitution. There is a difference between courts that deal with case law and determine constitutionality within a case law framework (e.g., supreme courts) and courts that deal only with constitutional interpretation (e.g., constitutional courts), however. In the United States, for example, the Supreme Court deals with issues of constitutional import only when they are brought as a matter of case law. Conversely, constitutional courts typically review laws before they are enacted, or might take up challenges to particular laws outside of regular lawsuits.

As the foregoing discussion suggests, the concepts of judicial independence and judicial review are closely aligned. The practice of judicial review is clearly influenced by judicial independence. And it makes intuitive sense that one measure of de facto judicial independence is judicial review: if the judiciary is willing and able to judge the constitutionality of legislative and

---

[8] Tom Ginsburg and Tamir Moustafa (eds.), *Rule by Law: The Politics of Courts in Authoritarian Regimes* (Cambridge, UK: Cambridge University Press, 2008).
[9] Helmke and Rosenbluth, 'Regimes and the Rule of Law'.

executive acts, this could be evidence that the judiciary has indeed achieved independence.[10]

Judicial supremacy, our ultimate object of concern, means that the other branches of government will abide by the judiciary's decision to nullify their acts. The judiciary, whether it takes the form of a supreme or constitutional court, is the final interpreter of the constitution. While the executive and legislative branches of government may also be engaged in interpreting the constitution – indeed, their work is usually framed by the constitution's provisions – they must back down in the face of a judicial veto. This means that their enforcement of any statute or rule has to come to a full stop if the judiciary deems it to be unconstitutional. Therefore, judicial supremacy implies some form of judicial review. It also seems to imply an independent judiciary: if the judiciary is not truly independent, its judgments might reflect the will of the executive or legislative branch and thus connote executive or parliamentary supremacy working thorough a co-opted judiciary.

The example par excellence of judicial supremacy is the U.S. system. For example, in *Bush v. Gore* [2000], the Supreme Court ruled on the constitutionality of a case that had an impact on both the executive and legislative branches. The Court ultimately awarded the contested presidential election to George W. Bush. Al Gore's political party (the Democrats) held the presidency during this decision; yet, even though the decision cut against its interests, the executive abided by the court's decision instead of appealing to the popular will – Gore had won the popular vote.

The great puzzle of judicial supremacy is how and why the other branches of government abide by the judgments of the judicial branch. The legislature has the money, the executive the military might. What stops them from brushing aside the pesky rulings of an antagonistic court?

Curiously, there is little in the positive literature that addresses this puzzle directly.[11] Most explanations focus on the United States. One perspective holds that American judicial supremacy emerged due to the recognition of the Constitution as the vessel of common law. Noting that elements of judicial

[10] Theodore L. Becker, *Comparative Judicial Studies* (Chicago: Rand McNally and Co, 1970), cited in Erik S. Herron and Kirk A. Randazzo, 'The Relationship between Independence and Judicial Review in Post-Communist Courts', *Journal of Politics* 65(2) (2003): 422–38.

[11] There are several normative arguments in favour of and against judicial supremacy. There are two possible alternatives in a constitutional democracy. The first is popular constitutionalism, where the 'people' are the ultimate interpreters of the constitution. Popular constitutionalism has received attention in recent years, as it has been espoused by politicians and activists associated with the Tea Party (see Adam Nagourney, 'A Defiant Rancher Savors the Audience That Rallied to His Side', *New York Times*, 23 April 2014). Another is departmentalism, the theory that all three government branches should have equal authority to interpret the constitution.

review and supremacy existed in the pre-constitution colonies, Haines argues that the legacy of British common law may have incentivised the framers (particularly Alexander Hamilton) to advocate for judicial dominance.[12] Dicey presents a similar view, though his focus is more on how the cultural and national aspects of American Federalism lead naturally to the creation of judicial review and judicial supremacy in the Constitution.[13] Counter-intuitively, both Dicey and Haines are swayed by U.S. Chief Justice John Marshall's interpretation of the Constitution as representing the true will of the people against the fickle nature of electoral mandates despite the fact that the only branch of government that is not elected at the federal level is the judiciary, which is responsible for interpreting that charter.[14] Some cross-national evidence supports this type of argument; La Porta et al. show that a history of common law explains the rise of judicial review and independence.[15]

Another set of theories on judicial supremacy fall under what Helmke and Rosenbluth label 'delegative models of judicial independence'.[16] These are centred on strategic decisions made by political actors who delegate governing responsibilities to the judicial branch as a way of advancing their partisan or material interests. The so-called insurance theory draws on such an assumption.[17] It holds that where levels of political pluralism are high, actors will be incentivised to support judicial review and judicial independence as insurance against undue prosecution should they be ousted from power by the opposition. Investing in a supreme judiciary – which takes a slow, measured and theoretically objective look at legislation and binds the other branches – might protect the legislators and their work from future dismantling.[18] Finally, legislators and executives may also support an independent judiciary as a way of avoiding controversial issues, letting justices make policy decisions that would otherwise carry heavy political costs.[19]

[12] *The American Doctrine of Judicial Supremacy.*
[13] *Introduction to the Study of the Law of the Constitution.*
[14] Bruce Ackerman, *The Failure of the Founding Fathers: Jefferson, Marshall, and the Rise of Presidential Democracy* (Cambridge, MA: Belknap Press of Harvard University Press, 2005).
[15] Rafael La Porta et al., 'Judicial Checks and Balances', *Journal of Political Economy* 1112(2) (2004): 445–70.
[16] 'Regimes and the Rule of Law', 349.
[17] Tom Ginsburg, *Judicial Review in New Democracies: Constitutional Courts in Asian Cases* (Cambridge, UK: Cambridge University Press, 2003).
[18] Of course, it might not be the case that pluralism is either a necessary or sufficient cause of judicial independence. For example, Marian Popova notes that in Ukraine, pluralism has not led to judicial independence: 'Political Competition as an Obstacle to Judicial Independence: Evidence from Russia and Ukraine', *Comparative Political Studies* 43(10) (7 May 2010): 1202–29.
[19] Mark A. Graber, 'The Nonmajoritarian Difficulty: Legislative Deference to the Judiciary', *Studies in American Political Development* 7 (1993): 875–901; Eli M. Salzberger, 'A Positive

Applications of these strategic theories are diverse. Knight and Epstein use game theory to model the short-run political choices that faced both the Jefferson administration and the Marshall court in the United States during the early nineteenth century.[20] They argue that in this case, the unique interactions between executive and judicial branches unintentionally created important precedents, including the seminal *Marbury v. Madison*, which unexpectedly gave birth to judicial review. Generalizing beyond the U.S. case, Landes and Posner argue that judicial independence extends the time horizons and commitment-making abilities of legislators by demonstrating to supporters that their hard-fought legislative work will not be undone by fickle courts.[21]

Barry Weingast and co-authors also provide valuable insights into judicial supremacy. Judicial review and judicial vetoes might provide both focal and trigger points to actors with de facto power who fear being side-lined in the future.[22] Focal points help actors coordinate action; trigger points send signals as to when actors have overstepped their bounds, breaking their commitments. Constitutions, when brought to the fore through constitutional conventions or other founding moments, act as focal points for actors to consolidate power. Similarly, judicial supremacy, through the mechanism of judicial review, produces trigger points by setting boundaries for the other two branches. For example, if the executive does not abide by the ruling of the court, the public and elites might perceive the executive as having overstepped their constitutional mandate. Thus, judicial supremacy creates moments around which diverse actors can coordinate, perhaps to punish the overreach of powerful central actors.[23]

Last, to motivate an explanation for the failure of judicial supremacy to emerge out of a constitution, we build on the literature on the strategic adoption of constitutions and legislatures by dictators.[24] Constitutions can

Analysis of the Doctrine of Separation of Powers, or: Why Do We Have an Independent Judiciary?' *International Review of Law and Economics* 13 (1993): 340–79; Keith E. Whittington, *Constitutional Construction: Divided Powers and Constitutional Meaning* (Cambridge, MA: Harvard University Press, 1999).

[20] 'On the Struggle for Judicial Supremacy'.

[21] 'The Independent Judiciary in an Interest-Group Perspective', *Journal of Law and Economics* 18 (1975): 875–901.

[22] Sonia Mittal and Barry R. Weingast, 'Constitutional Stability and the Deferential Court', *Journal of Constitutional Law* 13(2) (2010): 337–52; North and Weingast, 'Constitutions and Commitment'; Barry R. Weingast, 'The Political Foundations of Democracy and the Rule of Law', *American Political Science Review* 91 (1997): 245–63.

[23] Mittal and Weingast, 'Constitutional Stability and the Deferential Court'.

[24] North and Weingast, 'Constitutions and Commitment'; Roger B. Myerson, 'The Autocrat's Credibility Problem and Foundations of the Constitutional State', *American Political Science Review* 102(01) (13 February 2008): 125–39; Jennifer Gandhi, *Political Institutions under Dictatorship* (New York: Cambridge University Press, 2008).

serve as commitments to a launching organisation and placate supporters who might otherwise distrust a new sovereign. Albertus and Menaldo demonstrate that rulers who adopt constitutions receive significant boosts to their tenure.[25] These top-down, strategic commitments may not promote democratic reforms, but they may create real limits on executive power, albeit not ones imposed by a powerful judiciary.

A THEORY OF JUDICIAL SUPREMACY

Disparate actors – whether they are states, barons or warlords – sometimes seek to pool their military and financial power to enforce their rights and advance their interests. While diffuse actors may be able to command and marshal violence via militias or similar technologies, their individual power may not be sufficient for them to effectively exert their political will. Therefore, dispersed actors may find it expedient to pool their power and coordinate their actions; this can allow them to exercise their *aggregate power* to discipline other powerful actors with armies and deep pockets, thus deterring the latter from violating their rights and interests.

Most generically, this requires two things. The first is a focal point which allows them to enshrine their rights. The second is the ability to delegate authority to political actors who can serve as a vehicle to help them enforce their rights in the future.

For our purposes, we are interested in how a constitution organised according to the principle of judicial supremacy may provide a means for disparate actors with diffuse financial and military power to pool their resources, coordinate, and set up institutional vehicles that allow them to enforce their rights and advance their interests in the future. The constitutional moment can create focal points that motivate the original coordination of these diffuse actors. The judiciary can be constructed during a constitutional convention to serve as a means for setting future trigger points that can allow these diverse actors to mobilise beyond the constitutional moment.

If this is to happen, four things must occur. First, the decentralised actors must be numerous, so that coordination between them is critical. Second, the aggregate coercive power of these diverse actors must be relatively high, so that when pooled they have a credible threat against incumbents. Third, the

---

[25] Michael Albertus and Victor Menaldo, 'The Political Economy of Autocratic Constitutions', in *Constitutions in Authoritarian Regimes*, ed. Tom Ginsburg and Alberto Simpser (Cambridge, UK: Cambridge University Press, 2014), 53–82; Michael Albertus and Victor Menaldo, 'Dictators as Founding Fathers? The Role of Constitutions under Autocracy', *Economics & Politics* 24(3) (2 November 2012): 279–306.

coercive power at the constitutional moment should not only be diffused among several political agents, but the balance of power between these agents must also be relatively uniform. In other words, none of these decentralised political actors is powerful enough to threaten the others. Fourth, they must be able to come together to enshrine future trigger points that promote the enforcement of their rights and interests.

A constitutional convention and the institutions it creates can accomplish all of these tasks. A convention allows diffuse actors to congregate for the purpose of discussing and debating how the distribution of power between the branches of government can create venues for them to protect their rights and advance their interests. Abstract political principles such as pluralism, liberalism and accountability can serve as focal points that allow these actors to coordinate. In turn, coordination during constitutional construction can allow the actors to bestow tangible institutions, such as the judiciary, with the power to set future trigger points that can mobilise the diffuse actors, allowing them to re-coordinate at moments in time well beyond the founding constitutional moment. Specifically, a violation of a judicial veto by the other branches of government can trigger a reaction – perhaps even an insurrection – by decentralised actors against the centre.

Given this framework, one can re-conceptualise what judicial supremacy is as well as gain traction on the puzzle of why it may hold indefinitely despite the fact that the central executive commands the armed forces and police while the central legislature has the power of the purse. Judicial supremacy is the institutionalised production of trigger mechanisms after a constitutional moment to the benefit of decentralised actors who were strong enough to pool their resources and coordinate to create a judicial vehicle capable of helping them to enforce their rights and advance their interests. And the reason other government branches abide by judicial supremacy afterward despite their superiority in both military and financial power is that they know that if they disregard the court's decisions, they might trigger a costly reaction by these decentralised actors, if not new constituents who are activated by judicial trigger points. This picture can help us re-conceptualise judicial review as the continual production of trigger points, through the court's decisions, that lets decentralised actors know under what circumstances they might need to act against the executive and legislature to enforce their rights.

This situation contrasts strongly with the situation surrounding constitutions that are top-down, hand-tying devices. These constitutions are used by sovereigns to, at worst, buy time when they face a challenge to their rule and, at best, circumscribe their power in very limited ways. Constitutions of this type, designed without the strong backing of an enforcing group of diverse actors, are not the product of coordination by decentralised actors. Moreover, they do not produce devices, such as judicial review, for future enforcement through a trigger mechanism. Instead, they serve as a calculated bid by a sovereign to placate specific actors for the purpose of preserving the individual ruler's reign. In this case, decentralised actors are not numerous enough, strong enough or coordinated enough to pool their power together; by extension, they cannot cultivate a judiciary that will serve as a vehicle to protect their rights and interests by continually producing trigger points down the road, after the constitutional moment.

Testable Implications and Research Strategy

The majority of the empirical portion of this chapter deals with the first clause of the theoretical framework described in the previous section: the coordination of actors around a constitutional moment, whether top-down or bottom-up, that lays the groundwork for future cultivation of a trigger-setting judicial branch. However, we also move away from the constitutional moment at times in order to address the second, more future-oriented, portion of the theory: does the constitution serve as the basis for judicial supremacy in the future and, if so, what is its ultimate function? We expect that variation in the number, power and coordination potential of diffuse actors can explain the rise and consolidation of judicial supremacy or its absence.

To subject our theoretical intuitions about the advent and perpetuation of judicial supremacy to empirical scrutiny, we primarily compare the political history of the United States to England's during and after Magna Carta's sealing. Moreover, as an illustrative contrast to Magna Carta, we draw on similar 'feudal' constitutions of the era. Specifically, we examine other thirteenth-century charters whose creation was engineered by a sitting monarch. These include the 1222 Hungarian Golden Bull, the 1231 Sicilian Constitutions of Melfi and the 1272 Castilian Seven Divisions (Las Siete Partidas).

Why do we focus attention on old, and in some cases quite obscure, charters? The primary reason is that these cases occurred before there were veritable examples of democratic government in its modern form. This allows us to neutralise alternative factors that might influence judicial supremacy: for example, a free press that can report in real time, an educated electorate, a host of global examples about how to run courts in a modern republic and the ubiquity of norms that promote liberalism and individual rights. It also allows us to evaluate our theory against cases in which naked military power and coercion were very salient and palpable.

Finally, despite the vast amount of time that elapsed between the promulgation of Magna Carta and the adoption of the U.S. Constitution, two factors make this particular comparison useful. First, neither document explicitly calls for judicial review or judicial supremacy, ruling out a teleological explanation in which judicial supremacy emerges fully formed out of a constitution, like Athena springing forth from Zeus's brow. This means that it is more likely that the culprit behind judicial supremacy lies with strategic interactions between powerful actors and the messy world of politics. Second, the cultural and legal contexts surrounding these documents are quite similar, allowing us roughly to control for the effect of these variables on judicial supremacy.

THEORY MEETS EVIDENCE

Historical documents and narratives about the U.S. Constitutional Convention and American judicial history, as well as the birth and influence of Magna Carta, appear to support our framework. The actors who were behind the creation of the U.S. Constitution were diffuse but relatively strong: they possessed significant coercive forces. During the Philadelphia Convention, they were able to pool their power and coordinate to pursue their interests. Magna Carta, conversely, was a top-down, strategic reaction by a sovereign. King John sought to ameliorate the threat posed by a tiny elite who were relatively weak and lacked the ability to coordinate. The stories of feudal constitutions similar to Magna Carta also support our framework: they fit the model of top-down constitutions enacted for strategic purposes, as opposed to bottom-up constitutions enforced by diffuse actors. Judicial supremacy qua judicial review did not emerge in these instances.

The U.S. Case

To explain why it was possible for judicial supremacy to emerge in the United States, we focus on the creation and ratification of the U.S. Constitution. The Constitution was approved by a constituent assembly on September 17, 1787. It was then sent to state assemblies for ratification – nine of the thirteen states were required to approve the new constitution. The document was ultimately ratified by each state and came into effect in 1789.

One of the striking things about judicial supremacy in the U.S. case is its lack of explicit provision in the Constitution itself. Madison's notes from the convention indicate that little discussion was given to the issue.[26] However, and tellingly, pamphlets about the Constitution that were intended to sway voters to support its ratification *did include discussions of judicial review and judicial independence*.[27] In other words, one of the selling points of the new constitution to the decentralised actors at the forefront of our framework was the federal judiciary's ability to signal when the other branches were over-stepping their bounds vis-à-vis constitutional interpretation or modification. To give only one example, Alexander Hamilton's Federalist No. 78, written to sway public opinion in New York, extols the benefits of judicial review:

> It is far more rational to suppose that the courts were designed to be an intermediate body between the people and the legislature in order, among other things, to keep the latter within the limits assigned to their authority. The interpretation of the laws in the proper and peculiar province of the courts . . . the Constitution ought to be preferred to the statute, the intention of the people to the intention of their agents.[28]

Most commentaries on the origin of judicial supremacy highlight the *Marbury v. Madison* case of 1803. Although judicial review and judicial supremacy did not enter the standard lexicon of politics and judicial decision-making in America until many years after *Marbury*, the case was a key touchstone. Here, we present the history in broad brushstrokes.[29]

The facts are well known. The departing Adams administration pushed the Federalist-controlled legislature to adopt a statute in 1801 that expand the federal court system by creating a new, intermediate layer of appellate courts. Adams then appointed a slew of new judges on the eve of exiting office; however, not all of these judicial commissions were delivered before the handoff of power. The new, more populist Jefferson administration was less inclined towards federal power, and concomitantly the federal courts, and thus ordered that the remaining commissions not be sent. It also advocated on behalf of legislation to repeal the 1801 statute. William Marbury, who was supposed to have received one of these federal commissions, litigated for its

---

[26] David W. Tyler, 'Clarifying Departmentalism: How the Framers' Vision of Judicial and Presidential Review Makes the Case for Deductive Judicial Supremacy', *William & Mary Law Review* 50(6) (2009): 2219.

[27] This is consistent with the fact that concepts of higher law, including those espoused by Edward Coke, would have probably been salient in the colonies at the time. Among those concepts was judicial review. See Philip Hamburger, *Law and Judicial Duty* (Cambridge, MA: Harvard University Press, 2008).

[28] Alexander Hamilton, James Madison and John Jay, *The Federalist Papers*, original circa 1788, ed. Clinton Rossiter (New York: Signet Classic, 2003), 446.

[29] For a much more detailed analysis of the strategic interactions surrounding *Marbury v. Madison*, see Knight and Epstein, 'On the Struggle for Judicial Supremacy'.

instatement, naming Jefferson's Secretary of State, James Madison, in the suit, since he had been tasked by Jefferson with enacting an embargo on the remaining commissions.

The court's decision walked a careful political tightrope and in the process set a huge precedent. While the Supreme Court's Chief Justice, John Marshall, argued that Marbury indeed had a right to his commission, he also determined that the Supreme Court did not actually have the jurisdiction to force Madison to deliver the commission. Appealing to judicial review, the court ironically found that whereas the 1801 statute had ostensibly granted the court jurisdiction over judicial commissions, the provision of the 1789 Judiciary Act that empowered Marbury to bring his claim to the Supreme Court was itself unconstitutional, as it was in conflict with Article III of the Constitution. Marshall declared the 1789 law invalid on these grounds, limiting the court's own – legislatively provided – jurisdiction over the matter in the process.[30] Indeed, the decision was quite sweeping in that the court circumscribed its own authority within the parameters of the Constitution, as well as the discretion of the other two branches of government.[31]

Despite the fact that judicial supremacy was not prescribed in the Constitution per se, the court deduced this authority directly from the charter, which identified itself as the country's supreme law. In another irony for the birth of judicial review, the executive branch was the short-term victor: as Jefferson had wished, Marbury was denied his commission.[32] However, in the long term, Marshall's clever and seminal decision provided formal institutional backing for judicial supremacy, which would in the future clash with the preferences of the executive branch on many occasions; and although it never conspicuously curtailed Jefferson's power during his presidential term, Pandora's box was irrevocably opened.[33]

Yet we submit that it was only a matter of time, and that had the institutionalization of judicial review not arrived via the Trojan horse that was *Marbury v. Madison*, it would have eventually arrived in some other way, as the division of powers between freestanding government branches inevitably gave way to

---

[30] Ibid., 98.

[31] Ibid. Therefore, this was hardly the type of dramatic striking down of a law or constraint on executive authority that one may typically associate with judicial review; nonetheless, it was a patent nullification of an act of Congress.

[32] In another Jefferson victory from a separate case, *Stuart v. Laird*, the Court upheld the repeal of the 1801 Judiciary Act.

[33] For example, during the late 19th and early 20th centuries, the Supreme Court invalidated many laws at both the congressional and state level that were also supported by the executive branch, but deemed too populist. In *Lochner v. New York*, the Court struck down a New York law that limited the workday to ten hours on the grounds that it abrogated the liberty of contract under the due process clause of the Fourteenth Amendment.

conflicts and controversies. Indeed, going back to the 1787 Philadelphia Convention itself, the delegates highlighted judicial review in their efforts to persuade the states to ratify the constitution. Moreover, while the states had effectively undertaken judicial review prior to 1803 by invalidating state statutes that contradicted the federal constitution, there are also examples in which the federal court invalidated state statutes for the same reason.[34] Finally, in the lead-up to *Marbury v. Madison*, President Jefferson himself worried 'that the Court might strike down the Repeal Act as a violation of the Constitution'.[35]

We do not find these many precursors to *Marbury v. Madison* all that surprising. The U.S. Constitution was a bottom-up compromise – one that required the ratification by each individual state before it was enacted. The continued power of the states over the Constitution, ever after it was ratified, is evidenced by the rule that a two-thirds majority of state support is required to amend the Constitution. And an independent judiciary with the power to interpret the Constitution promised to protect the rights of the states by signalling when rebellion was necessary.

This innovation was possible because the states had coercive power and were able to pool their power and coordinate to pursue their interests. The states at the time of the U.S. constitutional ratification were organised around state constitutions. The states also had champions: individuals elected to the constituent assembly, many of whom believed strongly in the rights of states in the face of centralised power. These champions had not gathered to try to oust, or at least wring concessions from, a sitting king. Instead, they were charged with hammering out a document that would please the diverse actors at work in the states. Despite differences of opinion between members of the constituent assembly, they were able to create a constitution that the majority of citizens in their states would support.

The primary source of coercive power in the thirteen states came from militias.[36] Having participated in the Revolutionary War, most of those militias were battle-hardened and universally viewed as legitimate. Although it is impossible to place an exact figure on the number of militia members in each state in the aftermath of the Revolutionary War, it is clear that a large portion of the population could be mobilised along militia lines. McAllister argues that there were around 45,000 militiamen in Virginia alone.[37] This figure can

---

[34] See William Treanor, 'Judicial Review before Marbury', *Stanford Law Review* 58 (2005): 455–562.
[35] Knight and Epstein, 'On the Struggle for Judicial Supremacy', 95.
[36] John K. Mahon, *History of the Militia and the National Guard* (New York: Macmillan Publishing Co, 1983).
[37] J. T. McAllister, *Virginia Militia in the Revolutionary War* (Hot Springs, VA: McAllister Publishing Co, 1913).

be compared to estimates of the total number of U.S. military forces engaged in the Revolutionary War, which range from 184,000 to 250,000.[38]

Once the Revolutionary War ended and the Continental Army was disbanded, militias were recognised and respected by the federal government. Consistent with our framework, the 1792 Militia Act enjoined state militias to assist the federal government in enforcing compliance with the Constitution and mandated that all men should be required to join state militias, which distributed coercive power broadly among the states.[39] Militias were well organised and could pose a threat to the central government when mobilised, as evidenced by the 1791 Whiskey Rebellion in Pennsylvania. Indeed, state militias were a major source of coercive power in the United States through the Civil War.

Of course, the Civil War itself stands out as an important illustration of both the power and limits of judicial supremacy. In the *Dred Scott v. Sandford* case (1857), the Supreme Court's verdict created the basis for slavery to continue in the western territories, because the court ruled that blacks, regardless of whether they were slaves or not, were not American citizens and therefore could not bring lawsuits in federal courts. President Abraham Lincoln subsequently rode to power on his opposition to the decision. During his campaign for the U.S. Senate, which he lost to Stephen Douglass, he rose to national fame after engaging in a series of eponymous debates with his opponent. Lincoln then made the 'Slavery Question' and opposition to *Dred Scott* central to his presidential campaign.

We hasten to emphasise, however, that upon taking power, and despite the fact that he was suspicious of judicial supremacy, Lincoln eschewed adopting policies that would subvert the *Dred Scott* decision. Although we cannot know whether he was deterred by the fear of retaliation by Southern states or not, as is predicted by our framework, that is somewhat of a moot point. Lincoln's vocal opposition to the *Dred Scott* decision during his campaign; the ascendance of his political party, the Republicans, which opposed the spread of slavery in the West; and several attempts by state legislatures in the North to challenge *Dred Scott's* implications proved sufficient grounds for Southern states to secede from the Union.[40]

---

[38] Anne Leland and Mari-Jana Oboroceanu, *American War and Military Operations Casualties: Lists and Statistics* (Washington, DC, 2010).

[39] The Militia Act was continually renewed until 1903, when it was superseded by the creation of the National Guard.

[40] An example in which judicial supremacy was actually challenged occurred when President Andrew Jackson disobeyed the Supreme Court and implemented the Indian Removal Act, ushering in the infamous 'Trail of Tears' in which Native Americans were relocated west of the Mississippi. Specifically, in 1831 the Court declared sovereign the Cherokee tribe living in

Magna Carta

Magna Carta was sealed in 1215 by both England's King John and a bevy of English barons. Many of its clauses served to codify and clarify feudal policies. More importantly, it laid out a series of expectations and political rights. While its rights related primarily to the king's responsibilities to the nobility and clerical classes, Magna Carta also included clauses addressing merchants, burgesses, villeins and liberi homines (freemen).[41] The three clauses addressing the freemen have received the most attention from this document, though there is debate as to whom exactly the term 'freemen' encompasses.[42]

Magna Carta did not, as did the U.S. Constitution, culminate in judicial supremacy, however. Instead, parliamentary supremacy arose as the ultimate curb of monarchical authority, albeit belatedly. This development was not inevitable, however. Magna Carta had the potential to instantiate judicial supremacy.

Yet, the promulgation of Magna Carta and allusions to it throughout English history were instead relegated to the status of a strategic, and usually feckless, ruse in a repetitive contestation for power between sovereigns and groups that were predated upon by the former. In retrospect, the Charter was primarily a weapon of the weak. Originally, Magna Carta served two purposes. First, it was a means for King John to buy time. Second, and relatedly, it was a face-saving token used to placate some of the more recalcitrant barons in exchange for them to abandon their resistance to the King.

Although Magna Carta contains clauses regarding the enforcement of its commitment by a proto-judicial board of twenty-five barons, the barons were unable to enforce this clause.[43] To the contrary, King John undertook a renewed counter-offensive against the barons shortly after signing Magna Carta, which led them to reach out to the French for support. As Holt notes, 'In 1215 Magna Carta was a failure. It was intended as a peace and it provoked war.'[44]

Historically, attempts to revive Magna Carta – it was reissued a total of thirty-seven times – served as a rallying cry that galvanised disenfranchised or

Georgia and rejected as unconstitutional the state government's efforts to remove them from their land.

[41] Not all of these clauses extended rights to every class, and some classes receive only the briefest of attention. Villeins, for example, are mentioned only in clause 20, with reference to amercement. For more on Magna Carta and villeins, see Derek O'Brien's chapter in this volume (Ch. 6).

[42] Edward Jenks, *The Myth of the Magna Carta* (London: Independent Review, 1904), 14.

[43] Another possible enforcement agent could have been the fledgling legal professionariate, including lawyers and judges, noted by Ralph V. Turner, *The English Judiciary in the Age of Glanvill and Bracton* (New York: Cambridge University Press, 1985).

[44] J. C. Holt, *Magna Carta* (Cambridge, UK: Cambridge University Press, 1965), 1.

aggrieved groups to press their claims and challenge royal authority.[45] But this was usually only *after* English kings had transgressed without compunction against the rights outlined in the Charter.

There is abundant evidence supporting this view. Hantos notes that the first reissue of Magna Carta excised the clauses regarding baronial enforcement.[46] Moreover, this occurrence came after the Pope had resoundingly rejected the Charter's provisions and after King John had shown his willingness to continue to wage war, despite Magna Carta's sealing. And in a pair of documents from circa 1250, collected and translated by Martha Carlin and David Crouch, two knights exchanged correspondence about the King's infringement upon one of the clauses of Magna.[47] They were concerned that the King would marry their noble daughters to non-noblemen (an action known as disparagement). While Carlin and Crouch note that this correspondence may not be authentic,[48] they propose that these letters can be used as a bellwether about the issues of the day. If that is the case, then the knights in question planned to enforce their rights in a very non-coercive fashion. Instead of conspiring to take up arms against the King, resoundingly disciplining him for overstepping his bounds by defiling their daughters, the first knight instead suggested that they try bribery. The second knight seemed amenable to this suggestion.

We again hasten to emphasise that this turn of events was not inevitable; juridically speaking, there is no reason to believe that Magna Carta did not contain seeds that could blossom into judicial supremacy. Indeed, the famed jurist Edward Coke maintained that Magna Carta implies that the law is above the king, and that the role of the judiciary is to nullify acts of the king that go against this charter. This interpretation of Coke's ruling in the 1610 *Dr Bonham's Case* is presented by Raoul Berger, among others.[49]

Moreover, Coke is widely accepted as having laid the philosophical groundwork for judicial supremacy in the United States. For example, the timeline of key events that accompanies Steve Sheppard's edited volume of *The Selected Writings of Sir Edward Coke* has as its final entry the 1803 decision of the Supreme Court in *Marbury v. Madison*.[50]

[45] See Jenks, *The Myth of the Magna Carta*.

[46] Elemer Hantos, *The Magna Carta of the English and of the Hungarian Constitution: A Comparative View of the Law and Institutions of the Early Middle Ages*, 2005 ed. (Clark, NJ: Lawbook Exchange, Ltd, 1904), 149–51.

[47] Martha Carlin and David Crouch (ed.), *Lost Letters of Medieval Life: English Society, 1200–1250* (Philadelphia: University of Pennsylvania Press, 2013), 130–39.

[48] Ibid., 133.

[49] 'Doctor Bonham's Case: Statutory Construction or Constitutional Theory?' *University of Pennsylvania Law Review* 117(4) (1969): 521–45.

[50] Steve Sheppard (ed.), *The Selected Writings of Sir Edward Coke* (Indianapolis, IN: Liberty Fund, 2003), lxxi.

Explaining England's Lack of Judicial Supremacy

Why did Magna Carta not give birth to judicial supremacy in England despite its potential to do so? We submit that it is because the constitutional moment surrounding this charter was fundamentally different from the American one. It was not characterised by a coalition of diffuse actors who sought to deputise a judicial branch to produce future trigger points. There were no coercive forces at the ready, willing to enforce Magna Carta when overstepping by the king was indicated by justices. To the contrary, the barons lacked numbers, had weak coercive power, were unable to pool whatever power they had and did not find a way to successfully coordinate during or after the document was crafted. They were therefore unable to cultivate a judiciary that would set trigger points against the current and future kings that would allow the barons to enforce their rights.

Instead, Magna Carta was a strategic gambit by King John to placate restless elites. And it served, years and even centuries later, as a rallying cry for groups preyed upon by English monarchs. Thus, when Coke made exhortations for judicial review 400 years after Magna Carta was promulgated, they fell on deaf ears. He received no historically notable backing for his judicial solution to the question of how to constrain the sovereign, and the king was able to brush him aside.[51]

The barons who negotiated with King John to create Magna Carta in 1215 were relatively weak and uncoordinated. As Poole notes:

> It would seem that the demand for the Charter was a mere subterfuge; and what they really wanted was to rid themselves of King John. They had failed, and they realised that the only way by which they might achieve their object was by undisguised rebellion. *But they were disunited*, and some were half-hearted. They had *overestimated the strength of their position* and they were compelled, like the king, to look abroad for assistance.[52]

Sidney Painter, working from a host of primary documents, has attempted to accurately describe the size and strength of the baronial forces arrayed against King John. One interpretation of his data is relatively generous to the barons: he suggests that there was a small group of rebelling barons, a small group of barons supporting the King, and a majority of barons who 'stayed out of the

---

[51] The calculus of support for Coke changed, it should be noted, when he began to argue more clearly for parliamentary supremacy as in the 1628 Petition of Right. This argument, too, was based on a reading of Magna Carta.

[52] Austin Lane Poole, *From Domesday Book to Magna Carta 1087–1216*, 2nd ed. (London: Oxford University Press, 1951), 479 (emphasis added).

affair altogether'.[53] Another interpretation, however, suggests that if all of the barons did indeed pick sides in the conflict, the majority of the coercive forces were aligned *with King John* prior to Magna Carta's sealing. Painter finds that the thirteen major rebelling barons held 1,475 knight's fees, while the King held 1,580.[54] As a knight's fee (or fief) was required to maintain a knight, this proxy indicates that the King maintained the allegiance of more than half the available feudal forces. Painter also points out that the barons lacked siege engines and that their first siege attempt at Northampton was a failure.[55] In short, the coercive force shared by the barons seems to have been relatively weak during the original uprising that gave birth to Magna Carta.

In addition, the coercive force available to the barons in order to subsequently enforce their claims was relatively low. After the signing of Magna Carta, both the King and the barons asked for military assistance from beyond their borders: 'Both parties anticipating a hard struggle sought aid from abroad. The barons were in close touch with Philip Augustus who promised to help them as far as he could, and actually sent to England Eustace, the renegade monk turned pirate, with siege-engines.'[56] It therefore seems unlikely that the barons would have been able to enforce interpretations of Magna Carta that might run against the interests of English monarchs once their foreign supporters had departed.

The barons were not particularly unified either, as the following quote from McKechnie claims, with a citation to one of the more well-known interpretations of the history of Magna Carta, Stubbs's *Constitutional History of England*:

> Delay was doubly in [King John's] favor; *since the combination formed against him was certain, in a short time, to break up*. It was, in the happy phrase of Dr. Stubbs, a mere 'coalition,' not an 'organic union' – a coalition, too, in momentary danger of dissolving into its original factors. The barons were without sufficient sinews of war to carry a protracted struggle to a successful issue.[57]

Their disunity is also demonstrated by the departure from Runnymede of a number of the barons before Magna Carta had even been completed.[58] Furthermore, the ostensible coalition of barons aligned against the King

[53] Sidney Painter, *The Reign of King John* (Baltimore, MD: Johns Hopkins Press, 1949), 297.
[54] Ibid., 296.
[55] Ibid., 302.
[56] Poole, *From Domesday Book to Magna Carta 1087–1216*, 470.
[57] William Sharp McKechnie, *Magna Carta: A Commentary on the Great Charter of King John*, 2nd ed., vol. 1 (New York: Burt Franklin, 1914), 44 (emphasis added).
[58] Poole, *From Domesday Book to Magna Carta 1087–1216*, 477–78.

may have masked a generational gap. Young adventurers without the full backing of the more established, older generation may have been the ones to impetuously lead the charge against King John: 'It sometimes happened that the older and more experienced barons remained with the king, while their hotheaded sons joined the ranks of the insurgents. . . . The leaders of the revolt do not inspire confidence.'[59]

Other European Cases

In the thirteenth century, the experience represented by Magna Carta was replicated across a variety of European contexts. Written charters and compiled legal codes outlining the relationships between rulers and the ruled, in particular nobles, appeared in Hungary (Golden Bull, 1222), Sicily (Constitutions of Melfi, 1231) and Castile (Las Siete Partidas, circa 1256–1265). These charters, often building as Magna Carta did on earlier agreements, set out the rights and privileges of both sovereigns and social groups. On balance, however, these charters were even more exemplary top-down exercises than was Magna Carta. They were invariably initiated by the sovereign himself, and their timing and conditions dictated by his goals and needs. Often the charters appeared linked to wars abroad, with returning sovereigns setting down new plans and expectations.[60]

Many sovereigns in this era struggled with 'the root problem underlying the crisis of the monarchy in the early thirteenth century: the fragmentation of power at the expense of the king'.[61] Like Magna Carta, these other documents created frameworks for interaction between the sovereign and the elite, diverse actors with coercive power. Magna Carta emerged when these actors flexed their muscle, though their strength ultimately was not enough to pin down monarchs indefinitely. In the Hungarian, Sicilian and Castilian cases, the diverse actors were even less powerful and less organised. It is therefore unsurprising that judicial supremacy also failed to emerge in these situations.

The Golden Bull (Bulla Aurea) of Hungary is often described in relation to Magna Carta. Sealed by King Andrew II (Andreas) in 1222, it addressed the privileges of the nobility before the sovereign. In a memorable account, Elemer Hantos summarises the scene:

The nobility were determined to enforce their demands, and, gathering around the heir to the throne, they presented themselves in arms before the

---

[59] Ibid., 470.
[60] Holt, *Magna Carta*, 20–21.
[61] James M. Powell, *The Liber Augustalis or Constitutions of Melfi Promulgated by the Emperor Frederick II for the Kingdom of Sicily in 1231* (Syracuse, NY: Syracuse University Press, 1971), xxix.

king, and preferred [sic] their claim. There was a moment when Andreas –
like King John – found himself with a few mercenaries at his back, and before
him a nation in arms. Nursing wrath in his heart, he bowed to necessity and
called the nobility to the meeting of a diet in 1222.[62]

Although this passage provides a compelling narrative, we take issue with this
account on two points. First, regarding the comparison to England, we are more
convinced by the evidence presented previously, which suggests that King John
faced not a nation in arms, but a few elites with fleeting organisational unity.
Second, that Andrew called the nobility to meet suggests that *he* compelled
the creation of the Golden Bull, not the diverse actors themselves. Third, we
might question how coordinated and independent the nobility were: how could
they reasonably imbue the charter with limits on the future king if the future
king himself (Andrew's son) was conducting their negotiations?

Pal Engel's history of Hungary, while presenting more concrete evidence
that a revolt against Andrew II did occur in 1222,[63] also suggests that the
nobility were not well organised or possessing deep wells of coercive support.
The highest ranks of the nobility, the barons, were appointed by the King and
generally supported him.[64] The petty nobility, however, were shaken by
property reforms in the early thirteenth century. To be sure, these nobles did
have some military bona fides, many having risen through the ranks of castle
warriors.[65] But the largest mass of nobles involved in the 1222 revolt were
relatively weak. Moreover, they lacked focal points, or a leader for that matter –
besides perhaps the King's son, as just mentioned – that could help them pool
their power and influence the terms of the charter.

It is therefore no surprise that provisions for enforcement of the Golden Bull
were weak. The final clause allows for nobles to resist, jointly or singly, if they
feel the monarch has overstepped the charter.[66] Similar to Magna Carta, the
provision on enforcement by the diverse noble actors was absent in a subsequent version of the charter.[67] Pal Engel confirms that the enforcement clause
'was hardly even invoked throughout the rest of the Middle Ages'.[68] Without a
judiciary to signal when the sovereign had overstepped his bounds, support to

---

[62] *The Magna Carta of the English and of the Hungarian Constitution*, 21.
[63] He cites a letter to the Pope describing the scene: a large crowd making demands of the King;
see *The Realm of St Stephen: A History of Medieval Hungary, 895–1526* (London: I. B. Tauris,
2001), 94.
[64] Ibid., 92–93.
[65] Ibid., 94.
[66] Hantos, *The Magna Carta of the English and of the Hungarian Constitution*, 149–51.
[67] Though the clause was later reinstated, this was likely due to the efforts of the Church, not of
the nobility (see ibid., 149–51).
[68] *The Realm of St Stephen*, 94.

enforce the charter was difficult to garner. And although the Hungarian constitution now prescribes judicial review through a constitutional court, this compact has only been in force since the fall of the Berlin Wall.[69]

The Constitutions of Melfi (or the Liber Augustalis), promulgated in 1231 in Sicily under the rule of Frederick II, is another example of early charters laying out rights and responsibilities. Consistent with our framework, James Powell notes that Frederick II was acting from a position of strength, having already 'crushed the power of the rebellious nobility' and 'negotiated differences over royal rights with churches and monasteries'.[70] The motivation for the document came from 'the relentless concern of the crown for its rights and services'.[71] Regarding the nobility:

> It requires a careful reading of the constitutions to see the manner in which the interests of the nobles received the support of the monarchy. As an ideal for a turbulent society prone to solution of problems by physical violence, the monarch proposed the solution of orderly and impartial royal courts, while preserving for the nobility trial by peers.[72]

Far from conceding in the face of a coordinated group of actors, therefore, the Liber Augustalis is more concerned with reigning in the overly uncoordinated actors prone to feuds and internal violence. The nobility did not, apparently, have much of a say in the constitutions. The courts mentioned in the quote are intended to police the nobility, not the sovereign. The Constitutions of Melfi reflect a dynamic of interaction and mutual support between elites and sovereign, both endowed with coercive power.[73] But in the face of a strong king and weakly coordinated elites, it was the king who was able to set and enforce limits. The king was the final arbitrator of the legal code and was responsible for the appointment of judges. Unsurprisingly, judicial supremacy over the edicts of the sovereign did not grow from this document. Judicial review did not enter the Italian constitution until the mid twentieth century, under American influence in the wake of World War II.

Similar to the Liber Augustalis, Las Siete Partidas (the Seven Divisions) also represent a compilation of laws drawn up at the king's behest. Alfonso X, having combined Castile and Leon in 1230, supported the creation of Las Siete

---

[69] Andras Sajo, 'Reading the Invisible Constitution: Judicial Review in Hungary', *Oxford Journal of Legal Studies* 15(2) (1995): 253–67.

[70] *The Liber Augustalis or Constitutions of Melfi*, xxvi.

[71] Ibid., xxxv.

[72] Ibid., xxxiv.

[73] And the nobility in Sicily did have coercive power: 'The nobility was the military class. Members retained this position under Frederick II.' See ibid., xxxii. Their problem was in coordination.

Partidas to clarify the legal code of his kingdom.[74] The first version of the text was likely completed between 1256 and 1265.[75] This code served as the basis for Spanish law for centuries. In contrast to other compilations of law from this era, the sovereign – in this case Alfonso X – seems to have had a more direct role, likely serving as an editor.[76]

This mostly top-down code was not without influence from the nobility, however. O'Callaghan notes that Las Siete Partidas underwent revisions after the 1272 Cortes de Burgos, in which nobles protested some of Alfonso's legal innovations. As a result, the King allowed for the nobility to be tried 'according to their traditional customs'.[77]

Given the relatively strong position of Alfonso X, which we assume as a function of his ability to unite Castile and Leon, it is unsurprising that Las Siete Partidas did not develop the basis for judicial supremacy. This code was not a capitulation to noble clamouring or rebellion, though, as just shown, it was not created entirely without an eye towards the acquiescence of the elite. According to Las Siete Partidas, when questions of interpretation surrounding the law arise, 'they should be properly explained and their truth made manifest, this must be done by him who made them or by another who occupies his place, and who has the power to make new laws, and to preserve those already made'.[78] As only the king has the power to make or preserve laws, it is clear that the executive interpretation reigns supreme under this system. A contemporary constitutional court with de jure independence and judicial review power emerged only in the wake of the Francisco Franco regime.

CONCLUSION

Judicial supremacy, judicial review and judicial independence are now widely incorporated into constitutions throughout the world. Understanding how they first emerged and how they evolve over time can provide insights into these important linchpins of democratic rule.

A central contribution of this chapter is the insight that Magna Carta helps us better understand judicial supremacy.

---

[74] Joseph F. O'Callaghan, 'Alfonso X and the Partidas', in *Las Siete Partidas Volume 1: The Medieval Church: The World of Clerics and Laymen*, ed. Robert I. Burns (Philadelphia: University of Pennsylvania Press, 2001), xxx, xxxii.

[75] Ibid., xxxv.

[76] Ibid., xxxvii., citing Evelyn Proctor.

[77] Ibid., xxxix.

[78] Robert I. Burns and Samuel Scott Parsons (ed.), *Las Siete Partidas Volume 1: The Medieval Church: The World of Clerics and Laymen* (Philadelphia: University of Pennsylvania Press, 2001). Part 1, Title I, Law XIV, 5.

Judicial independence and judicial review are not always hardwired in a constitution. Indeed, this is true both of the U.S. case, where judicial supremacy evolved in short order, and Magna Carta, where it did not, despite its potential to do so. A delicious irony is that while we detect the fingerprints of Magna Carta and its potential for judicial review in the politics surrounding the U.S. Constitution, England itself never developed judicial supremacy – even though the native champions of higher law invariably pointed to the Great Charter as the source of executive restraint. Although Edward Coke claimed that he had discovered the basis for English judicial review in Magna Carta, this claim was left twisting in the wind. We suggest that Coke's philosophy was doomed in England not because it was illogical or lacked a legal basis – there are persuasive accounts on both sides of this debate – but because the Charter did not represent high degrees of coercive force spread uniformly across diverse actors. Indeed, cognate failures of judicial supremacy to take root were unfolding throughout Europe in the thirteenth century for the same reason.

Instead, Magna Carta allowed King John to buy time while dealing with rebellious elites. Although the barons, diverse actors with some coercive power, were able to extract Magna Carta from the King as a temporary commitment to their feudal rights and privileges, they did not possess either a strong coercive base or a significant source of coordination that would have allowed them to develop the type of institutional support that could limit future excesses by the sovereign. They were therefore unable to support the enforcement of Magna Carta.

In contrast, the process of creating the U.S. Constitution involved representatives from states that possessed significant levels of coercive power and coordination through state constitutions and militias. These powerful decentralised actors incentivised the creation of an independent judiciary and judicial review, which eventually crystallised into the doctrine of judicial supremacy. These actors continued to support the judiciary, with the intent that the Supreme Court could set trigger points for future action. By cultivating the judiciary, these actors developed an institution, judicial supremacy, which could send signals if the central government overstepped its bounds.

10

More Magna Than Magna Carta: Magna Carta's Sister – the Charter of the Forest*

Geraldine Van Bueren QC

> What art thou Freedom? ...
> For the labourer thou art bread, ...
> Thou art clothes and fire and food.
> — Shelley[1]

THE MAGNA CARTA, HUMAN RIGHTS THEORY AND THE ORIGIN OF POSITIVE AND COMMUNAL CONSTITUTIONAL RIGHTS

Although the original 1215 Magna Carta applied only to rights of 'freemen' and not to those less wealthy,[2] the legacy of Magna Carta on international human rights law is significant. It was acknowledged by Eleanor Roosevelt during the adoption by the United Nations of the Universal Declaration of Human Rights, which she described as the international magna carta for humanity.[3] The comedian Tony Hancock uses comedy to expose truth with his questions: 'Does Magna Carta mean nothing to you? Did she die in vain?'[4] This brings up a good point, because the original Magna Carta endured for less than nine

---

* I am grateful to Nicholas Bennett, the archivist of Lincoln Cathedral, for his comments and for arranging a private view of the Charter of the Forest.

[1] *The Masque of Anarchy*, 1819.

[2] The original issue of Magna Carta was limited to barons and freemen, and it was not until 1354 that the due process of law found in clause 39 was extended to any man 'of whatever estate or condition he may be'.

[3] 'We stand today at the threshold of a great event both in the life of the United Nations and in the life of mankind. This declaration may well become the international Magna Carta for all men everywhere.' On 10 December 1948, commemorated by the United Nations as Human Rights Day.

[4] Hancock (as foreman of the jury): 'Does Magna Carta mean nothing to you? Did she die in vain? Brave Hungarian peasant girl who forced King John to sign the pledge at Runnymede and close the boozers at half past ten!' 'Hancock's Half Hour', *Twelve Angry Men*, BBC, 16 October 1959.

weeks.[5] The socio-economic rights provisions of the Magna Carta have been overlooked, and the effect of this historical amnesia is death – that is, of the memory of the origin of socio-economic rights. Hence an analysis of the history of Magna Carta ought not to be limited to the history of a specific legal document, but should also be a re-examination of the history of human rights. Close examination of the text of Magna Carta reveals six points of importance for the foundations of human rights theory in general, and for socio-economic rights in particular.

Arguments which focus on the legacy of socio-economic rights protection must, however, first consider whether Magna Carta created rights or only liberties. Although some regard the legacy of Magna Carta as bequeathing liberties[6] rather than rights, as in 'customs and liberties',[7] such a conclusion omits consideration of the final clause of Magna Carta, which provides that 'men in our kingdom shall have and keep all these liberties, rights and concessions'.[8] Hence the concept of rights for others than monarchs was acknowledged in constitutional laws at least as far back as thirteenth-century England.

Magna Carta, as is widely acknowledged, provided the basis for the idea of a higher constitutional law, one that could not be altered by either executive mandate or legislative acts. It was not only that the divine right of kings was their God-given right to rule, but that their right to rule had no limits. This is the reason that the Pope declared the Charter an abomination,[9] as the divine right of kings could not be limited by mortal human beings. However, the medieval chipping away of the ancient and medieval religious constitutionalism in England also provides the basis of human rights. The first issue of Magna Carta, in establishing a committee of implementation, the Committee of Twenty Five,[10] placed the authority of the monarch in implementing the Charter under a higher authority, similar to the monitoring mechanisms of

---

[5] In the opening words of Magna Carta, King John had declared that it was 'by the honour of God' that he would abide by its terms; hence only the Pope could excuse him from this sacred oath. King John wrote to Pope Innocent III requesting to be released from the oath extracted from him by force. Pope Innocent III's reply reached England in September. King John had previously broken his oath in, for example, retaining castles which under the terms of Magna Carta ought to have been relinquished.

[6] See, e.g., J. Holt, *Magna Carta*, 2nd ed. (Cambridge University Press, 1992) at 5.

[7] Clause 60.

[8] Clause 63.

[9] The papal opposition to Magna Carta was included in the lecture of C. Cheney, 'The Eve of Magna Carta', lecture delivered in the John Rylands Library, University of Manchester, 11 May 1995.

[10] Clause 61.

the international human rights treaties at the United Nations, which seek to ensure implementation by sovereign states.

Magna Carta also protected the rights of women, albeit with regard to the limited group of ennobled men and freemen, a limited group of women and for a limited period of time. Magna Carta of 1215 built upon the Coronation Oath of Henry I,[11] which recognised specific women's rights, and Magna Carta also guaranteed to widows that they could retain their marriage portion and inheritance after the death of a husband, with a right to the family home for forty days. Although it cannot be claimed that the barons were in any way concerned with women's equal status, in addition to Holt's assertion that this 'was one of the first great stages in the emancipation of women',[12] the provision is significant because it is one of the earliest enshrinements of the constitutional economic rights of women.

The protection of the economic rights of women, however, is only one facet of Magna Carta's protection of socio-economic rights. Although it is widely acknowledged that Magna Carta laid the foundations of constitutional democracy by limiting the powers of the sovereign, it is not commonly realised that positive obligations flowing from states also have their origins in Magna Carta. The fundamental principle enshrined but rarely acknowledged is that under Magna Carta the sovereign could be subject to both negative and positive obligations. However, traditionally Magna Carta has been linked only to negative obligations, thus depriving positive rights such as socio-economic rights of their equally valuable and ancient and legitimate heritage.

Magna Carta also illustrates that there has been from medieval times an indivisibility of rights, as the civil and political rights appear side by side with socio-economic rights in the Charter. Hence the later division into civil and political rights and socio-economic rights has been a move away from heritage rather than a matter of history.

In addition to enshrining both positive and negative rights, Magna Carta enshrined one of the earliest acknowledgments of the universality of rights. Magna Carta incorporates a guarantee that the provisions of the charter are applicable in 'all places forever'.[13] This is at least a theoretical acknowledgement of the concept of universality, even though this recognition did not endure, because clause 63 did not appear in later reissues of Magna Carta.

---

[11] Administered in 1100. The Coronation Oath also provided that widows should be permitted the lands set aside for them by their husbands and that they should not be forced to remarry without their consent.

[12] Holt, *Magna Carta*, at 46.

[13] Clause 63.

Magna Carta also demonstrates that from the medieval period constitutional law is both individual and relational, and that those who criticise human rights as being Western and individualistic[14] have overlooked the significance of one of the principal originating documents of human rights. The communing provisions of both Magna Carta and the Charter of the Forest are ignored, perhaps as 'out of date feudal relics',[15] but, as is demonstrated in the paragraphs that follow, they incorporate the kernels of socio-economic rights. Socio-economic rights at their heart focus on rights held in common by communities, as well as rights held by individuals.[16] From medieval time, the two have co-existed, and law has been capable of dealing with this bifurcation. Hence the problem is not the modernity of socio-economic rights and the creation of new challenges for courts and governments, but rather the lack of inquiry about their ancient medieval heritage.

Santayana's warning that 'Those who cannot remember the past are condemned to repeat it'[17] endows historical amnesia with tragic consequences. However, there are other important consequences. A loss of heritage memory of medieval English and Welsh constitutional history has meant that there has been a significant erroneous limitation on the capacities of courts to help alleviate poverty. This is evidenced by Sunstein's observation that states with an English common law background are 'far less likely' to include socio-economic rights than those with a French civil law background.[18] The recognition that human rights originally embraced human rights concepts wider than solely civil and political rights is important because it would assist in making human rights in the United Kingdom more popular.[19] It would also assist in opening up the political debate, allowing the political parties, if they wished, to embrace rights such as the right to food[20] as being part of English heritage and not alien or only appropriate for some developing states. Finally,

---

[14] See, e.g., the discussion in Randall Nadeau, 'Confucianism and the Problem of Human Rights', *Intercultural Communication Studies* XI(2) (2002): 107; see also Goodhart, 'Origins and Universality in the Human Rights Debates: Cultural Essentialism and the Challenge of Globalization', *Human Rights Quarterly* 25 (2003): 935–64.

[15] Peter Linebaugh, *The Magna Carta Manifesto: Liberties and Commons for All*, at 11.

[16] See discussion following.

[17] George Santayana, 'Reason in Common Sense', Vol. I, *The Life of Reason*, 1905, at 284.

[18] Cass Sunstein, *The Second Bill of Rights*, 2004, at 105.

[19] See, e.g., the Centre for Analysis of Social Exclusion, 'Research Report to Inform the Debate about a Bill of Rights and a Written Constitution, Case Research Report 61', 2010, which reported that 87 per cent were in favour of a right to hospital treatment within a reasonable time and 60 per cent in favour of a right to housing for the homeless to be included in a bill of rights. The figures were consistently high from 2000.

[20] It is also a right which is found in 22 per cent of 195 constitutions, and is a justiciable right in 13 per cent of constitutions. See Jung, Hirschl and Rosevear, 'Economic & Social Rights in National Constitutions', at 11; electronic copy available at http://ssrn.com/abstract=2349680.

as the United Kingdom has a strong welfare state, the question has to be raised whether an historical legacy of socio-economic entitlement is a relevant path of enquiry. There is, however, a fundamental difference between the extent of the protection of a welfare state, with its party political–determined safety nets subject to alteration, and the legally required minimum standards of socio-economic rights, which would make it unlawful for a government to dilute. This distinguishing factor has also been recognised by the United Nations.[21] As two new food banks are launched by the Trussell Trust every week, and the resources for the National Health Service and the welfare state continue to be discussed at a political level, the acknowledgement of a medieval legacy of socio-economic entitlement in England and Wales becomes even more critical.[22]

The making of human rights more popular is an urgent task in light of the likelihood of a leaked proposed policy from one major political party, the Conservative Party, to make both the repeal of the Human Rights Act 1998 and the withdrawal from the European Convention on Human Rights 1950 a manifesto commitment in the next general election.[23]

MAGNA CARTA AND THE CONSTITUTIONAL CREATION
OF SOCIO-ECONOMIC RIGHTS

The constitutional creation of socio-economic rights by Magna Carta arose from the provisions focusing on forest law. The historical concept of 'forest' can be distinguished from contemporary definitions of wooded areas, in that the Norman concept of forest, which was introduced into England in the eleventh century, protected areas for hunting for the exclusive use of the monarch. These areas included not only woodland but also heath, marsh and villages in or nearby woodland. At its most extensive, in the late twelfth and early thirteenth century, approximately one-third of the land of southern England was established as royal forest, and one-quarter of the land in all of England; its impact therefore on medieval life cannot be underestimated.[24] The forest was used for medicine, hunting and grazing, and the timber was used both for shelter and for essential warmth and cooking. The forest streams

---

[21] UN Doc E/C.12/GBR/C)/5, 12 June 2009, para. 13.

[22] Magna Carta and the Charter of the Forest applied only to England, and in Wales, the Laws of Hywel Dda also enshrined provisions concerning socio-economic entitlement. A. Wade-Evans, *Welsh Medieval Law: Being a Text of the Laws of Howel the Good* (Oxford: Clarendon Press, 1909).

[23] See 'Cameron sets his sights on human rights court', 17 July 2014, BBC online at http://www.bbc.co.uk/news/uk-politics-28339263.

[24] There were 143 forests in England in 1215. See Linebaugh, *The Magna Carta Manifesto*, at 34.

and rivers were used for drinking and cooking and for fishing, and access to unblocked rivers was important, as rivers were one of the principal methods of transporting essential goods.

Royal afforestation meant that at a time of increasing population there was less land available to sustain the population. Hence the increasing desperation faced by those living in afforested areas, as they were no longer able to live off the land. Once afforested, it became illegal to hunt for food, firewood and building materials on the land – three essentials for life in medieval England. Viewed from this perspective, the importance of Ch. 47 of Magna Carta becomes apparent:

> All forests that have been created in our reign shall at once be disafforested.
> River-banks that have been enclosed in our reign shall be treated similarly.

The term 'disafforest' refers to the reversion from the legal status of a forest claimed by the monarch to that of ordinary land subject again to common law and no longer subject to the arbitrary will of the monarch. The disafforesting restored rights to people who were accustomed to enjoying such socio-economic rights before earlier kings' seizure of land.

There is, however, a problem in arguing that the socio-economic rights provisions of modern constitutions can be traced to Magna Carta. It is a mod-ification of the problem of the unwitnessed falling tree. It is not that Magna Carta itself was unwitnessed but that there has been a subsequent lack of reference to the socio-economic rights of Magna Carta in the preambles of democratic constitutions which do not cite English medieval legislative legacies. The same problem of visibility also applies to the civil and political rights in Magna Carta, which also are not cited by contemporary democratic constitutions. This is not surprising, because states newly independent from Great Britain would hardly have sourced their constitutional powers as deriving from colonial legislation, even where they retain some colonial legislation.[25] In addition, democratic states which were never under British colonial rule would have no reason to cite Magna Carta, preferring the roots of their own national political heritages.

It is clear, however, that the constitutional recognition of socio-economic rights is neither new, radical nor revolutionary. Socio-economic rights are not, as is commonly asserted, the creation of Marxist thought, but the exact opposite – the constitutional creation of a king and the nobility.

---

[25] Whilst not expressly referring to the title, Magna Carta, its language is used, for example, in the Massachusetts Body of Liberties 1641, Virginia Bill of Rights 1776 and the Fifth and Fourteenth Amendments of the U.S. Constitution. It was, however, cited in legislation; e.g. a colonial law of 1712 abolishing primogeniture was declared void in 1792, citing Magna Carta expressly – *Bowman v. Middleton*, 1 Bay 252 (SC 1792).

THE CHARTER OF THE FOREST – MORE MAGNA
THAN THE MAGNA

Magna Carta was not called 'Magna' until its reissue in 1217. The later name was only a comparative Magna: not because of the inherent greater nature of its substantive provisions of civil and political rights over socio-economic rights, but because Magna Carta was larger than its companion, the Charter of the Forest. As Holt observes, Magna Carta was only 17.75 inches wide and 18.25 inches long, and was only 'great' in a comparative sense of size when compared to the Charter of the Forest.[26] In constitutional history, size clearly matters.

In terms of its impact, the Charter of the Forest was more magna than the Magna Carta. The nature of the rights enshrined in the Charter of the Forest had a far greater beneficial impact on the daily lives of a greater number of people than did Magna Carta, because the Charter of the Forest not only affected the nobility, the church and freemen, but was beneficial also to the lower feudal classes living in disafforested areas.

On the death of John, William Marshall, who was appointed to govern during the minority of Henry III, reissued a revised version of the Magna Carta on 12 November 1216, and another on 6 November 1217, in attempt to restore peace. In the second reissue, the clauses relating to the royal forests were removed, expanded and issued in a separate Charter of the Forest.[27]

The Charter of the Forest, in contrast to the focus on the baronial and freemen entitlements of the 1215 Magna Carta,[28] re-established rights of access to the forest for freemen and provided entitlements and protections for a greater range of citizens of both genders, albeit within the existing feudal relationships. Prior to the Charter of the Forest, those whose animals grazed in forested land or hunted in the forest were subject to severe penalties, including dismemberment or death.[29] The Charter of the Forest reduced these penalties, removed the death penalty and reclaimed some of the land from the Crown. Therefore, although it has become traditional to characterise Magna Carta as a bastion against terror and violence, as Linebaugh comments, '[s]ometimes a local tyrant established a veritable reign of terror',

---

[26] Holt, *Magna Carta*, 275.

[27] The Charter of the Forest was sealed by King Henry III's chief minister William Marshal, the Earl of Pembroke and the papal legate, Giula Bicchieri, on 6 November 1217.

[28] The copy of Magna Carta belonging to Lincoln Cathedral is annotated with 'agreement between King John and the Barons'. After its renunciation by King John and Pope Innocent III, it was reissued to placate the barons.

[29] C. Young, *The Royal Forests of Medieval England* (Philadelphia: University of Pennsylvania Press, 1979), at 324.

from which the Charter of the Forest also provided liberation.[30] Hence the Charter of the Forest links socio-economic entitlement and civil rights protection against arbitrary and cruel punishment.[31]

The extent of the geographic reach of the Charter of the Forest can be seen despite the fact that the Charter contained no method of implementation. This situation led to localised self-help, and counties such as Nottinghamshire and Huntingdonshire initiated their own inquires, which effectively disafforested the entire counties.[32]

The Charter of the Forest also impacted beneficially on the rights of women. The seizure of traditional common land significantly reduced the economic livelihood of women, because estovers, or the gathering of fuel, was principally done by women and children. In addition, the common rights of herbage, or grazing rights, which permitted the keeping of cows, providing both for milk and cheese and manure, was also traditionally the work of all members of the family.[33]

Each of the medieval rights in the Charter of the Forest has its counterparts in treaties focusing on human rights.[34] The first chapter of the Charter of the Forest protected common pasture for all those 'accustomed to it', which is found in Article 11 of the International Covenant on Economic, Social and Cultural Rights, protecting the right to an adequate standard of living. The seventh chapter prohibited beadles or foresters from seizing lambs, piglets, sheaves of corn or oats in lieu of scotale,[35] as established in Article 11(1) of the Covenant, protecting the right to food. The ninth chapter of the Charter provided for 'agistement'[36] and 'pannage'[37] to freemen; and the thirteenth chapter established that all freemen should have their honey, which again is found in Article 11(1) of the Covenant. The prohibition on the seizure of livestock and crops and the protection of honey are clear forerunners of the right to adequate nutrition and the right to an adequate standard of living.

The importance of the right to water, as highlighted in the Charter of the Forest with the right to make ponds providing water for both animals and

---

[30] Linebaugh, *The Magna Carta Manifesto*, 41.

[31] See further, Van Bueren, 'Socioeconomic Rights and a Bill of Rights – An Overlooked British Tradition', *Public Law* (2013), at 826.

[32] Peter Coss, *The Origins of the English Gentry* (Cambridge University Press, 2003), at 116.

[33] J. M. Neeson, *Commoners: Common Rights, Enclosure and Social Change in England, 1700–1820* (New York: Cambridge University Press, 1993), 163.

[34] See further, Van Bueren, 'Socioeconomic Rights and a Bill of Rights'.

[35] A feudal tax.

[36] The proceeds of pasture in the royal forest.

[37] The right to allow pigs to forage for acorns.

people,[38] is not expressly recognised in either the Universal Declaration of Human Rights or in the International Covenant, but the UN Human Rights Committee, the implementing body of the International Covenant on Civil and Political Rights, has stated that it is an aspect of the right to life. Both the later Convention on the Rights of the Child and the Convention on the Elimination of All Forms of Discrimination Against Women also expressly protect the right to water.[39]

In medieval England from 1217 and for the next four centuries, whilst Magna Carta was principally concerned with political and juridical entitlement, the Charter of the Forest restored the traditional rights of the people where the land had once been held in common, restrained landowners from inflicting harsh punishments and was concerned with economic and social entitlement which affected people's daily lives.

Both Magna Carta and the Charter of the Forest were re-confirmed more than thirty times during the fourteenth century and eight times in the fifteenth, but during the sixteenth century the Charters appear to have been forgotten. It is only in the seventeenth century that the 1225 reissue of Magna Carta began to be reclaimed, whilst the Charter of the Forest appears to have disappeared from the constitutional memory. The historical importance of Magna Carta, as distinct from the equal historical importance of the Charter of the Forest, owes much to its Magna name, which has enhanced its significance.

The later amnesia clouding the Charter of the Forest ought not to minimise its original fundamental importance for socio-economic rights jurisprudence. Both charters were signed by a feudal king acceding to the demands of barons, but it is arguable that one of the reasons that the Charter of the Forest has been largely overlooked – and this is evidenced by the rare appearance of the Charter of the Forest in constitutional law discourse or indeed in political and constitutional law teaching – is the unfamiliarity of many contemporary scholars with medieval legal language. In addition, in Western contemporary life the focus on wood, and honey, for example, seems trivial and even irrelevant. This may have masked the importance of these products for medieval society, in which the structure, hierarchy and life itself depended on wood for both food and shelter and honey for basic nutrition. The right to

---

[38] Paragraph 12 of the Charter of the Forest provides that 'Every free man may henceforth without being prosecuted make in his wood or in land he has in the forest a mill ... a pond. ... on condition that it does not harm any neighbour.'

[39] The right to clean drinking water is found in Art. 24(2) of the Convention on the Rights of the Child 1989, and Art. 14(2) of the Convention on the Elimination of All Forms of Discrimination Against Women expressly provides that adequate living conditions include water supply.

water is also something which much of contemporary Britain takes for granted, and the right to the vert for healing and medicinal remedies appears outdated to states with Western health systems.

In addition the medieval title, the Charter of the Forest, to twentieth- and twenty-first-century ears is misleading. The title seems in modern times to speak of woods and trees. If it had been entitled Charter of the Commons or Charter for the Essentials of Life, it is possible that its longevity in constitutional memory would have been extended.[40]

THE IMPORTANCE OF MAGNA CARTA AND THE CHARTER OF THE FOREST FOR CONTEMPORARY HUMAN RIGHTS

One unintended consequence of the 800th anniversary of Magna Carta is that it can be used as a catalyst to focus on the lengthy history of socio-economic rights as well as on the Charter of the Forest itself. Both Magna Carta and the Charter of the Forest originally were regarded as two facets of the constitutional diamond. In 1297, King Edward I sent letters to all English counties with both charters, and the charters were read out aloud in public – a principal form of transmission in largely illiterate medieval England. Later Coke emphasised the equal importance of both instruments, describing them together as 'Chartae Libertatum Angliae', the great English Charters, and both were considered sufficiently important to be read aloud four times each year.[41] By 1369, the two were treated as a single statute, and both charters were printed together, forming the opening of the English Statutes-at-Large.[42] Hence Magna Carta and the Charter of the Forest were intended to be complementary and equally important constitutional law.

In contrast to the Cold War's ideological domination during the drafting of what became two separate human rights covenants,[43] medieval England provides an early source for the complementarity of civil and political and economic, social and cultural rights.[44] Magna Carta alone, and in its reading

---

[40] I am very grateful to Professor Anthony King for suggesting that I use as my title here 'The Charter of the Commons', renaming the Charter of the Forest. His suggestion is persuasive. However, because socio-economic rights are the subject of some discussion amongst the legal community in the United Kingdom, it may be better to use the original title rather than be accused of myth-making.

[41] On St Michael's, Christmas, Easter and St John's Day.

[42] Linebaugh, *The Magna Carta Manifesto*, at 3.

[43] The original intent, similar to that of the Universal Declaration of Human Rights 1948, was to have one treaty.

[44] This is evidenced by clause 20 of Magna Carta, which shows that its drafting occurred after the decision had been reached to make a separate charter for forest matters; see H. Rothwell, *English Historical Documents* (London: Eyre and Spottiswoode, 1975), 337.

together with the Charter of the Forest, debunks as historically inaccurate arguments by some that socio-economic rights are second-generation rights following after the first-generation civil and political rights. In Magna Carta they appear side by side, intra-generational rather then inter-generational.

The Charter of the Forest also provides evidence that from the thirteenth century, constitutional socio-economic rights were capable of being justiciable. In 1290, for example, the 'men' of Stoneleigh in Warwickshire petitioned the king because they had lost estovers[45] and pasturage and could no longer survive.[46] This reinforces arguments that the characterisation of socio-economic rights as non-justiciable is a matter of policy preference rather than fact. Twenty-first-century questioning about judicial competence in socio-economic rights litigation – which is raised in the United Kingdom[47] and in the United States relating to the limits of judicial skill in socio-economic rights or the problems posed by Fuller's polycentricity[48] – ignores medieval history. Admittedly some contemporary socio-economic rights litigation may be more complex than thirteenth-century disputes, but, as Fuller concedes, there are polycentric aspects to many disputes.

Ironically, socio-economic rights jurisprudence may appear prima facie to be more complex, but this is in part because the questions asked to the court appear to be new, and many lawyers feel more comfortable with the historical status quo. It is ironic because, as a study of Magna Carta and the Charter of the Forest demonstrates, it is the perceived status quo which is new.

Courts which are recognised for their use of comparative law do not refer to the history of socio-economic rights, as in the *Certification of the Constitution Case* in the South African Constitutional Court, where the Court ruled that justiciable socio-economic rights did not undermine a constitutional separation of powers.[49] Yet the Warwickshire and other petitioners also demonstrate that the constitutional protection of socio-economic rights, far from undermining democracy, assists in developing constitutional democracy. The medieval pleas show that socio-economic rights jurisprudence provided an opportunity for the disempowered to seek relief and therefore contributed to

---

[45] Timber.
[46] J. Birrel, 'Common Rights in the Medieval Forest: Disputes and Conflict in the Thirteenth Century', *Past and Present* 17 (1987), at 48.
[47] For a contemporary criticism of justiciable socio-economic rights, see Gearty in C. Gearty and V. Mantouvalou, *Debating Social Rights* (Hart, 2011).
[48] L. L. Fuller, 'The Forms and Limits of Adjudication', 92 Harvard LR (1978), 353, 397–98, acknowledges this. Allison, 'Fuller's Analysis of Polycentric Disputes and the Limits of Adjudication', 53 Cambridge LJ (1994), 367, 371.
[49] *Certification of the Constitution of the Republic of South Africa* (CCT 23/1996); see particularly paras. 77 and 78.

a rebalancing of power and to the development of constitutional checks and balances.

Magna Carta and the Charter of the Forest also illustrate that the importance to women of socio-economic rights has been recognised from the medieval period. This is not to deny medieval woman's chattel status in feudal society, but both charters are an early acknowledgment both of the feminisation of poverty and that the language of constitutional rights could offer protection to women.

The potential protection of socio-economic rights for women living in poverty is evidenced by the significant number of women who have either been party to leading socio-economic rights jurisprudence or who have directly benefitted from it.[50] The economic inheritance rights of women are still subject to constitutional challenge. In South Africa the Constitutional Court in *Bhe* considered the constitutional validity of the principle of primogeniture in the context of the customary law of succession, where the general rule is that only a male relative is considered an intestate heir.[51] The Court ruled that 'the official system of customary law of succession is incompatible with the Bill of Rights',[52] an approach which can be traced back to both Magna Carta and the Charter of the Forest.

The right to health, one of the socio-economic rights most commonly included in bills of rights, also can be traced back to Magna Carta and the Charter of the Forest.[53] U.S. President Franklin D. Roosevelt proposed in his second Bill of Rights '[t]he right to adequate medical care and the opportunity to achieve and enjoy good health' for 'every American'.[54] Although this particular bill of rights did not see legislative enactment, by the beginning of the twenty-first century, the right to health was incorporated into 133 national constitutions.[55] At first sight, however, the right to health seems to have been

---

[50] In South Africa, for example, leading cases include *Government of the Republic of South Africa, the Premier of the Province of the Western Cape, Cape Metropolitan Council, Ostenberg Municipality v. Irene Grootboom and Others* [2001], (1) SA 4 (CC) 2000 (11) BC LR 1 16) (CC); *Minister of Health and Others v. Treatment Action Campaign and Others* [2002], (5) SA 721 (CC) 2002 (!o) BCLR 1033 (CC).

[51] 'Women do not participate in the intestate succession of deceased estates. In a monogamous family, the eldest son of the family head is his heir. If the deceased is not survived by any male descendants, his father succeeds him. If his father also does not survive him, an heir is sought among the father's male descendants related to him through the male line.' Olivier et al., *Indigenous Law* (Durban: Butterworths, 1995), 147 at para. 142.

[52] At para. 97.

[53] See in Van Bueren, *Law's Duty to the Poor*, UNESCO, 2010.

[54] His speech was delivered on 11 January 1944; see Sunstein *The Second Bill of Rights*.

[55] E. D. Kinney, 2001, 'The International Human Right to Health: What Does This Mean for Our Nation and World?' *Indiana Law Review* 34, 1457 at 1465.

omitted from the Charter of the Forest. However, the Charter included the right to the vert,[56] the plants and greenery under the trees, which were also used for the treatment of disease. The importance of vert for health is not only an ancient tradition but continues both in indigenous cultures and in their use by major pharmaceutical companies.

The focus on the right to health through right of access to the vert is not of course as broad as the right to health incorporated into the Constitution of the World Health Organisation 1946, with its emphasis on a holistic physical, mental and social well-being. The charters focused on the treatment of disease, an approach found expressly in Article 12 of the International Covenant on Economic, Social and Cultural Rights; the UN Committee on Economic, Social and Cultural Rights has now adopted a more expansive approach.[57] Despite modern-day progress in this area, the medieval origin of the right to health is rarely if ever acknowledged.

MAGNA CARTA, THE CHARTER OF THE FOREST AND THEIR IMPACT ON A NEW SOCIAL CONTRACT FOR THE TWENTY-FIRST CENTURY

The advantage of a new social contract approach is that it assists in enforcing the ought: the social contract provides the parties with a 'special source of reassurance that obligations owed to them will be discharged',[58] and in so doing, it can assist in strengthening the relationship between the constitutional obligations of states and the combating of poverty. The impact of the two charters on the social contract is that they assist, together with contemporary international human rights law, in translating moral and social demands into legal entitlements, moving socio-economic rights from the relatively unhampered political discretion to a transparent and accountable process where decisions must be justified in a mutually acceptable legal language and weighting.

The impact of the socio-economic rights provisions of Magna Carta and the Charter of the Forest on the social contract is that it assists in transforming the social contract approach by recognising that in incorporating socio-economic rights, the social contract can be instrumental in overcoming some of the

---

[56] See, e.g., clause 8 in the Charter of the Forest.
[57] The UN Committee on Economic, Social and Cultural Rights, in common with the other human rights treaty monitoring bodies, adopts General Comments which are of persuasive value in interpreting the ambit of treaty rights. It expanded the disease lens approach to health in its General Comment 14. UN Doc E/C.12/2000/4.
[58] Kimel, *From Promise to Contract, towards a Liberal Theory of Contract* (2003), at 57.

justifiable objections of disadvantaged and formerly disadvantaged groups to a social contract.[59]

The essence of socio-economic rights is the protection of individual rights through creating a sense of community,[60] as successful socio-economic rights litigation is rarely action taken by isolated individuals[61] but is more frequently brought by group actions which benefit both individuals and the community as a whole.[62] A similar approach can be seen in the medieval pleas of the Men of Warwick.

Historically, the essence of the social contract was based on a recognition of the inherent dignity of 'man', or more accurately of 'some men', and was unacceptably limited.[63] Yet social contract theory was an attempt to enshrine an inherent kernel of equality, which contrasted with the earlier approaches based on the divinity of monarchs. It may at first appear strange to apply a theory which has been described as non-factual, 'historically and sociologically implausible',[64] and not a historical event but an intellectual experiment. But social contract theory is, as Lessnoff argues, 'intuitively attractive', as it holds the promise of equal protection to the possibly conflicting interests of all, and therefore ought to be of universal application.[65]

This is the reason that, looking beyond the lens of Anglo-American jurisprudence, progress in socio-economic jurisprudence, despite its infancy, has been so swift. The latter half of the twentieth century and the opening decades of the twenty-first century have witnessed the development of the equality aspect of the social contract, not only guaranteeing the traditional liberties recast as rights, but also including socio-economic rights.

---

[59] See, e.g., Pateman, who persuasively argues that contemporary subordination is created through contract: Pateman, *The Sexual Contract* (Polity Press, 1988).

[60] Socio-economic rights overcome Marx's concern that labour isolates the worker from the community: Marx, *Karl Marx and Frederick Engels: Collected Works*, Vol. 28 (Lawrence and Wishart, 1986), at 17.

[61] See the unsuccessful attempt in South Africa *Soobramoney v. Minister of Health (Kwazulu-Natal)*, (CCT32/97) [1997], ZACC 17; 1998 (1) SA 765 (CC); 1997 (12) BCLR 1696 (27 November 1997). On a very different level in India, see *re State of Himachal Pradesh v. Parents of A Student of Medical College, Simla* [1985], 3 SCC169.

[62] Van Bueren, 'Housing' in Cheadle et al., *South African Constitutional Law* (2002), at 473.

[63] One glaring example is the decision of the Supreme Court in *Scott v. Sandford*, 60 U.S. 19 How. 393 (1856).

[64] Waldron, 'John Locke – Social Contract versus Political Anthropology', in Boucher and Kelly, *The Social Contract from Hobbes to Rawls* (1994), at 54 and 55. Waldron regards the social contract as a process evolving over time rather than any one specific event to which all have to consent, because 'No society can ... be a scheme of cooperation which men enter voluntarily in a literal sense: each finds himself placed at birth in some particular position in some particular society.'

[65] Lessnoff, *Social Contract* (1986), at 159–60.

Although it may seem a leap to argue that the evolution of the social contract requires justiciable socio-economic rights, if it is accepted that socio-economic rights are part of the new social contract and that the human rights initially set out in Magna Carta are holistic and indivisible, then the same appropriate tools are required to enforce the socio-economic provisions of the social contract as the right to life, liberty and property. In the United Kingdom this would require the enactment of a socio-economic rights act or incorporation into a legally binding and justiciable bill of rights.

The drafting of Magna Carta and the Charter of the Forest could not in any sense be described as inclusive or participatory; however, socio-economic rights jurisprudence is capable of developing and opening up the courts to a more participatory form of justice. In *Occupiers of 51 Olivia Road, Berea Township and Another v. City of Johannesburg and Others*, before the Constitutional Court gave judgment it ordered the parties to address the possibilities of short-term steps to improve the living conditions and alternative accommodation for those who would be rendered homeless. The parties reached consensus that the city would not eject the occupiers, that it would upgrade the buildings and that it would provide temporary accommodation. In addition, the parties agreed to meet and discuss permanent housing solutions. An agreement was reached by the parties and made an order by the Court.[66] Thus the parties' own agreement was made into hard law by the Court. Such an approach is consistent with 'deliberative democracy' and with Habermas's call for a renewed democratisation of public institutions and spaces.[67] It is a development of institutional conversations being not only conversations between the seats of power – which in the medieval period were between the king, the Church and the freemen[68] – but, in the nature of the evolution of the social contract, a genuine participatory conversation between government, the courts and the people.

It is through the participatory nature of the twenty-first-century social contract that the issues surrounding polycentricity no longer require centre stage. The approach of the Constitutional Court avoids Fuller's concerns that polycentric issues would give rise to unintended consequences and would encourage the judiciary to consult with non-represented parties and guess

---

[66] Case CCT 24/07, judgment of the Constitutional Court of South Africa, 19 February 2008.

[67] Habermas, *Structural Transformation* (1989), 284.

[68] See *Viceconte v. Ministry of Health and Social Welfare*, Poder Judicial de la Nación, Causa no. 31 777/96, judgment of 2 June 1998 in which the Argentine Court of Appeals ordered the state to manufacture sufficient vaccine for haemorrhagic fever according to a prescribed schedule.

at facts, etc.[69] It is bitterly ironic that despite the medieval constitutional settlement of England and the influence of British social contract theorists on the Constitution of the United States, the United Kingdom and the United States have now fallen behind in the protection of the socio-economic rights of the vulnerable members of their communities.

CONCLUSION

The concept that constitutions and constitutionalism can help fundamentally to change societies is one familiar to states emerging from oppression at the end of the twentieth century in Latin America and southern Africa.[70] However, Magna Carta and the Charter of the Forest are two of the earliest examples of transformative constitutionalism, in that they created legal possibilities not only for moving forward but also for addressing issues of the past.[71]

There was an opportunity for the United Kingdom to recognise its English and Welsh heritage of socio-economic rights with the ratification of the European Union's Charter of Fundamental Rights. The Charter of Fundamental Rights was first adopted by the Treaty of Nice but was specifically not justiciable; however, the Treaty of Lisbon made the Charter justiciable. The United Kingdom, together with Poland, attached a protocol to their ratifications, which claims that Title IV of the Charter – containing economic and social rights – does not create justiciable rights.[72] The British negotiated the protocol during the Lisbon negotiations, which, according to the then British Minister for Europe, would ensure that the Charter would not extend the powers of the European Court of Justice over United Kingdom law.[73] This

---

[69] India has resolved the gathering of facts by courts appointing their own fact-finding committees, which report back to both parties and to the court, thus augmenting the institutional capacities of the courts; see, e.g., *Mehta v. State of Tamil Nadu* [1996], 6 SCC 756.

[70] See, e.g., Sandra Liebenberg, *Socioeconomic Rights: Adjudication under a Transformative Constitution* (2010).

[71] Issues such as the royal seizure of the forests.

[72] The United Kingdom and Poland's protocol provides that 'The Charter does not extend the ability of the Court of Justice of the European Union, or any court or tribunal of Poland or of the United Kingdom, to find that the laws, regulations or administrative provisions, practices or action of Poland or of the United Kingdom are inconsistent with the fundamental rights, freedoms and principles that it reaffirms. In particular, and for the avoidance of doubt, nothing in Title IV of the Charter creates justiciable rights applicable to Poland or the United Kingdom except in so far as Poland or the United Kingdom has provided for such rights in its national law. Article 2. To the extent that a provision of the Charter refers to national laws and practices, it shall only apply to Poland or the United Kingdom to the extent that the rights or principles that it contains are recognised in the law or practices of Poland or of the United Kingdom.'

[73] 'EU Reform Treaty Abandons Constitutional Approach', Foreign Office, 22 August 2007.

approach has been undermined both by the Court of Justice of the European Union[74] and by an English court.[75]

However, in plans to celebrate Magna Carta, the focus has exclusively been on its civil and political rights to the exclusion of socio-economic rights. Admittedly, the four surviving copies of Magna Carta have been awarded 'Memory of the World' status by UNESCO.[76] (A similar status has yet to be given to the Charter of the Forest.) Although there is a risk with all medieval documents of over-claiming the past, there is an equally important danger of overlooking their significance. Once the forest provisions were removed from Magna Carta, it was, on a simple numerical basis, the Charter of the Forest which greatly improved the lives of the general population living in afforested areas, whereas the 1215 Magna Carta primarily benefitted a smaller number – barons and freemen. In 1215 there were 143 forests in England, and at its most extensive, in the late twelfth and early thirteenth centuries, approximately one-quarter of the land in England was afforested;[77] therefore the impact of disafforesting upon daily life cannot be underestimated. Although there was resistance from Henry III in seeking to reclaim land,[78] the same resistance was displayed by King John, who wrote to the Pope requesting that he condemn the Magna Carta as an abomination. Nevertheless, constitutionally if the Magna Carta is regarded as the cornerstone of English liberty, then there ought to be a similar acknowledgement of the contribution of the Charter of the Forest to the development of socio-economic rights. A similar status

---

[74] In *N.S. v. Home Secretary*, the Court of Justice of the European Union declared that: 'Article 1(1) of [the seventh] protocol explains article 51 of the Charter with regard to the scope thereof and does not intend to exempt the Republic of Poland or the United Kingdom from the obligations to comply with the provisions of the Charter or to prevent a court of one of those member states from ensuring compliance with those provisions. C-411/10, C-493/10 [2011] CJEU, 21 December 2011, at para. 120.

[75] In *AB, R (on the application of) v. Secretary of State for the Home Department*, Mostyn J. said: 'The constitutional significance of this decision can hardly be overstated. . . . Notwithstanding the endeavours of our political representatives at Lisbon it would seem that the much wider Charter of Rights is now part of our domestic law. Moreover, that much wider Charter of Rights would remain part of our domestic law even if the Human Rights Act were repealed. So it can be seen that even if the Human Rights Act were to be repealed, with the result that article 8 of the European Convention on Human Rights was no longer directly incorporated into domestic law, an identical right would continue to exist under the Charter of Fundamental Rights of the European Union, and this right is, according to the Court in Luxembourg, enforceable domestically.' [2013] EWHC 3453 (Admin), at para. 14.

[76] They belong to Lincoln Cathedral, Salisbury Cathedral and the British Library, which has two copies. There are only two remaining copies of the Charter of the Forest, belonging to Lincoln and Durham Cathedrals.

[77] P. Linebaugh, *The Magna Carta Manifesto* (University of California Press, 2008), 34.

[78] Bazeley, 'The Extent of the English Forest in the Thirteenth Century' (1921), 140 Transactions of the Royal Historical Society 153, citing as an example land in Nottingham.

conferred on the Charter of the Forest may seem a trivial approach, but the symbolic significance ought not to be underestimated. An international acknowledgement of the historical legacy of the two charters together, if fully recognised, would encourage more states to incorporate socio-economic rights in their constitutions and constitutional settlements.

In the United Kingdom socio-economic rights are popular with the people[79] but often resisted by legislatures. This is echoed in Ireland, where in 2014 the Constitutional Convention, with a majority of 85 per cent, recommended that protection of these rights be strengthened in Bunreacht na hÉireann,[80] the Constitution of Ireland. Because of the make-up of the Constitutional Convention, such a recommendation would not have been possible without the support of the public, as distinguished from the political members of the Constitutional Convention.

At the beginning of *The Federalist Papers*, Alexander Hamilton enquires whether people are 'forever destined to depend, for their political constitutions, on accident'.[81] It is an accident of history that the United Kingdom and the United States have forgotten the Charter of the Forest, but the amnesia surrounding the history of socio-economic rights ought not to determine the future.

---

[79] See, e.g., the report of the Social Exclusion Unit, n. 19.
[80] These are currently only directive principles of the social policy; see Art. 45.
[81] Alexander Hamilton, The Federalist No. 1; asked in the opening paragraph.

11

Michael Oakeshott, the Legendary Past
and Magna Carta

Natalie Riendeau

On the 750th anniversary of Magna Carta, the English philosopher Michael Oakeshott published a review of J. C. Holt's seminal work, *Magna Carta*. Oakeshott begins his review by stating that 'the historical understanding of the Great Charter, like that of nearly every important event or occasion, has emerged gradually out of the quite different enterprise of assigning it a significant place in the legend of English life'.[1] This is but one of numerous, yet sporadic, allusions Oakeshott makes to legend and myth in general, and to the English legend in particular, in his works. In spite of the intermittent nature of such references by Oakeshott, it is nevertheless possible to gather from his limited writings on the subject that this type of narrative plays a fundamental role in relation to the political.

Oakeshott holds that the political enterprise of legend-making – that is, of 'constructing and confirming a social identity and consciousness by establishing a significant relationship between present moods and past events [–] is a perennial practical necessity'.[2] This statement suggests that legend and myth play a foundational role in relation to a political society's identity and sense of self-consciousness. Moreover, the distinction Oakeshott draws between the historical understanding of Magna Carta and the legend-making enterprise intimates that a different sort of past, a legendary past, is involved in legend-making and that it is indispensable for the political. However, despite the central role Oakeshott attributes to legend and myth, he never fully theorises their political function. In this sense, commentators have noted that the idea that a society requires a foundational myth if it is to have the requisite social cohesion is 'one that [Oakeshott] never really worked out in detail; it is the

---

[1]   M. Oakeshott, *The Vocabulary of a Modern European State: Essays and Reviews 1952–88* (Exeter and Charlottesville: Imprint Academic, 2008), 194.
[2]   Oakeshott, *Vocabulary European State*, 194.

source of some unresolved tensions in his thought'.[3] Although he never fully worked out his concept of legends of political life, he nevertheless asserts that the English legend of political life, in which Magna Carta occupies a significant place, constitutes a necessary political and practical enterprise.

Contributors to this volume also note the legendary or mythical interpretation of Magna Carta. For instance, Anthony King describes the signing of Magna Carta – the King being subdued by victorious barons – as an image that most English schoolchildren have imprinted on their minds.[4] Geraldine Van Bueren underlines the symbolic role played by the 'Magna' name in enhancing the significance of the medieval charter.[5] Vernon Bogdanor reminds us that in the seventeenth century Magna Carta became a myth, if not to say 'something of a cult'.[6] Craig S. Lerner traces the myth of Magna Carta to the seventeenth-century jurist Sir Edward Coke, stating that Coke 'dusted off Magna Carta and created a mythology that proved useful in parliamentary attacks on royal authority'.[7] In sum, as argued by Craig S. Lerner, Magna Carta's significance today is in mythologizing the law.[8]

Magna Carta has undeniably become a 'sacred text'.[9] Remarking upon this development, Claire Breay, in a volume published by the British Library, maintains that 'despite all the claims which have been made for it since, the charter was not intended to be the cornerstone of English democracy'.[10] It is interesting to observe, however, that on its website, the British Library states that 'Magna Carta is often thought of as the corner-stone of liberty and the chief defence against arbitrary and unjust rule in England'.[11] While not quite a claim for democracy, nevertheless the British Library's statement not only indicates that Magna Carta has come to symbolise liberty, but that this mythical interpretation of the meaning of the charter has come to form part of the national consciousness. Thus, over the centuries, Magna Carta has come to be enveloped in myth.[12]

---

[3] T. Nardin and L. O'Sullivan, Introduction in: T. Nardin and L. O'Sullivan (eds.), M. Oakeshott, *Lectures in the History of Political Thought* (Exeter and Charlottesville: Imprint Academic, 2006), 15.

[4] See Anthony King's chapter (Ch. 3).

[5] See Geraldine Van Bueren's chapter (Ch. 10).

[6] J. P. Kenyon, *Stuart England*, 2nd ed. (London: Penguin Books, 1985), 38, quoted by Vernon Bogdanor, Ch. 2.

[7] See Craig S. Lerner's chapter (Ch. 8).

[8] Despite this myth, survey data demonstrates the 'apparent lack of any national myth around the existence and significance of Magna Carta'. See Roger Mortimore's chapter (Ch. 4).

[9] J. C. Holt, *Magna Carta*, 2nd ed. (Cambridge: Cambridge University Press, 1992), 21.

[10] C. Breay, *Magna Carta: Manuscripts and Myths* (London: The British Library, 2002), 7.

[11] The British Library, *Magna Carta*, http://www.bl.uk/onlinegallery/onlineex/histtexts/magna/.

[12] Breay, *Magna Carta*, 48.

Although scholars refer to the myths surrounding Magna Carta, much of the focus is on how the charter's true origin, its content and its significance have become obscured by these myths and misunderstandings.[13] In other words, the concern is with the perceived distortion of the authentically historical understanding of the medieval charter and not with the myth itself and its meaning. Albeit historically inaccurate, mythical and legendary interpretations of Magna Carta are not in and of themselves illegitimate and should not be rejected outright. These interpretations are important, I suggest, as they fulfil a fundamental political role. The aim of this chapter is to examine this role and, more specifically, the function of the legendary past in relation to the political.

My objective is to understand Magna Carta both politically and historically. To this end, Oakeshott's political philosophy and philosophy of history are fruitful in helping to understand the political role of legend and its past. Oakeshott's political philosophy allows us to understand the English political legend and its function, while his philosophy of history enables us to specify the type of thinking about the past involved in certain interpretations of Magna Carta. As we will see, underlying the analyses of J. G. A. Pocock and Holt is the idea that in certain cases there is a different, non-historical past involved in interpreting Magna Carta. In this respect, Pocock and Holt recognise that certain seventeenth-century interpretations of Magna Carta were used to support arguments about the present.[14] Although Pocock and Holt never make this argument, it may be suggested that the identification of past and present is not historical thinking, as it serves a political purpose. This is precisely the idea which is at the heart of Oakeshott's philosophical distinction between history and the legendary past. The identification of past and present serves a practical, political purpose and therefore does not constitute history such as Oakeshott defines it. Hence, the legendary past allows us not only to understand the political function of Magna Carta, but also how the myth works.

The chapter's starting point is Oakeshott's position that Magna Carta occupies a significant place in the legend of English political life. I begin by theorising his concept of legends of political life. Following this, I focus specifically on the legendary past and Oakeshott's philosophical distinction between history and the legendary past, which helps us understand the emergence of an historical understanding of Magna Carta. I then proceed to explore the English political legend which places Magna Carta at its core. I

[13] See Breay, *Magna Carta*, 7.
[14] J. G. A. Pocock, *The Ancient Constitution and the Feudal Law* (New York: W.W. Norton & Company, Inc, 1967), 45, and Holt, *Magna Carta*, 9.

make the case that the English legend of political life endows the English polity with an identity and consciousness founded on the idea of liberty as well as the fundamental principle which, as Bogdanor explains in this volume, makes Magna Carta so important – that is, the principle that government is subject to the law.[15] I then look at how seventeenth-century jurists, and Sir Edward Coke in particular, made use of Magna Carta and the legendary past in order to support their political claims against the Stuart kings. Finally, I conclude that there are two lessons learned from studying Magna Carta's legendary past: (1) legend plays an essential political role, and (2) there are different types of past. Thus, the Great Charter's influence is symbolic and direct because the legendary interpretation of the document constructs and confirms the English identity and consciousness.

LEGENDS OF POLITICAL LIFE

In his *Lectures on the History of Political Thought*, Oakeshott states that the ties that bind members of a state to one another are the least tangible of the themes of modern European political thought.[16] It is important to keep in mind that Oakeshott defends a conception of the state understood as an historic society. To this end, he argues that 'the somewhat novel associations of human beings which came to be called the states of modern Europe emerged slowly, pre-figured in earlier European history, but not without some dramatic passages in their emergence. Each was the outcome of human choices, but none was the product of a design'.[17] For Oakeshott, what binds members of an historic society to one another is 'the memory of shared experiences' and 'the total of contingent circumstances', by which he means 'a common language, a literature, common laws, folk-tales and legends, songs'.[18] In other words, Oakeshott understands the modern European state as a collection of human beings who chance has brought together and 'who have acquired a sentiment of solidarity from having enjoyed, over the years, a common and continuous 'historical' experience'.[19] This idea of solidarity based on a memory of shared experiences, it may be argued, leads a collection of human beings to forge a common identity. That is, from the long enjoyment of a common experience of living together there emerges a shared sense of identity which unites members of a state.

---

[15] See Vernon Bogdanor's chapter (Ch. 2).
[16] M. Oakeshott, *Lectures in the History of Political Thought* (Exeter and Charlottesville: Imprint Academic, 2006), 425.
[17] M. Oakeshott, *On Human Conduct* (Oxford: Oxford University Press, 1975), 185.
[18] Ibid., 422.
[19] Ibid.

The question that arises is how precisely is a political society's identity forged? The answer, I argue, lies with Oakeshott's concept of a legend of political life. Oakeshott's writings on legends are sporadic; he never devotes himself to a systematic discussion or analysis of the subject. Whenever he introduces the concept, it is usually while discussing the modes of experience and philosophy. Briefly, following the idealist tradition, Oakeshott posits that experience is thought and as such constitutes a world of ideas.[20] Modifications may be distinguished within experience. These are modes, and they may be thought of as the whole of experience perceived from a limited standpoint. Alternatively, Oakeshott also refers to modes of experience as arrests in experience. He contends that at the point of the arrest, a separate world of ideas is constructed, thus constituting a mode of experience.[21] As for philosophy, it is 'experience without reservation or presupposition'.[22] It is experience which is self-conscious, self-critical and is pursued for its own sake.[23] Although Oakeshott asserts that the number of potential modes of experience is unlimited, he identifies four: practice (practical experience or activity including the modulation of politics), science, poetry and history. Because modes of experience are abstract, homogeneous worlds of ideas, it therefore follows for Oakeshott that each mode is 'wholly and absolutely independent of any other'.[24] In other words, there is no direct relationship between the modes of experience, and consequently it is impossible to pass in argument from one mode of experience to another.[25] This idea is key to understanding Oakeshott's concept of the legendary or practical past. History is modally irrelevant to practice. When history is assimilated to practice, Oakeshott's position is that this constitutes a different sort of past – the practical past. In the practical past, history is subordinated to practice. As we will see in relation to Magna Carta, due to the primordial human need to make ourselves at home in the world, it has proven particularly difficult for history to emancipate itself from the authority of practice – that is, for history to emerge from myth.

Oakeshott mentions legend and myth when discussing history, poetry and philosophy in order to distinguish them from what they are not. A close study of the relationship of legends to history, poetry and philosophy, I suggest, reveals that Oakeshott's concept of legends of political life is composed of three constitutive elements: foundational reflection upon the political (as

---

[20] M. Oakeshott, *Experience and its Modes* (Cambridge: Cambridge University Press, 1995), 27.
[21] Ibid., 73–74.
[22] Ibid., 82.
[23] Ibid.
[24] Ibid., 75.
[25] Ibid., 76.

opposed to philosophy), the practical past (as opposed to history) and poetry. I posit that political legends are poetic constructs which tell the story of a past event, such as Magna Carta, and allow political societies to understand their political fortunes, whether actual or imaginary, in the idiom of general ideas. As to the content of legend and myth, they are prescriptive narratives in that they carry and transmit an explicit moral and message and, as such, serve as an authority for the political. In sum, legends of political life endow political societies with their identity and sense of self-consciousness, thereby ensuring solidarity amongst strangers.[26]

THE LEGENDARY PAST

In his review of Holt's *Magna Carta*, Oakeshott distinguishes between two different understandings of the past in relation to Magna Carta: the historical past and the legendary past. Oakeshott emphasises the difficult emancipation of the historical past from the authority of the legendary past. That being said, he does not for this reason deem the legendary past to be illegitimate. On the contrary, Oakeshott states that it is an 'indispensable ingredient of an articulate civilized life', as it is this past which constructs and confirms a society's identity.[27]

Oakeshott argues the point vigorously throughout his extensive writings on the philosophy of history. In this regard, he maintains that speaking about the past in the practical idiom cannot be dismissed as merely illegitimate, nor can it be forbidden, as this would amount to proscribing the 'primordial activity of making ourselves at home in the world by assimilating *our* past to *our* present'.[28] For Oakeshott, the practical past is 'not the enemy of mankind, but only the enemy of "the historian"'.[29] In this sense, the story of Magna Carta is a prime example of history's difficult emancipation from the authority of practice. In *On History*, Oakeshott defines history and its concomitant past as 'the conclusion of a critical enquiry of a certain sort; it is to be found nowhere but in a history book'.[30] The philosopher identifies this enquiry as one in which survivals from the past are dissolved into their component features and are

---

[26] For the theorisation of Oakeshott's legends of political life and an exposition of the argument that they serve as constructed foundations for the political, see N. Riendeau, *The Legendary Past: Michael Oakeshott on Imagination and Political Identity* (Exeter and Charlottesville: Imprint Academic, 2014).

[27] M. Oakeshott, *On History and Other Essays* (Indianapolis: Liberty Fund, 1999), 48.

[28] M. Oakeshott, *Rationalism in Politics and Other Essays: New and Expanded Edition* (Indianapolis: Liberty Fund, 1991), 180, original emphasis.

[29] Ibid., 180.

[30] Oakeshott, *On History*, 36.

used as circumstantial evidence from which to infer a past which has not survived. This past is composed of passages of related historical events which are assembled as answers to questions formulated by an historian.[31] These historical events have no message since their meanings lie in their unrepeatable conditions. That is, they cannot be detached from their circumstantial conditions without losing their meanings.[32] The meanings of historical events are neither universal nor timeless, but rather contingent and circumstantial.

The very opposite is true of events and objects that have survived from a near or distant past and which comprise legends of political life, such as the story of Magna Carta. In this respect, Oakeshott defines the legendary past as 'what is "read" and what may be read with advantage to ourselves in our current engagements'.[33] That is, the purpose of the practical past is to be of worth to the current practical engagements of the practical present. Thus, objects and events which are valued for their usefulness in current practical engagements are divorced from their circumstantial conditions. Oakeshott asserts that they are 'abstracted from record in a reading which divests them of their contingent circumstances and their authentic utterance'.[34] From authentic and circumstantial historical meanings, survivals are transformed into emblematic characters and episodes, symbolic and stereotypic *personae*, actions, exploits and situations.[35] In this sense, the legendary past is composed of objects recognised 'not as survivals but merely to have survived'.[36] The legendary past, therefore, involves creation. For this reason, Oakeshott describes the legendary past as evoked, a work of art. In this respect, it has to be 'created, learned, cared for and cultivated'.[37] In creating, learning, caring and cultivating the legendary past, humans assimilate the past to the present.

Oakeshott posits that the past is assimilated to the present in a procedure of recollection. By this, he means that objects or events of worth which have survived from the past become available to agents in a procedure of recall to mind.[38] The procedure of recollection, as it is understood by Oakeshott, is 'joining a puzzling or intractable present with a known and unproblematic past to compose a less puzzling or more manageable practical present'.[39] This

[31] Ibid., 36.
[32] Ibid., 41–42.
[33] Ibid., 19.
[34] Ibid., 42.
[35] Ibid.
[36] Ibid., 41.
[37] M. Oakeshott, *What Is History? and Other Essays* (Exeter and Charlottesville: Imprint Academic, 2004), 347.
[38] Oakeshott, *On History*, 17–18.
[39] Ibid., 18.

is a significant assertion. Oakeshott claims that the practical past's usefulness is derived from the fact that it contributes to composing a less mystifying and unwieldy present. That is, the practical past offers stability and sense to the present-future of practical engagement. Oakeshott contends that the practical present contains an 'ever-increasing deposit' of fragments of past that have survived and which are available to be listened to and consulted.[40] These fragments are relevant to present circumstances and, as such, may be related to current conduct.[41] These recalled fragments consist in artefacts, recorded anecdotes and episodes of bygone human fortune used to elaborate stories of past human circumstance, exemplars of human character and images of human conduct.[42] The virtue of these fragments lies in their familiarity and usefulness to the practical present. They are useful in that they communicate useful information or advice and may be listened to, consulted and used. In this sense, authority may be attributed to these fragments which have survived from the past.[43] It is important to note, however, that Oakeshott ultimately finds that the legendary past is not significantly past at all. Rather, the legendary past is part of the present-future of practical engagement in which survived objects are stored.[44] He concludes that the legendary past comprises 'the present contents of a vast storehouse into which time continuously empties the lives, the utterances, the achievements and the sufferings of mankind'.[45]

Oakeshott asserts that every society has an inheritance of such survived objects. Whether these are actual or imaginary is irrelevant since what is important is what they can teach a society and tell its members about themselves.[46] Consequently, it follows for Oakeshott that 'whether or not these survivals are scenes from a mythology, products of poetic imagination or alleged bygone exploits is often a matter of indifference'.[47] Part of the living past is an actual or imaginary ancestral past in which members of a society locate the society to which they belong.[48] As regards the self-understanding of a society, Oakeshott argues that when considerable passages of the practical past are assembled by putting together fragmented survivals, they 'yield important conclusions about ourselves and our current circumstances'.[49] In

[40] Ibid.
[41] Ibid.
[42] Ibid.
[43] Ibid., 18–19.
[44] Ibid., 41.
[45] Ibid., 43.
[46] Ibid., 18–19.
[47] Ibid.
[48] Ibid., 19.
[49] Ibid., 21.

this sense, the constructed living past recalled by the political may take the form of a legend or a saga, a kind of past which Oakeshott qualifies as poetic and defines as a 'drama from which all that is casual, secondary and unresolved has been excluded; it has a clear outline, a unity of feeling and in it everything is exact except place and time'.[50] As will be examined in greater detail, this is the very type of drama evoked by the legendary story of Magna Carta. Oakeshott's point is that humans, because of their primordial, practical attitude, assimilate the past to the present in order to build a world of sense for themselves and for generations to come. Therefore, the identity of a society and the knowledge its members have of it are directly related to the practical past. The legendary past, through the process of recollection to mind, endows political societies with 'unequivocal lineage and character'.[51] In sum, the legendary past's virtue is to make persons and association of persons 'at home in an otherwise mysterious and menacing universe'.[52]

However, Magna Carta is not only recalled by the practical past. Before broaching the legend of Magna Carta, I want to examine how it has been understood historically. In his review of Holt's *Magna Carta*, Oakeshott charts the gradual and imperfect emergence of an historical understanding of Magna Carta. In this sense, Oakeshott observes that the first version of an historical understanding of Magna Carta still contained relics of the legend-making enterprise. He argues that the baronial opponents of King John, now 'deposed from their legendary role of champions of liberty', were recast for another role – that of 'self-seeking dissidents and the opponents of administrative efficiency'.[53] However, in spite of these legendary relics, Oakeshott notes that this first version – which he refers to as 'retrospective modernism' and associates with nineteenth-century historians – by concentrating upon the 'feudal' and 'legal' character of the document, demonstrates, in his opinion, that a serious attempt at historical understanding was under way.[54] For this reason, Oakeshott concludes that 'retrospective modernism' may now be recognised, not as historical error, but rather as evidence of the imperfect emergence of an historical understanding from the legend-making enterprise.[55]

This, according to Oakeshott, is the starting point of the historical understanding of Magna Carta, and the story of this understanding, from the early

---

[50] Oakeshott, *Rationalism in Politics*, 182.
[51] Oakeshott, *What Is History?* 347.
[52] Ibid., 347.
[53] Oakeshott, *Vocabulary European State*, 194.
[54] Ibid., 194.
[55] Ibid.

twentieth century onwards, has been one of 'endless and fascinating elabora-tion'.[56] The manner in which the story has been elaborated makes the distinction Oakeshott establishes between the historical and the practical past all the more clear. In this regard, Oakeshott argues that the relics retained by the 'retrospective modernist' interpretation have since been detached from it in order for their own history to be written as elements in their own right. Thus, Oakeshott asserts that the context in which Magna Carta is read has been both extended and deepened.[57] Whereas the early 'retrospective moder-nist' version, with its stated aim of extracting Magna Carta from the legend of English politics, interpreted it severely in its thirteenth-century context, the context in which it was read in the later versions was pushed back into early Norman England and enlarged to include twelfth-century Europe.[58] Put another way, the historical understanding of Magna Carta has ceased to be 'predominantly "feudal" and "legal"'.[59] Moreover, the generalities of the legend have been replaced by specificalities. In this sense, Oakeshott points out that 'actual discontents and their magnitudes have been distinguished'.[60] As for the legendary barons and their fiefs, castles and rights, they have been replaced with 'named persons, with discernible characters, with individual interests and the usual mixture of motives, and named properties'.[61] Thus, a 'situation composed of complicated tensions has replaced the old simplicities', following Oakeshott.[62] This has allowed for a new outline composed of 'more appropriate general statements' to emerge.[63] In short, Oakeshott maintains that the passage of the past surrounding Magna Carta has become 'historically more intelligible'.[64] Significantly, Oakeshott considers the process in which an historical understanding of Magna Carta emerged to be a 'remarkable example of historical thought'.[65] However, Oakeshott emphasises that like all enterprises of historical understanding, the history of Magna Carta is unfinished. His point isn't simply that historical thought is forever generating new enquiries, but that the historical understanding of Magna Carta makes us capable of entertaining and assimilating new representations of it and of the whole period to which this event belongs.[66]

[56] Ibid., 195.
[57] Ibid.
[58] Ibid., 194–95.
[59] Ibid., 195.
[60] Ibid.
[61] Ibid.
[62] Ibid.
[63] Ibid.
[64] Ibid.
[65] Ibid.
[66] Ibid.

MAGNA CARTA AND THE ENGLISH LEGEND
OF POLITICAL LIFE

The English, like every people possessed of communal self-consciousness, have invoked the legendary past and constructed a myth or legend which imaginatively interprets how their political self-consciousness emerged. In this sense, Oakeshott declares that 'every people awakened to political self-consciousness constructs a myth, an imaginative interpretation of how this came about. The myth of modern English politics, for example, began to be constructed in the seventeenth century'.[67] As will be examined further on, Oakeshott is most certainly referring to the myth constructed by seventeenth-century jurists and historians, of whom the leading figure was Sir Edward Coke.[68] In this section of the chapter, however, I want to explore the 'significant place' assigned to Magna Carta in the English legend of political life. While in *Lectures on the History of Political Thought* Oakeshott asserts that the myth of modern English politics began to be constructed in the seventeenth century, in his review of Holt's *Magna Carta*, he argues that in respect of the Charter the enterprise has been pursued since the fourteenth century.[69] Oakeshott appears to be referring to Holt's argument that the decisive period in the development of the myth of Magna Carta was the fourteenth century when many of the features of the seventeenth-century interpretation of the Charter were embodied in parliamentary statute.[70] In this respect, Holt notes that between 1331 and 1368, in six acts, Parliament passed statutory interpretations of chapter 29, which 'went far beyond any of the detailed intention and sense of the original Charter'.[71] Whether the legend-making enterprise began in the fourteenth or seventeenth century, it is Magna Carta, a 'thirteenth-century document which has survived', which, I argue, is the event recalled to mind from the legendary past in order to form the basis of the English political legend.[72]

The myth of modern English politics recounts England's political fortunes and, Oakeshott asserts, is 'something to which our current political arguments and attitudes are always returning, and which is always in a process of enlargement and revision'.[73] In other words, current political conduct is

---

[67] Oakeshott, *Lectures*, 46.
[68] Breay, *Magna Carta*, 46.
[69] Oakeshott, *Vocabulary European State*, 194.
[70] Holt, *Magna Carta*, 9.
[71] Holt, *Magna Carta*, 10. Note that Art. 29 in the currently in-force Magna Carta was Art. 29 and 30 in the original Magna Carta sealed in 1215.
[72] Oakeshott, *On History*, 46.
[73] Oakeshott, *Lectures*, 46.

bound or tied to the myth of English politics. Change, political decisions and legislation must be congruent with the myth which is itself thereby preserved and augmented. Although Oakeshott never explicitly details what these fortunes may be, I posit that poetry constructs a legend or myth which recounts the story of English freedom. The legend awakens the English people to its political inheritance and guards its tradition of freedom by means of its message – that is, that English freedom depends upon the maintenance of rights and procedures for redress. Fundamental to the moral of the legend is the principle that authority is subject to the law.

Central to Oakeshott's interpretation of Magna Carta is the conception of freedom it embodies. In this sense, in the essay 'Power and Freedom', Oakeshott argues that Magna Carta is a charter of liberties and, as such, is a record of liberties which are already enjoyed.[74] Its content, he maintains, comes from a deep stratum of social thought which, ultimately, was little influenced by the superficial political action of politicians, here understood as the King and the barons.[75] He is adamant that it is not a bill of rights, the content of which begins with an abstract idea of freedom and ends with a list of freedoms and devices for securing these freedoms. Put another way, the exercise of freedom is not first experienced and then recorded as it is with a charter such as Magna Carta.[76] Freedom, for Oakeshott, 'is not a bright idea'.[77] While this may indeed be true, above and beyond whether Magna Carta is a record of already-enjoyed liberties or is a list of abstract freedoms which need to be instituted, what is important is the function it serves in relation to the political as well as in relation to the English political imagination and sense of self-consciousness. Oakeshott broaches the subject of the role Magna Carta plays in the *Lectures in the History of Political Thought* in the context of his discussion of Roman law. One of the most important episodes of the Roman legend of politics was when the ancient, customary and unwritten law of Rome was written down and published. In the history of Roman law, Oakeshott claims, this was the 'one great event which overshadowed all others'.[78] The demand behind this event was one of the earliest made by the *concilium plebis*, who, according to Livy, wished that the law 'cease to be kept secret among the mysteries and sacraments of the immortal gods'.[79] The result of the demand was the *decemviri*, a commission of ten patricians whose duty it

---

[74] Oakeshott, *What Is History?* 240.
[75] M. Oakeshott, *Religion, Politics, and the Moral Life* (New Haven: Yale University Press, 1993), 93.
[76] Oakeshott, *What Is History?* 239–40.
[77] Oakeshott, *Rationalism in Politics*, 54.
[78] Oakeshott, *Lectures*, 242.
[79] Oakeshott citing Livy, *Lectures*, 243.

was to reduce the law in order to write it down and publish it. What they produced was the 'famous' twelve tables of the Roman law, which was 'engraved on panels of metal and set up in the forum. And it was for ever cherished as the fundamental, original, sacred law of the Romans'.[80] All subsequent laws and legislation, or *leges*, were thought of as 'additions to or amplifications of this fundamental law'.[81] Oakeshott's position is that Magna Carta is akin to the twelve tables of Roman law in that it also has been forever cherished by the English as their fundamental, original and sacred law. Nardin and O'Sullivan, the editors of the *Lectures in the History of Political Thought*, point out that Oakeshott made a marginal note in the manuscript in relation to the sentence explaining how the Romans cherished the twelve tables of the Roman law, stating 'Cp. Magna Carta'.[82] Finally, following the Roman example, all subsequent English laws and legislation are thought of as amplifications of Magna Carta.

Magna Carta, then, is the recalled artefact which stabilises the problematic present of English politics, and it is from this legal charter that the English legend flows. The legendary story of Magna Carta relates the tense and difficult relations between King John and the barons of England, the principal actors of the drama. Among the episodes which compose the drama is the one in which the King was at the temple in London in January 1215 when the barons arrived, armed, and demanded 'the grant of a charter confirming the ancient "liberties" of the realm'.[83] Later on that year, when the barons were encamped at Staines and the King at Windsor Castle, they agreed to meet 'half way' at Runnymede on 15 June 1215, and King John made 'a formal grant of the "liberties" which he had conceded'.[84] This formal grant of liberties was Magna Carta, of which copies were made for distribution throughout England.[85] In this regard, Magna Carta takes on a significant symbolic quality. The fact that two copies of the document are on permanent display at Salisbury and Lincoln Cathedrals reflects the document's elevation to iconic status. Furthermore, sculptures and statues of the protagonists adorn cathedrals throughout England. These are elements of a legend in that they are symbolic images and not mere images and, as such, transmit a message regarding the meaning of freedom in England. Oakeshott asserts that Magna Carta was a reaffirmation of feudal rights which had been infringed by King John and thus

---

[80] Oakeshott, *Lectures*, 243.
[81] Ibid., 243.
[82] Ibid., note 2. Editorial note.
[83] D. I. Stroud, *Magna Carta* (Southampton: Paul Cave Publications Ltd, 1998), 3.
[84] Ibid., 4.
[85] Ibid.

established the right of vassals to extract redress from the King.[86] The liberties of the English barons were maintained, and a procedure for the redress of wrongs was ensured. It is this idea which is preserved and augmented in the drama of English politics.

Thus, the legendary past, by recalling Magna Carta and its message to mind, plays a fundamental political role. It endows English society with is political identity and sense of self-consciousness. The legend of English politics, such as Oakeshott understands it, I argue, relates the story of English freedom and of the institutions which emerged to ensure its continuity. He asserts that current political arguments and attitudes are always returning to the legend in order to understand English freedom, as well as to revise and enlarge its meaning. Put another way, the English political legend is at once preserved and augmented. Political conduct returns to the legend as a source of authority and political change is bound to the story in that it must be congruent with it. Change is augmentation or amplification of the legend. Permanence and change are, consequently, tied together. What is in effect preserved and augmented is the English political identity.

SIR EDWARD COKE AND THE LEGENDARY PAST

In this final section of the chapter, I want to put forward the argument that when seventeenth-century jurists and historians argued in opposition to the Stuart kings that Magna Carta stated fundamental principles of law – more than this, that it constituted a declaration of individual liberty and formed part of an ancient constitution – they were in fact invoking the legendary past and resorting to its storehouse of 'alleged past performances reduced to exemplary characters, utterances and situations'.[87] To this end, both Pocock and Holt emphasise that Coke and his allies assimilated the past to the present by recalling Magna Carta for specific political ends. Thus, I propose that they were not engaged in history, but in a legend-making enterprise.

As previously mentioned, Oakeshott believes that the legend of English politics began to be constructed in the seventeenth century. Although he does not elaborate beyond this, we may gather from the essay the 'Rule of Law' that he has Coke in mind. He notes in the essay that 'some English writers in the seventeenth century attributed to Magna Carta or to an imaginary Ancient Constitution the character of a Fundamental Law'.[88] As we saw, Oakeshott

---

[86] Oakeshott, *Lectures*, 311.
[87] Oakeshott, *On History*, 47.
[88] Ibid., 170, note 12.

does not believe that Magna Carta constitutes a 'charter of unconditional "liberties"', much less a fundamental or foundational law.[89] Therefore, he arguably agrees with Holt's definition of the myth of Magna Carta as 'that interpretation of it which gives it qualities which the men of 1215 did not intend'.[90] Historians agree that Magna Carta was never intended as a statement of fundamental law nor of legal principle or theory.[91] Rather, it was 'a practical solution to a political crisis'.[92]

Breay emphasises that Magna Carta's status and significance underwent a profound shift in the seventeenth century.[93] To fully grasp this shift, it is important to understand the common law interpretation of history as well as the myth of the ancient constitution 'which bulked so large in the political thought of the seventeenth century', according to Pocock.[94] Oakeshott hints at the common law interpretation of history when he explains that some seventeenth-century writers understood Magna Carta or an imaginary ancient constitution as a formulation of principles of justice insulated from change.[95] Following Pocock, the common law interpretation of history received its classic formulation from Coke.[96] This interpretation defined the law as immemorial custom.[97] For Pocock, the clue to understanding this paradoxical definition of the common law lies in the ambiguity of the concept of custom. He argues that while custom can indeed refer to the idea of constant adaptation and thus be understood historically, it can equally be regarded as 'that which has been retained throughout the centuries and derives its authority from its having survived unchanged all changes of circumstances'.[98] Thus, custom was unchanging and immemorial. For the common law interpretation of history to work, however, it had to overcome 'the one great apparent breach' in the continuity of English history: the Norman Conquest and importation of the new law.[99] In order to resolve this difficulty, Pocock argues that Coke and his allies were aided by the Normans themselves, who maintained that they governed England

---

[89] Ibid., 170.
[90] Holt, *Magna Carta*, 9.
[91] Breay, *Magna Carta*, 7.
[92] Ibid., 7.
[93] Ibid., 45.
[94] Pocock, *Ancient Constitution*, 36.
[95] Oakeshott, *On History*, 169–70.
[96] Pocock, *Ancient Constitution*, 31.
[97] Ibid., 37.
[98] Ibid.
[99] Ibid., 42.

according to the laws of Edward the Confessor.[100] Thus, by the seventeenth century, the belief that the laws of the last Anglo-Saxon king had been confirmed by the Conqueror and his successors was orthodox history.[101] In this context, then, Magna Carta was linked by Coke with the successive confirmations of the Confessor's law. In this respect, the myth of the confirmations culminated with Magna Carta, which Coke asserted had itself been confirmed by more than thirty parliaments.[102] This is the first element of Coke's interpretation of Magna Carta.

In the second process, Coke, Pocock maintains, studied the medieval charter clause by clause to prove that it enacted the main principles of seventeenth-century common law and parliamentary liberty.[103] Put another way, Coke discovered the rights of parliament and property in a thirteenth-century document.[104] Therefore, following the common law interpretation that the law was immemorial and declared what has always been law, Coke was able to identify the law of his own day with the law of the earliest records.[105] At this point, as Pocock underscores, 'the identification of past and present was complete'.[106]

The identification of past and present in the seventeenth century by Coke, common lawyers and parliamentarians also had a political aspect. The belief in the antiquity of the common law had encouraged belief in the existence of an ancient constitution which could be used for political ends against the Stuart kings and their doctrine of the Divine Right of Kings.[107] Thus, for a constitution to be truly immemorial, it could not be subject to a sovereign.[108] In other words, a right rooted in custom rendered it independent of the sovereign's interference since custom was immemorial and could not be traced to an original act of foundation, founder or king.[109] A sovereign could not revoke rights rooted in unchanging, immemorial custom.

Like Pocock, Holt also emphasises that Coke's aim was 'to call in the past in order to support his arguments about the present'.[110] In this sense, any judgment Coke made about medieval society was entirely subsidiary to this[111] – that

[100] Ibid., 42–43.
[101] Ibid., 43.
[102] Ibid., 44.
[103] Ibid., 45.
[104] Ibid.
[105] Ibid.
[106] Ibid.
[107] Ibid., 46.
[108] Ibid., 51.
[109] Ibid., 37.
[110] Holt, *Magna Carta*, 9.
[111] Ibid., 9.

is, subsidiary to his claim that Magna Carta 'was an affirmation of fundamental law and the liberty of the subject'.[112] In order to defend his position, Coke fought for carefully selected chapters from the Charter and for his own interpretation of that selection.[113] Holt compares Coke's approach to history and his interpretation of Magna Carta to the analysis of modern historians. To this end, Holt points out that modern historians interpret Magna Carta as a statement of liberties, as does Oakeshott, and not as an assertion of liberties.[114] Moreover, and contrary to Coke, Holt explains that modern historians seek the precise contemporary meaning of the Charter – its intent, its vocabulary and its effects.[115] For modern historians, all else is distortion, according to Holt, an 'imposition on its "real" content of anachronistic and perhaps politically motivated misinterpretations'.[116] Holt is cautious when treating the subject of distortion in Coke's historical thought. Firstly, he argues that it is impossible to establish the exact contemporary sense of Magna Carta as canon.[117] In this respect, Holt reminds us that Magna Carta was a political document produced in a crisis and consequently that it was not an exact statement of law and that many of its provisions had no precise meaning.[118] Secondly, Holt holds that there is often no hope of establishing a precise contemporary meaning of particular phrases or clauses.[119] Thus, he asserts that there exists an admissible range of opinion on Magna Carta, and the question is whether Coke's interpretation falls within that range.[120]

In addition, Holt asserts that distortion was inherent in Magna Carta itself. In this sense, Holt notes that just as Coke himself used Magna Carta as a defence of 'ancient liberties' against the Stuart kings, the barons appealed to the laws of Edward the Confessor and Henry I to maintain what they alleged was ancient custom against the government of King John.[121] For Holt, the barons are just as guilty of distortion as Coke – perhaps even more so.[122] Hence, for Holt, it is not helpful to accuse Coke of distortion, because to distort a distortion is 'little more than venial' in his opinion.[123] In sum, then,

---

[112] Ibid., 4.
[113] Ibid.
[114] Ibid., 4–5.
[115] Ibid., 5.
[116] Ibid.
[117] Ibid., 5–6.
[118] Ibid., 6.
[119] Ibid., 6–7.
[120] Ibid., 7–8.
[121] Ibid., 20.
[122] Ibid.
[123] Ibid., 21.

following Holt, it is unjustified to treat Magna Carta as a kind of datum from which all subsequent departure is unjustified.[124]

While not accusing Coke of distortion, we can legitimately ask whether his politically motivated interpretation of Magna Carta constitutes history. Both Pocock and Holt show that Coke and his allies assimilated the past to the present by recalling to mind Magna Carta with the intention of joining an intractable present with a known and unproblematic past in order to stabilise the practical present. This should not be understood solely in terms of active politics. Coke's interpretation also provided stability as to the meaning of the law and liberty and created a world of sense. Thus, following Oakeshott's admittedly sharp distinction between history and the practical past and apply-ing Oakeshott's analysis of a barrister's use of Magna Carta to Coke's inter-pretation, we can conclude that he was not appealing to an 'historically understood recorded past, an utterance whose authentic meaning is hidden in long-defunct local circumstance'.[125] Rather, Coke sought in Magna Carta 'something that could be represented as a relevant and persuasive analogy to support his case'.[126] In other words, Coke, like the barons and Normans before him, had recourse to the storehouse of emblems, and, according to Oakeshott, 'as a storehouse of emblems of just procedure [Magna Carta] has long been credited with almost magical authority'.[127]

In his defence of Coke's interpretation of Magna Carta, Holt seems to be suggesting that the seventeenth-century chief justice did not make illegitimate use of Magna Carta. Nevertheless, historians note that Coke's commentary on Magna Carta 'had a number of erroneous or exaggerated statements in it'.[128] In this sense, there was 'often too much of Coke in Coke's jurisprudence'.[129] It is my position that Oakeshott's concept of the practical past is helpful in order to understand the nature and purpose of Coke's engagement with the past. Coke's use of Magna Carta is not illegitimate; it is only that his interpretation of the document is not historical. It is important to emphasise that this in no way diminishes Coke's thinking and work. The practical past is not an inferior type of past – it is simply philosophically different from history. The practical or legendary past is indispensable to an articulate civilised life, as the legend of Magna Carta well shows. Magna Carta occupies a central place in the legend of English politics which tells the story of English freedom. Fundamental to

[124] Ibid., 20.
[125] Oakeshott, *On History*, 46.
[126] Ibid., 46.
[127] Ibid.
[128] W. F. Swindler, *Magna Carta: Legend and Legacy* (Indianapolis: Bobbs-Merrill Company, Inc, 1965), 195.
[129] Ibid., 166.

the story is the message transmitted by Magna Carta that government is subject to the law. By recalling Magna Carta to mind and assimilating the past to the present, Coke at once invoked and augmented the English political legend.

CONCLUSION

'The past is past only for history; elsewhere it is present. The event has gone; but it lives on in fable, in gesture, in turns of speech, in habit, and above all in myth'.[130] The event of Magna Carta has gone. The year 2015 marks 800 years since Pope Innocent III 'instructed John to come to an understanding with and make peace with the magnates of England in 1215'.[131] Magna Carta, however, lives on as myth and as the core element of the English legend of political life. The year 2015 also marks fifty years since the publication of J. C. Holt's *Magna Carta*, one of the most important contributions to Magna Carta scholarship, as well as of Oakeshott's review of the work. These anniversaries present us with the opportunity to reflect upon the Great Charter and consider its historical and political meanings.

By stating that the past is past only for history, Oakeshott establishes a sharp distinction between history and the legendary past. As the case of Magna Carta shows, such a sharp distinction makes it difficult for an authentically historical understanding to emerge from the authority of the legendary past. Nevertheless, Oakeshott is of the opinion that an historical understanding of Magna Carta did eventually emerge, but not without difficulty.

The variance Oakeshott establishes between history and the legendary past is philosophical and has no hierarchical implications. That is, the legendary past is not an inferior or illegitimate type of past. Only, as the legend of English political life demonstrates, it has a political function. In this sense, beginning in the seventeenth century, it is around the survived event and document of Magna Carta that the modern legend of English politics has been constructed. English society, like all societies awakened to political self-consciousness, has constructed 'a legend of its own fortunes which it keeps up to date and in which is hidden its own understanding of its politics'.[132] A political society such as England constructs its legend with the objective of understanding its political experience and its manner of political thinking by 'the underlinings it makes in the book of its history'.[133] Thus, the legendary story of Magna Carta is

---

[130] M. Oakeshott, *Notebooks, 1922–86* (Exeter and Charlottesville: Imprint Academic, 2014), 422.
[131] Oakeshott, *Lectures*, 275.
[132] Oakeshott, *Rationalism in Politics*, 63.
[133] Ibid.

an underlining in the book of English history. Ultimately, this poetic construct, by means of the story it tells of freedom and the moral it transmits regarding the principle that authority is subject to the law, endows English society with its identity and a sense of self-consciousness and guards them thereafter. Therefore, the myth or legend of Magna Carta plays a fundamental political role in that it ensures solidarity amongst strangers by binding members of a political society to one another. To understand Magna Carta in this manner, as invoking the legendary past, in is no way pejorative.

Finally, as the example of the use made of Magna Carta by seventeenth-century jurists and historians led by Sir Edward Coke in their opposition to the Stuart kings demonstrates, the legendary past can also be invoked in the context of active politics. For this purpose, Magna Carta is by far the most successful and influential of emblems kept in the storehouse of past events and exemplary characters, utterances and situations. Its message is indubitable: the king is subject to the law, and the limits of the king's authority can be defined by a written document.[134]

Hence, Magna Carta has been elevated to iconic status. Holt asks why it rather than any other document became a 'sacred text, glossed, interpreted and extended'.[135] While it is true that the thirteenth-century document has become famous because it is interpreted as the first to guarantee basic civil liberties and freedom for all under the law,[136] Oakeshott's concepts of legends of political life and of the legendary past allow us to understand that its political role goes much deeper than this. Magna Carta symbolises English freedom, and the English political legend founds the English tradition of politics by recounting the story of English freedom and of the institutions which emerged to ensure its continuity. In sum, one could surmise that Oakeshott would consider Magna Carta to be the legendary foundation of English freedom and politics.

---

[134] Breay, *Magna Carta*, 48.
[135] Holt, *Magna Carta*, 21.
[136] Breay, *Magna Carta*, 46.

English Translation of Magna Carta (1215)

Here, we reproduced the original version of Magna Carta. The translation is from the British Library and comes with the following introductory note:[1]

In the charter itself the clauses are not numbered, and the text reads continuously. The translation sets out to convey the sense rather than the precise wording of the original Latin.

Articles in italics were omitted from all subsequent versions of Magna Carta. Articles in bold are still in force according to legislative.gov.uk, albeit based on the 1297 reissue of Magna Carta.[2]

JOHN, by the grace of God King of England, Lord of Ireland, Duke of Normandy and Aquitaine, and Count of Anjou, to his archbishops, bishops, abbots, earls, barons, justices, foresters, sheriffs, stewards, servants, and to all his officials and loyal subjects, Greeting.

KNOW THAT BEFORE GOD, for the health of our soul and those of our ancestors and heirs, to the honour of God, the exaltation of the holy Church, and the better ordering of our kingdom, at the advice of our reverend fathers Stephen, archbishop of Canterbury, primate of all England, and cardinal of the holy Roman Church, Henry archbishop of Dublin, William bishop of London, Peter bishop of Winchester, Jocelin bishop of Bath and Glastonbury, Hugh bishop of Lincoln, Walter Bishop of Worcester, William bishop of Coventry, Benedict bishop of Rochester, Master Pandulf subdeacon and member of the papal household, Brother Aymeric master of the knighthood of the Temple in England, William Marshal earl of Pembroke, William earl of Salisbury, William earl of Warren, William earl of Arundel, Alan de Galloway constable of Scotland, Warin Fitz Gerald, Peter Fitz Herbert, Hubert de Burgh seneschal of Poitou, Hugh de Neville, Matthew Fitz Herbert,

---

[1] Available from http://www.bl.uk/magna-carta/articles/magna-carta-english-translation.
[2] Articles in force are available at http://www.legislation.gov.uk/aep/Edw1cc1929/25/9/contents.

Thomas Basset, Alan Basset, Philip Daubeny, Robert de Roppeley, John
Marshal, John Fitz Hugh, and other loyal subjects:

(1) **FIRST, THAT WE HAVE GRANTED TO GOD, and by this present
    charter have confirmed for us and our heirs in perpetuity, that the
    English Church shall be free, and shall have its rights undiminished,
    and its liberties unimpaired.** That we wish this so to be observed,
    appears from the fact that of our own free will, before the outbreak of
    the present dispute between us and our barons, we granted and con-
    firmed by charter the freedom of the Church's elections – a right
    reckoned to be of the greatest necessity and importance to it – and
    caused this to be confirmed by Pope Innocent III. This freedom we
    shall observe ourselves, and desire to be observed in good faith by our
    heirs in perpetuity.

TO ALL FREE MEN OF OUR KINGDOM we have also granted, for us
and our heirs for ever, all the liberties written out below, to have and to keep
for them and their heirs, of us and our heirs:

(2) If any earl, baron, or other person that holds lands directly of the Crown,
    for military service, shall die, and at his death his heir shall be of full age
    and owe a 'relief', the heir shall have his inheritance on payment of the
    ancient scale of 'relief'. That is to say, the heir or heirs of an earl shall pay
    £100 for the entire earl's barony, the heir or heirs of a knight 100s. at most
    for the entire knight's 'fee', and any man that owes less shall pay less, in
    accordance with the ancient usage of 'fees'.

(3) But if the heir of such a person is under age and a ward, when he comes of
    age he shall have his inheritance without 'relief' or fine.

(4) The guardian of the land of an heir who is under age shall take from it only
    reasonable revenues, customary dues, and feudal services. He shall do this
    without destruction or damage to men or property. If we have given the
    guardianship of the land to a sheriff, or to any person answerable to us for the
    revenues, and he commits destruction or damage, we will exact compensa-
    tion from him, and the land shall be entrusted to two worthy and prudent
    men of the same 'fee', who shall be answerable to us for the revenues, or to
    the person to whom we have assigned them. If we have given or sold to
    anyone the guardianship of such land, and he causes destruction or damage,
    he shall lose the guardianship of it, and it shall be handed over to two worthy
    and prudent men of the same 'fee', who shall be similarly answerable to us.

(5) For so long as a guardian has guardianship of such land, he shall main-
    tain the houses, parks, fish preserves, ponds, mills, and everything else

pertaining to it, from the revenues of the land itself. When the heir comes of age, he shall restore the whole land to him, stocked with plough teams and such implements of husbandry as the season demands and the revenues from the land can reasonably bear.

(6) Heirs may be given in marriage, but not to someone of lower social standing. Before a marriage takes place, it shall be made known to the heir's next-of-kin.

(7) At her husband's death, a widow may have her marriage portion and inheritance at once and without trouble. She shall pay nothing for her dower, marriage portion, or any inheritance that she and her husband held jointly on the day of his death. She may remain in her husband's house for forty days after his death, and within this period her dower shall be assigned to her.

(8) No widow shall be compelled to marry, so long as she wishes to remain without a husband. But she must give security that she will not marry without royal consent, if she holds her lands of the Crown, or without the consent of whatever other lord she may hold them of.

(9) Neither we nor our officials will seize any land or rent in payment of a debt, so long as the debtor has movable goods sufficient to discharge the debt. A debtor's sureties shall not be distrained upon so long as the debtor himself can discharge his debt. If, for lack of means, the debtor is unable to discharge his debt, his sureties shall be answerable for it. If they so desire, they may have the debtor's lands and rents until they have received satisfaction for the debt that they paid for him, unless the debtor can show that he has settled his obligations to them.

(10) *If anyone who has borrowed a sum of money from Jews dies before the debt has been repaid, his heir shall pay no interest on the debt for so long as he remains under age, irrespective of whom he holds his lands. If such a debt falls into the hands of the Crown, it will take nothing except the principal sum specified in the bond.*

(11) *If a man dies owing money to Jews, his wife may have her dower and pay nothing towards the debt from it. If he leaves children that are under age, their needs may also be provided for on a scale appropriate to the size of his holding of lands. The debt is to be paid out of the residue, reserving the service due to his feudal lords. Debts owed to persons other than Jews are to be dealt with similarly.*

(12) *No 'scutage' or 'aid' may be levied in our kingdom without its general consent, unless it is for the ransom of our person, to make our eldest son a knight, and (once) to marry our eldest daughter. For these purposes only a*

reasonable 'aid' may be levied. 'Aids' from the city of London are to be treated similarly.

(13) **The city of London shall enjoy all its ancient liberties and free customs, both by land and by water. We also will and grant that all other cities, boroughs, towns, and ports shall enjoy all their liberties and free customs.**

(14) *To obtain the general consent of the realm for the assessment of an 'aid' – except in the three cases specified above – or a 'scutage', we will cause the archbishops, bishops, abbots, earls, and greater barons to be summoned individually by letter. To those who hold lands directly of us we will cause a general summons to be issued, through the sheriffs and other officials, to come together on a fixed day (of which at least forty days notice shall be given) and at a fixed place. In all letters of summons, the cause of the summons will be stated. When a summons has been issued, the business appointed for the day shall go forward in accordance with the resolution of those present, even if not all those who were summoned have appeared.*

(15) *In future we will allow no one to levy an 'aid' from his free men, except to ransom his person, to make his eldest son a knight, and (once) to marry his eldest daughter. For these purposes only a reasonable 'aid' may be levied.*

(16) No man shall be forced to perform more service for a knight's 'fee', or other free holding of land, than is due from it.

(17) Ordinary lawsuits shall not follow the royal court around, but shall be held in a fixed place.

(18) Inquests of novel disseisin, mort d'ancestor, and darrein presentment shall be taken only in their proper county court. We ourselves, or in our absence abroad our chief justice, will send two justices to each county four times a year, and these justices, with four knights of the county elected by the county itself, shall hold the assizes in the county court, on the day and in the place where the court meets.

(19) If any assizes cannot be taken on the day of the county court, as many knights and freeholders shall afterwards remain behind, of those who have attended the court, as will suffice for the administration of justice, having regard to the volume of business to be done.

(20) For a trivial offence, a free man shall be fined only in proportion to the degree of his offence, and for a serious offence correspondingly, but not so heavily as to deprive him of his livelihood. In the same way, a merchant shall be spared his merchandise, and a villein the implements of his husbandry, if they fall upon the mercy of a royal court. None of these fines shall be imposed except by the assessment on oath of reputable men of the neighbourhood.

(21) Earls and barons shall be fined only by their equals, and in proportion to the gravity of their offence.

(22) A fine imposed upon the lay property of a clerk in holy orders shall be assessed upon the same principles, without reference to the value of his ecclesiastical benefice.

(23) No town or person shall be forced to build bridges over rivers except those with an ancient obligation to do so.

(24) No sheriff, constable, coroners, or other royal officials are to hold lawsuits that should be held by the royal justices.

(25) *Every county, hundred, wapentake, and riding shall remain at its ancient rent, without increase, except the royal demesne manors.*

(26) If at the death of a man who holds a lay 'fee' of the Crown, a sheriff or royal official produces royal letters patent of summons for a debt due to the Crown, it shall be lawful for them to seize and list movable goods found in the lay 'fee' of the dead man to the value of the debt, as assessed by worthy men. Nothing shall be removed until the whole debt is paid, when the residue shall be given over to the executors to carry out the dead man's will. If no debt is due to the Crown, all the movable goods shall be regarded as the property of the dead man, except the reasonable shares of his wife and children.

(27) *If a free man dies intestate, his movable goods are to be distributed by his next-of-kin and friends, under the supervision of the Church. The rights of his debtors are to be preserved.*

(28) No constable or other royal official shall take corn or other movable goods from any man without immediate payment, unless the seller voluntarily offers postponement of this.

(29) No constable may compel a knight to pay money for castle-guard if the knight is willing to undertake the guard in person, or with reasonable excuse to supply some other fit man to do it. A knight taken or sent on military service shall be excused from castle-guard for the period of this service.

(30) No sheriff, royal official, or other person shall take horses or carts for transport from any free man, without his consent.

(31) Neither we nor any royal official will take wood for our castle, or for any other purpose, without the consent of the owner.

(32) We will not keep the lands of people convicted of felony in our hand for longer than a year and a day, after which they shall be returned to the lords of the 'fees' concerned.

(33) All fish-weirs shall be removed from the Thames, the Medway, and throughout the whole of England, except on the sea coast.

(34) The writ called precipe shall not in future be issued to anyone in respect of any holding of land, if a free man could thereby be deprived of the right of trial in his own lord's court.

(35) There shall be standard measures of wine, ale, and corn (the London quarter), throughout the kingdom. There shall also be a standard width of dyed cloth, russet, and haberject, namely two ells within the selvedges. Weights are to be standardised similarly.

(36) In future nothing shall be paid or accepted for the issue of a writ of inquisition of life or limbs. It shall be given gratis, and not refused.

(37) If a man holds land of the Crown by 'fee-farm', 'socage', or 'burgage', and also holds land of someone else for knight's service, we will not have guardianship of his heir, nor of the land that belongs to the other person's 'fee', by virtue of the 'fee-farm', 'socage', or 'burgage', unless the 'fee-farm' owes knight's service. We will not have the guardianship of a man's heir, or of land that he holds of someone else, by reason of any small property that he may hold of the Crown for a service of knives, arrows, or the like.

(38) In future no official shall place a man on trial upon his own unsupported statement, without producing credible witnesses to the truth of it.

(39) No free man shall be seized or imprisoned, or stripped of his rights or possessions, or outlawed or exiled, or deprived of his standing in any other way, nor will we proceed with force against him, or send others to do so, except by the lawful judgement of his equals or by the law of the land.

(40) To no one will we sell, to no one deny or delay right or justice.

(41) All merchants may enter or leave England unharmed and without fear, and may stay or travel within it, by land or water, for purposes of trade, free from all illegal exactions, in accordance with ancient and lawful customs. This, however, does not apply in time of war to merchants from a country that is at war with us. Any such merchants found in our country at the outbreak of war shall be detained without injury to their persons or property, until we or our chief justice have discovered how our own merchants are being treated in the country at war with us. If our own merchants are safe they shall be safe too.

(42) *In future it shall be lawful for any man to leave and return to our kingdom unharmed and without fear, by land or water, preserving his allegiance to us, except in time of war, for some short period, for the common benefit of the realm. People that have been imprisoned or outlawed in accordance with the law of the land, people from a country that is at war with us, and merchants – who shall be dealt with as stated above – are excepted from this provision.*

(43) If a man holds lands of any 'escheat' such as the 'honour' of Wallingford, Nottingham, Boulogne, Lancaster, or of other 'escheats' in our hand that are baronies, at his death his heir shall give us only the 'relief' and service that he would have made to the baron, had the barony been in the baron's hand. We will hold the 'escheat' in the same manner as the baron held it.

(44) People who live outside the forest need not in future appear before the royal justices of the forest in answer to general summonses, unless they are actually involved in proceedings or are sureties for someone who has been seized for a forest offence.

(45) *We will appoint as justices, constables, sheriffs, or other officials, only men that know the law of the realm and are minded to keep it well.*

(46) All barons who have founded abbeys, and have charters of English kings or ancient tenure as evidence of this, may have guardianship of them when there is no abbot, as is their due.

(47) All forests that have been created in our reign shall at once be disafforested. River-banks that have been enclosed in our reign shall be treated similarly.

(48) *All evil customs relating to forests and warrens, foresters, warreners, sheriffs and their servants, or river-banks and their wardens, are at once to be investigated in every county by twelve sworn knights of the county, and within forty days of their enquiry the evil customs are to be abolished completely and irrevocably. But we, or our chief justice if we are not in England, are first to be informed.*

(49) *We will at once return all hostages and charters delivered up to us by Englishmen as security for peace or for loyal service.*

(50) *We will remove completely from their offices the kinsmen of Gerard de Athée, and in future they shall hold no offices in England. The people in question are Engelard de Cigogné, Peter, Guy, and Andrew de Chanceaux, Guy de Cigogné, Geoffrey de Martigny and his brothers, Philip Marc and his brothers, with Geoffrey his nephew, and all their followers.*

(51) *As soon as peace is restored, we will remove from the kingdom all the foreign knights, bowmen, their attendants, and the mercenaries that have come to it, to its harm, with horses and arms.*

(52) *To any man whom we have deprived or dispossessed of lands, castles, liberties, or rights, without the lawful judgement of his equals, we will at once restore these. In cases of dispute the matter shall be resolved by the judgement of the twenty-five barons referred to below in the clause for securing the peace. In cases, however, where a man was deprived or dispossessed of something without the lawful judgement of his equals by our father King Henry or our brother King Richard, and it remains in our*

hands or is held by others under our warranty, we shall have respite for the period commonly allowed to Crusaders, unless a lawsuit had been begun, or an enquiry had been made at our order, before we took the Cross as a Crusader. On our return from the Crusade, or if we abandon it, we will at once render justice in full.

(53) We shall have similar respite in rendering justice in connexion with forests that are to be disafforested, or to remain forests, when these were first afforested by our father Henry or our brother Richard; with the guardianship of lands in another person's 'fee', when we have hitherto had this by virtue of a 'fee' held of us for knight's service by a third party; and with abbeys founded in another person's 'fee', in which the lord of the 'fee' claims to own a right. On our return from the Crusade, or if we abandon it, we will at once do full justice to complaints about these matters.

(54) No one shall be arrested or imprisoned on the appeal of a woman for the death of any person except her husband.

(55) All fines that have been given to us unjustly and against the law of the land, and all fines that we have exacted unjustly, shall be entirely remitted or the matter decided by a majority judgement of the twenty-five barons referred to below in the clause for securing the peace together with Stephen, archbishop of Canterbury, if he can be present, and such others as he wishes to bring with him. If the archbishop cannot be present, proceedings shall continue without him, provided that if any of the twenty-five barons has been involved in a similar suit himself, his judgement shall be set aside, and someone else chosen and sworn in his place, as a substitute for the single occasion, by the rest of the twenty-five.

(56) If we have deprived or dispossessed any Welshmen of lands, liberties, or anything else in England or in Wales, without the lawful judgement of their equals, these are at once to be returned to them. A dispute on this point shall be determined in the Marches by the judgement of equals. English law shall apply to holdings of land in England, Welsh law to those in Wales, and the law of the Marches to those in the Marches. The Welsh shall treat us and ours in the same way.

(57) In cases where a Welshman was deprived or dispossessed of anything, without the lawful judgement of his equals, by our father King Henry or our brother King Richard, and it remains in our hands or is held by others under our warranty, we shall have respite for the period commonly allowed to Crusaders, unless a lawsuit had been begun, or an enquiry had been made at our order, before we took the Cross as a Crusader. But on our return from the Crusade, or if we abandon it, we will at once do full justice according to the laws of Wales and the said regions.

(58) *We will at once return the son of Llywelyn, all Welsh hostages, and the charters delivered to us as security for the peace.*

(59) *With regard to the return of the sisters and hostages of Alexander, king of Scotland, his liberties and his rights, we will treat him in the same way as our other barons of England, unless it appears from the charters that we hold from his father William, formerly king of Scotland, that he should be treated otherwise. This matter shall be resolved by the judgement of his equals in our court.*

(60) All these customs and liberties that we have granted shall be observed in our kingdom in so far as concerns our own relations with our subjects. Let all men of our kingdom, whether clergy or laymen, observe them similarly in their relations with their own men.

(61) SINCE WE HAVE GRANTED ALL THESE THINGS *for God, for the better ordering of our kingdom, and to allay the discord that has arisen between us and our barons, and since we desire that they shall be enjoyed in their entirety, with lasting strength, for ever, we give and grant to the barons the following security:*

The barons shall elect twenty-five of their number to keep, and cause to be observed with all their might, the peace and liberties granted and confirmed to them by this charter.

If we, our chief justice, our officials, or any of our servants offend in any respect against any man, or transgress any of the articles of the peace or of this security, and the offence is made known to four of the said twenty-five barons, they shall come to us – or in our absence from the kingdom to the chief justice – to declare it and claim immediate redress. If we, or in our absence abroad the chief justice, make no redress within forty days, reckoning from the day on which the offence was declared to us or to him, the four barons shall refer the matter to the rest of the twenty-five barons, who may distrain upon and assail us in every way possible, with the support of the whole community of the land, by seizing our castles, lands, possessions, or anything else saving only our own person and those of the queen and our children, until they have secured such redress as they have determined upon. Having secured the redress, they may then resume their normal obedience to us.

Any man who so desires may take an oath to obey the commands of the twenty-five barons for the achievement of these ends, and to join with them in assailing us to the utmost of his power. We give public and free permission to take this oath to any man who so desires, and at no time will we prohibit any man from taking it. Indeed, we will compel any of our subjects who are unwilling to take it to swear it at our command.

If one of the twenty-five barons dies or leaves the country, or is prevented in any other way from discharging his duties, the rest of them shall choose another baron in his place, at their discretion, who shall be duly sworn in as they were.

In the event of disagreement among the twenty-five barons on any matter referred to them for decision, the verdict of the majority present shall have the same validity as a unanimous verdict of the whole twenty-five, whether these were all present or some of those summoned were unwilling or unable to appear.

The twenty-five barons shall swear to obey all the above articles faithfully, and shall cause them to be obeyed by others to the best of their power.

We will not seek to procure from anyone, either by our own efforts or those of a third party, anything by which any part of these concessions or liberties might be revoked or diminished. Should such a thing be procured, it shall be null and void and we will at no time make use of it, either ourselves or through a third party.

(62) *We have remitted and pardoned fully to all men any ill-will, hurt, or grudges that have arisen between us and our subjects, whether clergy or laymen, since the beginning of the dispute. We have in addition remitted fully, and for our own part have also pardoned, to all clergy and laymen any offences committed as a result of the said dispute between Easter in the sixteenth year of our reign (i.e. 1215) and the restoration of peace.*

In addition we have caused letters patent to be made for the barons, bearing witness to this security and to the concessions set out above, over the seals of Stephen archbishop of Canterbury, Henry archbishop of Dublin, the other bishops named above, and Master Pandulf.

(63) IT IS ACCORDINGLY OUR WISH AND COMMAND *that the English Church shall be free, and that men in our kingdom shall have and keep all these liberties, rights, and concessions, well and peaceably in their fullness and entirety for them and their heirs, of us and our heirs, in all things and all places for ever.*

Both we and the barons have sworn that all this shall be observed in good faith and without deceit. Witness the above-mentioned people and many others.

Given by our hand in the meadow that is called Runnymede, between Windsor and Staines, on the fifteenth day of June in the seventeenth year of our reign.

Bibliography

AB, R (on the application of) v. Secretary of State for the Home Department [2013], EWHC (Admin).

Ackerman, Bruce, *The Failure of the Founding Fathers: Jefferson, Marshall, and the Rise of Presidential Democracy* (Cambridge, MA: Belknap Press of Harvard University Press, 2005).

Albertus, M. and Menaldo, Victor A., 'Dictators as Founding Fathers? The Role of Constitutions under Autocracy', *Economics & Politics* 24 (2011), 279–306.

'The Political Economy of Autocratic Constitutions', in *Constitutions in Authoritarian Regimes*, eds. Tom Ginsburg and Alberto Simpser (Cambridge: Cambridge University Press, 2014), 53–82.

Alexander, James, 'A Brief Narrative of the Case and Trial of John Peter Zenger' (1736), in Stanley N. Katz (ed.), *The Case and Trial of John Peter Zenger* (Cambridge, MA: Harvard University Press, 1989), 78, 100–01.

Ali v. State [2008], FJCA.

Allison, J. W. F., 'Fuller's Analysis of Polycentric Disputes and the Limits of Adjudication', *Cambridge Law Journal* 53 (1994), 367, 371.

Amar, Akhil Reed, 'Fourth Amendment First Principles', *Harvard Law Review* 107 (1994), 757, 775–78.

The Bill of Rights: Creation and Reconstruction (New Haven: Yale University Press, 1998).

Amnesty International, Amicus Brief filed in 2012 WL 174238 at 9.

Amnesty International, *Amnesty International Fair Trial Manual* (2014), available at http://www.amnesty.org/en/fairtrials.

Angelo, A. H. and Townend, Andrew, 'Pitcairn: A Commentary', *NZJPIL* 1 (2003), 229, 230.

The Antelope, 23 U.S. (10 Wheat) 66, 123 (1825).

Antigua Slave Code Act 1697.

'Appeal Judges Resign over Gates' Actions', *Fiji Times Online*, http://www.fijitimes.com/story/aspxid=69814 (accessed 7 February 2014).

Ashley, Maurice, *Magna Carta in the Seventeenth Century* (Charlottesville: University Press of Virginia, 1965).

Atkinson v. Namale West Inc [2012], FJHC.

Attlee Foundation, Lecture, 11 April 2006, 'Democracy, The Rule of Law and the Role of Judges', 20.

Australian Government, Department of Foreign Affairs and Trade, Website, http://aid.dfat.gov.au/countries/pacific/Pages/home.aspx (accessed 7 February 2014).

Australian Government, 'International Legal Assistance' run by Commonwealth Attorney-General's department, available at http://www.ag.gov.au/Internatonalre lations/InternationalLegalAssistance/Pages/default.aspx (accessed 23 March 2014).

Baar, Carl, 'Court Delay Data as Social Science Evidence: The Supreme Court of Canada and "Trial within a Reasonable Time"', *Justice System Journal* 19 (1997), 123–44.

Baker, John (ed.), *Oxford History of the Laws of England: 871–1216* (Oxford: Oxford University Press, 2013).

Barbados Slave Code Act 1661, Barbados MSS Laws, 1645–1682, Colonial Office Series, Public Record Office, 30/2/16–26.

Barbados Slave Code Act 1664.

Barbados Slave Code Act 1674, P.R.O. *CO* 139/3.

Bavoro v. State [2011], FJHC.

Bazeley, M. L., 'The Extent of the English Forest in the Thirteenth Century', in *Transactions of the Royal Historical Society*, vol. 4 (Cambridge: Cambridge University Press, 1921), 141–72.

Beckett, Gilbert à, *The Comic Blackstone*, new ed. (Chicago: Callaghan and Cockcroft, 1870).

Beckles, Hilary McD, 'The "Hub of Empire": The Caribbean and Britain in the Seventeenth Century' in *The Origins of Empire*, ed. N. Canny (Oxford: Oxford University Press, 1998), 218.

Bell v. Director of Public Prosecutions [1985], AC.

Berger, Raoul, 'Doctor Bonham's Case: Statutory Construction or Constitutional Theory?' *University of Pennsylvania Law Review* 117 (1969), 521–45.

Bhika v. State [2008], FJHC.

The Bill of Rights, 1689. Available at http://www.legislation.gov.uk/aep/WillandMar Sess2/1/2/introduction (last accessed 6 December 2014).

Birrel, J., 'Common Rights in the Medieval Forest: Disputes and Conflict in the Thirteenth Century', *Past and Present* 17 (1987), 48.

Black, Barbara A., 'The Constitution of Empire: The Case for the Colonists', *University of Pennsylvania Law Review* 124 (1976), 1198–203.

Blackburn, R., *The Overthrow of Colonial Slavery: 1776–1848* (London: Verso, 1988).

Blackstone, William, *Commentaries on the Laws of England*, 4 vols. (Oxford: Clarendon Press, 1765).

Blaydes, Lisa and Chaney, Eric, 'The Feudal Revolution and Europe's Rise: Political Divergence of the Christian West and the Muslim World before 1500 CE', *American Political Science Review* 107 (2013), 16–34.

Bogdanor, Vernon, *The New British Constitution* (Oxford: Hart, 2009).

Boman, Dennis K., *Hamilton Gamble: Dred Scott Dissenter and Missouri's Civil War Governor* (Baton Rouge: Louisiana State University Press, 2006).

Boolell v. State of Mauritius (2006) [2012], 1 WLR.

Botein, Stephen, *Early American Law and Society* (New York: Knopf, 1983).

Bowman v. Middleton, 1 Bay 252 (SC 1792).

Bracton, Henry de, *The Laws and Customs of England*, Bracton Online, 4 vols. (Harvard online library), vol. IV, available at http://bracton.law.harvard.edu/Unframed/English/v4/366.htm#TITLE501 (last accessed 9 December 2014).

Breay, C., *Magna Carta: Manuscripts and Myths* (London: British Library, 2002), 7.

Brennan, F. and Packer, J. (eds.), *Colonialism, Slavery, Reparations and Trade* (New York: Routledge, 2012).

British Library, *Magna Carta*, available at http://www.bl.uk/onlinegallery/onlineex/histtexts/magna/ (last accessed 10 December 2014).

Burns, Robert I. and Parsons, Samuel Scott (eds.), *Las Siete Partidas, Vol. 1: The Medieval Church: The World of Clerics and Laymen* (Philadelphia: University of Pennsylvania Press, 2001).

Butterfield, Herbert, *Magna Carta in the Historiography of the Sixteenth and Seventeenth Centuries* (Reading, UK: University of Reading, 1969).

Calvin v. Smith, in 7 Coke's Rep. 1a 77 Eng. Rep. 377, 401 (K.B. 1608).

The Cambridge History of the British Empire: Volume II The Growth of the New Empire 1783–1870 (London: Cambridge University Press, 1940).

Cameron, David, 'British values aren't optional, they are vital.' *Mail* on Sunday, 15 June 2014, available at http://www.dailymail.co.uk/debate/article-2658171/DAVID-CAMERON-British-values-arent-optional-theyre-vital-Thats-I-promote-EVERY-school-As-row-rages-Trojan-Horse-takeover-classrooms-Prime-Minister-delivers-uncompromising-pledge.html.

Carlin, Martha and Crouch, David (eds.), *Lost Letters of Medieval Life: English Society, 1200–1250* (Philadelphia: University of Pennsylvania Press, 2013).

Carmona v. Ward, 439 U.S. (1979).

Carter v. R [1986], 1 SCR.

Center for the Administration of Criminal Law, Amicus Brief filed in 2009 WL 2236773.

Centre for Analysis and Social Exclusion, 'Research Report to Inform the Debate about a Bill of Rights and a Written Constitution, Case Research Report 61' (2010).

Certification of the Constitution of the Republic of South Africa (CCT 23/1996).

Charles v. R [2000], 1 WLR (PC).

The Charter of the Forests 1217.

Chemerinsky, Erwin, 'The Constitution and Punishment', *Stanford Law Review* 56 (2004), 1049, 1063–65.

Cheney, C., 'The Eve of Magna Carta', Lecture delivered in the John Rylands Library, University of Manchester, on 11 May 1995.

Christian v. R [2007], 2 AC (PC).

Clark, Bradford R., 'The Eleventh Amendment and the Nature of the Union', *Harvard Law Review* 123 (2010), 1905–06.

Clark, D., 'The Icon of liberty: The Status and Role of Magna Carta in Australian and New Zealand Law', *Melbourne University Law Review* 24 (2000), 866.

Clayton, Ruby and Chaisson, Angela, 'Waiting for Justice', Precedent, 28 June 2013, available at http://lawandstyle.ca/waiting-for-justice/ (last accessed 14 April 2014).

Cohen, Elizabeth F., 'Jus Tempus in the Magna Carta: The Sovereignty of Time in Modern Politics and Citizenship', *PS: Political Science* 43 (2010), 463–66.

Coke, Edward, *The Reports of Sir Edward Coke, Knt. In Thirteen Parts Reprinted in New Edition*, 13 vols. (London: Joseph Butterworth and Son, 1826) (first published 1605).

Commons Debates 1628 (19 March–April 1628), Robert C. Johnson and Maija Jansson Cole (eds.), 4 vols. (New Haven: Yale University Press, 1977), vol. II, 357–58.

The Second Part of the Institutes of the Laws of England (London: M. Fleffer and R. Young, 1642).

Colbourn, H. Trevor, *The Lamp of Experience: Whig History and the Intellectual Origins of the American Revolution* (Chapel Hill: University of North Carolina Press, 1965).

Collins v. R [2008], NBPC 53 (New Brunswick Prov Ct)[8]–[9].

Columbia v. Okely, 17 U.S. (1819).

The Comparative Constitutions Project (CCP), available at http://comparativeconstitutionsproject.org/ (last accessed 24 November 2014)

Conor, Hanly, 'The Decline of Civil Jury Trial in Nineteenth-Century England', *Journal of Legal History* 26 (2005), 255–59, 269–78.

Constitution of Fiji 1970 as a Schedule to the Fiji Independence Order 1970 (UK), available from Heinonline at http://heinonline.org/HOL/Page?collection=cow&handle=hein.cow/ctituson0002&id=135 (last accessed 11 December 2014).

Constitution of Fiji 1988. Available from Heinonline at http://heinonline.org/HOL/COWShow?collection=cow&cow_id=144 (last accessed 11 December 2014).

Constitution of Fiji (Promulgation) Decree 1990. Available from Heinonline at http://heinonline.org/HOL/Page?handle=hein.cow/zzfj0001&collection=cow (last accessed 11 December 2014).

Constitution of Fiji 1997.

Constitution Of Fiji 2013, *Constitute*, available at https://www.constituteproject.org/constitution/Fiji_2013 (last accessed 10 December 2014).

Constitution of the Independent State of Samoa 1962 (rev. 2010), Constitute available at https://www.constituteproject.org/constitution/Samoa_2010 (last accessed 10 December 2014).

Constitution of Jamaica 1962 (rev. 1994), *Constitute*, available at https://www.constituteproject.org/constitution/Jamaica_1994 (last accessed 10 December 2014).

Constitution of Kiribati 1979 (rev. 1995), *Constitute*, available at https://www.constituteproject.org/constitution/Kiribati_1995 (last accessed 10 December 2014).

Constitution of Maryland 1776. Avalon Project, available at http://avalon.law.yale.edu/17th_century/ma02.asp (last accessed 6 December 2014).

Constitution of Massachusetts, 1780. Available at http://www.nhinet.org/ccs/docs/ma-1780.htm (last accessed 6 December 2014).

Constitution of Nauru 1968, *Constitute* available at https://www.constituteproject.org/constitution/Nauru_1968 (last accessed 10 December 2014).

Constitution of New Hampshire 1784. Available from the New Hampshire Government at http://www.nh.gov/constitution/billofrights.html (last accessed 6 December 2014).

Constitution of New York 1777, Avalon project, available at http://avalon.law.yale.edu/18th_century/ny01.asp (last accessed 6 December 2014).

Constitution of North Carolina, 1776. Available at http://www.ncga.state.nc.us/legislation/constitution/ncconstitution.html (last accessed 6 December 2014).

Constitution of Papua New Guinea 1975 (rev. 2014) *Constitute*, available at https://www.constituteproject.org/constitution/Papua_New_Guinea_2014 (last accessed 10 December 2014).

Constitution of the Republic of Vanuatu 1980 (rev. 1983), Constitute, available at https://www.constituteproject.org/constitution/Vanuatu_1983 (last accessed 10 December 2014).

Constitution of Solomon Islands 1978 (rev 2009). *Constitute*, available at https://www.constituteproject.org/constitution/Solomon_Islands_2009 (last accessed 10 December 2014).

Constitution of South Carolina 1778, Avalon project, available at http://avalon.law.yale.edu/18th_century/sco2.asp (last accessed 6 December 2014).

Constitution of South Carolina 1790. Available at http://emoglen.law.columbia.edu/twiki/pub/AmLegalHist/TheEstablishedChurchInSouthCarolina/S.C._Constitution_of_1790.pdf (last accessed 6 December 2014).

Constitution of the State of New York, 1938. Available from the New York State Library at http://www.nysl.nysed.gov/scandocs/nyconstitution.htm (last accessed 6 December 2014).

Constitution of Tuvalu 1986, Constitute, available at https://www.constituteproject.org/constitution/Tuvalu_1986?lang=en (last accessed 10 December 2014).

Constitution of the United States of America 1789 (rev. 1992), Constitute, available at: https://www.constituteproject.org/constitution/United_States_of_America_1992 (last accessed 6 December 2014).

Constitution of Virginia, 1776. Available at http://www.nhinet.org/ccs/docs/va-1776.htm (last accessed 6 December 2014).

Convention on the Elimination of All Forms of Discrimination Against Women.

Convention on the Rights of the Child 1989.

Coronation Oath of Henry I, 1100.

Corrin, Jennifer and Paterson, Don, *Introduction to South Pacific Law*, 3rd ed. (South Yarra, Vic: Palgrave MacMillan, 2011).

Coss, Peter, *The Origins of the English Gentry* (Cambridge: Cambridge University Press, 2003).

Criminal Procedure Decree 2009 (Fiji) s 290(1)(f).

'Crown apologizes for rape case delay', CBC News (Calgary) online, 3 December 2009 at http://www.cbc.ca/news/canada/calgary/crown-apologizes-for-rape-case-delay-1.822427 (last accessed 16 April 2014).

Dawson v. Public Prosecutor [2010], VUCA (Vanuatu CA).

de Freitas v. Benny [1976], AC.

de Tocqueville, Alexis, *Democracy in America*, J. P. Mayer (ed.), George Lawrence (trans.) (New York: Harper Perennial, 1969), 270–76.

Declaration and Resolves of the First Continental Congress in October 14, 1774. Avalon project, available at http://avalon.law.yale.edu/18th_century/resolves.asp (last accessed 6 December 2014).

The Delaware Bill of Rights of 1776. Available at http://www.jstor.org/stable/1834141 (last accessed 6 December 2014).

Dicey, A. V., *Introduction to the Study of the Law of the Constitution*, 10th ed. (London: Macmillan & Co Ltd, 1959).

DPP v. Nasralla [1967], 2 AC 238.

Draper, N., *The Price of Emancipation: Slave-Ownership, Compensation and British Society at the End of Slavery* (Cambridge: Cambridge University Press, 2010).

Drayton, William Henry, *A letter from freeman of South-Carolina, to the deputies of North-America, assembled in the high court of Congress at Philadelphia* (Charleston: Peter Timothy, 1774).

Dupont, J., *The Common Law Abroad: Constitutional and Legal Legacy of the British Empire* (Littleton, CO: Fred B. Rothman Publications, 2001.

Dyer, Justin Buckley, 'Slavery and the Magna Carta in the Development of Anglo-American Constitutionalism', *PS: Political Science* 43 (2010) 479–82.

Eckle v. Federal Republic of Germany [1982], 5 EHRR 1[72] cited in R v. Christian (No 2).

Elkins, Zachary, 2012, 'Magna Carta Abroad'. Presentation at the National Archives in Washington DC on 17 February 2012.

Elkins, Zachary, Ginsburg, Tom and Melton, James, 'Comments on Law and Versteeg: The Declining Influence of the U.S. Constitution', NYU Law Review 87 (2012), 2088–101.

Elliot, Jonathan (ed.), *The Debates in the Several State Conventions of the Adoption of the Federal Constitution*, 2nd ed., 5 vols. (1836), vol. III.

Engdahl, David E., 'Immunity and Accountability for Positive Government Wrongs', *University of Colorado Law Review* 44 (1972), 1, 14, 19.

Engel, Pál, *The Realm of St Stephen: A History of Medieval Hungary, 895–1526* (London: I.B. Tauris, 2001).

'English Translation of Magna Carta', British Library, available at http://www.bl.uk/magna-carta/articles/magna-carta-english-translation (last accessed 21 November 2014).

Equiano, Olaudah, *The Interesting Narrative of the Life of Olaudah Equiano, Or Gustavus Vassus the African* (1789).

Farrand, Max, *The Records of the Federal Convention of 1787*, 3 vols., New Haven: Yale University Press, 1911.

Fiddes, Edward, 'Lord Mansfield and the Somersett Case', 50 *LQR* (1934), 499–500.

Fiji Constitution Amendment Act 1997 Revocation Decree 2009 in Republic of Fiji Islands Government Gazette, 10 April 2009, No 1.

Fitzjames, Stephen James, *A History of the Criminal Law of England*, 3 vols. (London: Macmillan, 1883).

Flemming v. Talagi [2010], NUHC 1 (Niue HC).

Flint River Steamboat Co v. Foster, 5 Ga. (1848).

Four-dollar bill, Maryland Provincial Currency, issued 26 July 1775, Maryland State Archives, Annapolis, Maryland, Vosloh Collection, SC 1267.

Fox, John, *The History of Contempt of Court* (Oxford: Clarendon Press, 1927).

French Declaration of the Rights of Man 1789. Avalon Project, available at http://avalon.law.yale.edu/18th_century/rightsof.asp (last accessed 6 December 2014).

Fuller, L. L., 'The Forms and Limits of Adjudication', 92 *Harvard LR* (1978), 353, 397–98.

Furman v. Georgia, 408 U.S. (1972).

Gandhi, Jennifer, *Political Institutions under Dictatorship* (New York: Cambridge University Press, 2008).

Gearty, C. and Mantouvalou, V., *Debating Social Rights* (Hart, 2011).

Genesis 4:13, The Bible.

Ghai, Yash and Cottrell, Jill, 'A Tale of Three Constitutions: Ethnicity and Politics in Fiji', 5 *International Journal of Constitutional Law* (2007), 639–69.

Gibson v. Attorney General [2010], 5 LRC (Caribbean Ct of Justice).

Gibson, C., *Empire's Crossroads: A History of the Caribbean from Columbus to the Present Day* (Basingstoke and Oxford: Macmillan, 2014).

Gilbert, William Schwenck and Sullivan, Arthur Seymour, *The Complete Plays of Gilbert and Sullivan* (New York: W.W. Norton, 1997).

Ginsburg, Tom, *Judicial Review in New Democracies: Constitutional Courts in Asian Cases* (Cambridge: Cambridge University Press, 2003).

Ginsburg, Tom and Moustafa, Tamir (eds.), *Rule by Law: The Politics of Courts in Authoritarian Regimes* (Cambridge: Cambridge University Press, 2008).

Goodhart, M., 'Origins and Universality in the Human Rights Debates: Cultural Essentialism and the Challenge of Globalization', *Human Rights Quarterly* 25 (2003), 935–64.

Gough, J. W., *Fundamental Law in English Constitutional History* (Oxford: Clarendon Press, 1955).

Goveia, E. V., *The West Indian Slave Laws of the Eighteenth Century* (Mona, Barbados: Caribbean Universities Press, 1970).

Government of the Republic of South Africa, the Premier of the Province of the Western Cape, Cape Metropolitan Council, Ostenberg Municipality v. Irene Grootboom and Others [2001], (1) SA 4 (CC) 2000 (11) BC LR 1 16) (CC).

Graber, Mark A., 'The Nonmajoritarian Difficulty: Legislative Deference to the Judiciary', *Studies in American Political Development* 7 (1993), 875–901.

Graham v. Florida, 560 U.S. (2010).

Graham, Erin R., Shipan, Charles R. and Volden, Craig, 'The Diffusion of Policy Diffusion Research in Political Science', *British Journal of Political Science* 43 (2013), 673–701.

Granucci, Anthony F., 'Nor Cruel and Unusual Punishment Inflicted: The Original Meaning', *California Law Review* 57 (1969), 839, 844–47.

Greene, J. P., *Exclusionary Empire: English Liberty Overseas, 1600–1900* (Cambridge: Cambridge University Press, 2010).

Gregson v. Gilbert [1783], 3 Dougl. 233.

Habeas Corpus Act 1679. Available at http://www.legislation.gov.uk/aep/Cha2/31/2/contents (last accessed 6 December 2014).

Habermas, J., *The Structural Transformation of the Public Sphere* (Cambridge, MA: MIT Press, 1989).

Hadfield, Gillian K. and Weingast, Barry, 'Microfoundations of the Rule of Law', *Annual Review of Political Science* 17 (2014), 21–42.

Haines, Charles Grove, *The American Doctrine of Judicial Supremacy* (New York: Macmillan Company, 1914).

Hall, C. D. G. (ed.), *The Treatises on the Laws and Customs of the Realm of England Commonly Called Glanvill* (Oxford: Clarendon Press, 1993).

Halsall, Paul, 'The Text of Magna Carta', Internet History Sourcebooks Project, 2014, available at http://www.fordham.edu/halsall/source/magnacarta.asp (last accessed 21 November 2014).

Hamburger, Philip, *Law and Judicial Duty* (Cambridge, MA: Harvard University Press, 2008).

Hamilton, Alexander, *The Federalist Papers* (J. and A. Milan, 1788).

'The Federalist No. 83' (1788), reprinted in Rossiter (ed.), *The Federalist Papers* (New York: Penguin, 1961).

Hamilton, Alexander, Madison, James and Jay, John, *The Federalist Papers*, ed. Clinton Rossiter (New York: Signet Classic, 2003).

Hancock, Tony, 'Hancock's Half Hour', *Twelve Angry Men*, BBC, 16 October 1959.

Hantos, Elemer, *The Magna Carta of the English and of the Hungarian Constitution: A Comparative View of the Law and Institutions of the Early Middle Ages*, 2005 ed. (Clark, NJ: Lawbook Exchange, Ltd, 1904).

Harmelin v. Michigan, 501 U.S. (1991).

Harrington, Matthew P., 'The Economic Origins of the Seventh Amendment', *Iowa Law Review* 87 (2001), 173–76, 186, 187.

Hauer, Stanley R., 'Thomas Jefferson and the Anglo-Saxon Language', *PMLA* 98 (1983), 880–81.

Hazeltine, H. D., 'Magna Carta and the U.S. Constitution', in Henry E. Malden (ed.), *Magna Carta Commemoration Essays* (London: Royal Historical Society, 1917)

Helmholz, R. H., 'Magna Carta and the Ius Commune', *University of Chicago Law Review* 66 (1999), 297–371.

Helmke, Gretchen and Rosenbluth, Frances, 'Regimes and the Rule of Law: Judicial Independence in Comparative Perspective', *Annual Review of Political Science* 12 (2009) 345–66.

Herron, Erik S. and Randazzo, Kirk A., 'The Relationship between Independence and Judicial Review in Post-Communist Courts', *Journal of Politics* 65 (2003), 422–38.

Heuman, G., 'From Slavery to Freedom' in P. D. Morgan and S. Hawkins (eds.), *Black Experience and the Empire* (Oxford: Oxford University Press, 2004), 141.

Hicks, Paul D., *Joseph Henry Lumpkin: Georgia's First Chief Justice* (Athens: University of Georgia Press, 2002).

Higgs v. Minister of National Security [2000], 2 AC.

Hill, Christopher, *Intellectual Origins of the English Revolution Revisited* (Oxford: Clarendon Press, 1997).

   The Century of Revolution, 1603–1714, 2nd ed. (London: Routledge, 2001).

   (ed.), *The World Turned Upside Down: Radical Ideas during the English Revolution* (London: Penguin, 1991).

The History, Civil and Commercial of the British Colonies in the West Indies (4th ed.) (London: John Stockdale, 1807).

Holt, J. C., *Magna Carta*, 2nd ed. (Cambridge: Cambridge University Press, 1992).

Holt's quote in 1706, 2 Salkeld 666.

Howard, A. E. Dick, *The Road to Runnymede: Magna Carta and Constitutionalism in America* (Charlottesville: University of Virginia Press, 1968).

Hudson, John, *The Formation of the English Common Law: Law and Society in England from the Norman Conquest to the Magna Carta* (London: Longman, 1996).

Huebner, Timothy S., *The Southern Judicial Tradition: State Judges and Sectional Distinctiveness, 1790–1890* (Athens: University of Georgia Press, 1999).

Hulsebosch, Daniel J., 'The Ancient Constitution and the Expanding Empire: Sir Edward Coke's British Jurisprudence', *Law and History Review* 21 (2003), 439–82.

   Constituting Empire: New York and the Transformation of Constitutionalism in the Atlantic World, 1664–1830 (Chapel Hill: University of North Carolina Press, 2005).

Hyams, Paul R., 'Tales from the Medieval Courtroom: The Fall and Rise of Thomas of Elderfield' (1985), available from CaltechAUTHORS online database at http://authors.library.caltech.edu/18859/1/HumsWP-0107.pdf (last accessed 25 November 2014).

Imperial Laws Application Act No 112 1988. Available from New Zealand Parliamentary Office at http://www.legislation.govt.nz/act/public/1988/0112/latest/whole.html #DLM135091 (last accessed 21 November 2014).

In re Application by Nand [2008], FJHC.

In re Buo [2007], PGNC (Papua New Guinea National Court).

Ingivald v. The State [1996], FJHC.

International Commission of Jurists, 'Nauru: Removal of Judges Violates Independence of Judiciary', 21 January 2014, press release available at http://www.icj.org/nauru-removal-of-judges-violates-independence-of-judiciary/ (last accessed 7 February 2014).

International Covenant on Civil and Political Rights, 1966. Available at http://www.ohchr.org/en/professionalinterest/pages/ccpr.aspx (last accessed 6 December 2014).

Ipsos MORI, State of the Nation Survey for the Joseph Rowntree Reform Trust, 21 April–8 May 1995, http://www.ipsos-mori.com/researchpublications/researcharchive/2753/State-of-the-Nation-Survey-1995.aspx (accessed 28 July 2014).

1998 survey, human rights, http://www.ipsos-mori.com/researchpublications/researcharchive/2111/Human-Rights.aspx.

Irvine, Lord, 'The Legacy of Magna Carta', 119 *LQR* (2003), 227.

Jackson v. Attorney-General [2005], UKHL 56.

Jago v. District Court of New South Wales [1989], 168 CLR (HCA).

Jamaica Slave Code Act 1664.

Jay, John, 'The Federalist No. 2' (1787), reprinted in Clinton Rossiter (ed.), *The Federalist Papers* (New York: Penguin, 1961).

Jenks, Edward, *The Myth of the Magna Carta* (London: Independent Review, 1904).

Jung, Courtney, Hirschl, Ran and Rosevear, Evan, 'Economic and Social Rights in NationalConstitutions', *American Journal of Comparative Law*, forthcoming, electronic copy available at http://ssrn.com/abstract=2349680 (last accessed 9 December 2014).

Kasper, Eric T., 'The Influence of Magna Carta in Limiting Executive Power in the War on Terror', *Political Science Quarterly* 126 (2011), 547–78.

Kelly v. R [2006], SBCA.

Kenyon, J. P., *Stuart England*, 2nd ed. (London: Penguin Books, 1985).

Kimel, D., *From Promise to Contract, towards a Liberal Theory of Contract* (Oxford: Hart Publishing, 2003).

Kimisi v. DPP [1990], SBHC.

King v. The Queen [1969], 1 AC.

King, Anthony, *The British Constitution* (Oxford: Oxford University Press, 2007).

Kinney, E. D., 'The International Human Right to Health: What Does This Mean for Our Nation and World?' *Indiana Law Review* 34 (2001), 1457.

Knight, Jack and Epstein, Lee, 'On the Struggle for Judicial Supremacy', *Law and Society Review* 30 (1996), 90.

Krikler, J., 'The Zong and the Lord Chief Justice', *History Workshop Journal* 64 (2007), 29–47.

Kyio v. R [2004], SBHC.

Kynaston, David, *Austerity Britain, 1945–51* (London: Bloomsbury Publishing, 2007).

La Porta, Rafael et al., 'Judicial Checks and Balances', *Journal of Political Economy* 1112 (2004), 445–70.

Lambarde, William, *Eirenarcha, or, The Office of Justices of Peace* (London: Ra. Newbery and H. Bynneman, 1581).
　Eirenarcha, available from Wythepedia at http://lawlibrary.wm.edu/wythepedia/index.php/Eirenarcha (last accessed 10 December 2014).

Landes, William M. and Posner, Richard A., 'The Independent Judiciary in an Interest-Group Perspective', *Journal of Law and Economics* 18 (1975), 875–901.

Langbein, John H., 'Chancellor Kent and the History of Legal Literature', *Columbia Law Review* 93 (1993), 566–69.
　'The Disappearance of Civil Jury Trial in the United States', *Yale Law Journal* 122 (2012), 522, 542–72.

Langbein, John H., Lettow Lerner, Renée and Smith, Bruce P., *History of the Common Law: The Development of Anglo-American Legal Institutions* (New York: Aspen Publishers, 2009).

Lassalle v. AG [1971], (WIR).

Law Reform Commission of Canada, Working Paper No. 67, Trial Within a Reasonable Time (1994), 11–14.

Leland, Anne and Oboroceanu, Mari-Jana, *American War and Military Operations Casualties: Lists and Statistics* (Washington, DC, 2010).

Lerner, Craig S., 'Sentenced to Confusion, *Miller v. Alabama* and the Coming Wave of Eighth Amendment Cases', *George Mason Law Review* 20 (2012), 25.
　'Life Without Parole as a Conflicted Punishment', *Wake Forest Law Review* 48 (2013), 1101, 1127–31.

Lessnoff, Michael, *Social Contract* (Atlantic Heights, NJ: Humanities Press International, 1986).

Lettow, Renée B., 'New Trial for Verdict against Law: Judge/Jury Relations in Early Nineteenth-Century America', *Notre Dame Law Review* 71 (1996), 519–21.

Lettow Lerner, Renée, 'The Failure of Originalism in Preserving Constitutional Rights to Jury Trial', *William and Mary Bill of Rights Journal* 22 (2014), 845–69.

Levy, C., 'The Last Years of Slavery', *Journal of Negro History* 44 (1959), 308–18.

Levy, Leonard W., *Origin of the Bill of Rights* (New Haven: Yale University Press, 1999).

Lewis v. AG (Jamaica) [2000], 3 WLR.

Lewis v. Garrett's Adm'rs, 6 Miss. (5 Howard) (1841).

Liebenberg, Sandra, *Socioeconomic Rights: Adjudication under a Transformative Constitution* (Juta, 2010).

Lincoln, Abraham, Speech at Chicago, Illinois, 10 July 1858, in Roy P. Basler et al. (eds.), *The Collected Works of Abraham Lincoln*, 9 vols. (New Brunswick, NJ: Rutgers University Press, 1953), vol. II, 499–500.

Linebaugh, Peter, *The Magna Carta Manifesto: Liberties and Commons for All* (Berkeley: University of California Press, 2009).

Lochner v. New York (chapter 9, p13).

MacDonald, William, *Select Charters and Other Documents Illustrative of American History, 1606–1775* (New York: Macmillan Publishing Co, 1910).

Magna Carta 1215.

Magna Carta 1297, 25 Edw 1 cc 1 9 29, available at http://www.legislation.gov.uk/aep/ Edw1cc1929/25/9/contents (last accessed 24 November 2014).

Magna Carta 1352, 25 Edw. III, st. 5.

Magna Carta 1354, 28 Edw. III.

Magna Carta 1368, 42 Edw. III.

Magna Carta, 3 Edw. 1 (1275).

Mahon, John K., *History of the Militia and the National Guard* (New York: Macmillan Publishing Co, 1983).

Mailamua v. R [2009], TVHC (Tuvalu HC).

Marks, Kathy, *Pitcairn Paradise Lost: Uncovering the Dark Secrets of a South Pacific Fantasy Island* (Sydney: Fourth Estate, 2008).

Marshall, Henrietta Elizabeth, 'John Lackland – The Story of the Great Charter', in *An Island Story: A History of England for Boys and Girls* (New York: Frederick A. Stokes Co, 1920), 171–78.

Marx, Karl Marx and Engels, Frederick, *Collected Works*, vol. 28 (London: Lawrence and Wishart, 1986).

Maryland Act of November Session, 1793.

Massachusetts Body of Liberties 1641, available at http://www.constitution.org/bcp/ mabodlib.htm.

Mavor, Alicia, 'Magna Carta: A Bitter Indictment of King John's Rule?' *History Today* (2013), available at http://www.historytoday.com/alicia-mavor/magna-carta-bitter -indictment-king-johns-rule (last accessed 21 November 2013).

Mayer, Thierry and Zignago, Soledad, 'Notes on CEPII's Distances Measures: The GeoDist Database', CEPII Working Paper Series, 25 December 2011, available at http://www.cepii.fr/CEPII/en/bdd_modele/presentation.asp?id=6 (last accessed 21 November 2013).

McAllister, J. T., *Virginia Militia in the Revolutionary War* (Hot Springs, VA: McAllister Publishing Co, 1913).

McKechnie, William S., *Magna Carta: A Commentary on the Great Charter of King John*, 2nd ed. (Glasgow: James Maclehose and Sons, 1914).

McLean, Nicholas M., 'Livelihood, Ability to Pay, and the Original Meaning of the Excessive Fines Clause', *Hastings Constitutional Law Quarterly* 40 (2013), 833, 861.

McPherson, B. H., *The Reception of English Law Abroad* (Brisbane: Supreme Court of Queensland Library, 2007).

Mehta v. State of Tamil Nadu [1996], 6 SCC 756.

Miller v. Alabama, 132 S.Ct. 2455, 567 U.S. (2012).

Mills v. State [2005], FJCA.

Minister of Health and Others v. Treatment Action Campaign and Others [2002], (5) SA 721 (CC) 2002 (!o) BCLR 1033 (CC).

Minister of Home Affairs (Bermuda) v. Fisher [1980], AC.

Mittal, Sonia and Weingast, Barry R., 'Constitutional Stability and the Deferential Court', *Journal of Constitutional Law* 13 (2010), 337–52.

Montserrat Slave Code Act 1693.

Mungroo v. R [1991], 1 WLR (PC).

Myerson, Roger B., 'The Autocrat's Credibility Problem and Foundations of the Constitutional State', *American Political Science Review* 102 (2008), 125–39.

'A Field Manual for the Cradle of Civilization: Theory of Leadership and Lessons of Iraq', Journal of Conflict Resolution 53 (2009), 470–82.

N.S. v. Home Secretary the Court of Justice of the European Union, C-411/10, C-493/10 [2011] CJEU 21 December 2011.

N.Y. Sess. Laws c. 379, § 221 (1848).

Naba v. The State [2001], FJHC.

Nacagi v. State [2009], FJHC.

Nadeau, Randall, 'Confucianism and the Problem of Human Rights', *Intercultural Communication Studies* XI(2) (2002), 107.

Nalawa v. State [2010], FJSC 2.

Nagourney, Adam, 'A Defiant Rancher Savors the Audience That Rallied to His Side', *New York Times*, 23 April 2014.

Nardin, T. and O'Sullivan, L., Introduction in T. Nardin and L. O'Sullivan (eds.), *M. Oakeshott, Lectures in the History of Political Thought* (Exeter and Charlottesville: Imprint Academic, 2006), 15.

Nederman, Cary J., 'The Liberty of the Church and the Road to Runnymede: John of Salisbury and the Intellectual Foundations of the Magna Carta', *PS: Political Science* 43 (2010), 457–61.

Neeson, J. M., *Commoners, Commoners Rights Enclosure and Social Change in England 1700–1820* (New York: Cambridge University Press, 1993).

New Zealand Department of Foreign Affairs and Trade, New Zealand Aid Programme, http://www.aid.govt.nz/about-aid-programme/aid-statistics/aid-allocations-201213 -201415 (last accessed 7 February 2014).

New Zealand Ministry of Foreign Affairs and Trade, 'Strengthening Justice across the Pacific', October 2013, https://www.aid.govt.nz/media-and-publications/develop ment-stories/october-2013/strengthening-justice-across-pacific (last accessed 10 December 2014).

North, Douglass C. and Weingast, Barry R., 'Constitutions and Commitment: The Evolution of Institutions Governing Public Choice in Seventeenth-Century England', *Journal of Economic History* 49 (1989), 803–32.

Nur v. State [2009], FJHC.

O'Brien, Bruce, 'Forgers of Law and Their Readers: The Crafting of English Political Identities between the Normal Conquest and the Magna Carta', *PS: Political Science* 43 (2010), 467–73.

O'Brien, D., *Constitutional Law Systems of the Commonwealth Caribbean* (Oxford: Hart Publishing, 2014).

O'Callaghan, Joseph F., 'Alfonso X and the Partidas', in *Las Siete Partidas Volume 1: The Medieval Church: The World of Clerics and Laymen*, ed. Robert I. Burns (Philadelphia: University of Pennsylvania Press, 2001), xxx, xxxii.

O'Toole, Megan, 'Ontario mother's gang rape case thrown out because of "slow" and "inefficient" court system', *National Post* (Toronto) online, 27 September 2013, available at http://news.nationalpost.com/2013/09/27/ontario-mothers-gang -rape-case-thrown-out-because-of-ontarios-slow-and-inefficient-court-system/ (last accessed 16 April 2014).

Oakeshott, M., *Rationalism in Politics and Other Essays: New and Expanded Edition* (Indianapolis: Liberty Fund, 1991).

Religion, Politics, and the Moral Life (New Haven: Yale University Press, 1993).

Experience and Its Modes (Cambridge: Cambridge University Press, 1995).

On History and Other Essays (Indianapolis: Liberty Fund, 1999).

What Is History? and Other Essays (Exeter and Charlottesville: Imprint Academic, 2004).

The Vocabulary of a Modern European State: Essays and Reviews 1952–88 (Exeter and Charlottesville: Imprint Academic, 2008).

Notebooks, 1922–86 (Exeter and Charlottesville: Imprint Academic, 2014).

Observance of Due Process of Law Act 1368. Available at http://www.legislation.gov.uk/aep/Edw3/42/3/contents (last accessed 6 December 2014).

Occupiers of 51 Olivia Road, Berea Township and Another v. City of Johannesburg and Others, Judgement CCT 24/07 (2008).

Oldham, J., 'New Light on Mansfield and Slavery', *Journal of British Studies* 27 (1988), 45–53.

Olivier et al., *Indigenous Law* (Durban: Butterworths, 1995).

Ontario Supreme Court of Justice decision (2011), 109 OR (3d) 187[26].

An Ordinance for the Government of the Territory of the United States North West of the River Ohio,' adopted by the Confederation Congress on July 13, 1787. Available from the Library of Congress at http://www.loc.gov/rr/program/bib/ourdocs/north west.html (last accessed at 6 December 2014).

Pacific Islands Law Officer's Network (website), available at http://www.pilonsec.org/ (last accessed 7 February 2014).

Pacific Judicial Development Programme, 'Programme Background' (2010–2015), available at http://www.fedcourt.gov.au/pjdp (last accessed 7 February 2014).

Painter, Sidney, *The Reign of King John* (Baltimore: Johns Hopkins Press, 1949), 297.

Pallitto, Robert, 'The Legacy of the Magna Carta in Recent Supreme Court Decisions on Detainee Rights', *PS: Political Science* 43 (2010), 483–86.

Pateman, *The Sexual Contract* (Cambridge: Polity Press, 1988).

Paton, D., 'Punishment, Crime and the Bodies of Slaves in Eighteenth-Century Jamaica', *Journal of Social History* 34 (2001), 923–54.

Pearne v. Lisle, Amb 75, 27 ER 47.

Pease, T. C., *The Leveller Movement: A Study in the Historical and Political Theory of the English Great Civil War* (1916) (Gloucester, MA: Peter Smith, 1965).

The Petition of Right 1628. Available at: http://www.legislation.gov.uk/aep/Cha1/3/1 (last accessed 6 December 2014).

Pinker, Steven, *The Better Angels of Our Nature: Why Violence Has Decline* (New York: Viking, 2011).

Pitcairn Islands Constitution Order 2010, UK SI 2010 No 244, s 7(3). Available at http://www.government.pn/Pitcairn%20Islands%20Constitution%20Order%202010.pdf.

Pitcairn Trials Act 2002(NZ) Schedule. Available from the Parliamentary Counsel Office of New Zealand at http://www.legislation.govt.nz/act/public/2002/0083/latest/DLM169865.html (last accessed 10 December 2014).

Pocock, J. G. A., *The Ancient Constitution and the Feudal Law: A Study of English Historical Thought in the Seventeenth Century* (Cambridge: Cambridge University Press, 1957, reissued 1987).

The Ancient Constitution and the Feudal Law (New York: W.W. Norton & Company, Inc, 1967).

Police v. Falkner [2005], WSSC 4[7].

Police v. Ropati [2006], 2 LRC (Samoa SC).

Pollock, Frederick and Maitland, Frederic William, *History of English Law before the Time of Edward I*, 2 vols. (Cambridge: Cambridge University Press, 1898).

Poole, Austin Lane, *From Domesday Book to Magna Carta 1087–1216*, 2nd ed. (London: Oxford University Press, 1951).

Popova, Marian, 'Political Competition as an Obstacle to Judicial Independence: Evidence from Russia and Ukraine', *Comparative Political Studies* 43 (2010), 1202–29.

Powell, James M., *The Liber Augustalis or Constitutions of Melfi Promulgated by the Emperor Frederick II for the Kingdom of Sicily in 1231* (Syracuse, NY: Syracuse University Press, 1971).

Pratt and Morgan v. Attorney General of Jamaica [1994], 2 AC.

Public Prosecutor v. Benard [2006], 1 LRC (Vanuatu SC).

Public Prosecutor v. Emelee [2006], 2 LRC (Vanuatu CA).

Public Prosecutor v. Emelee [2006], 3 LRC (Vanuatu CA).

Qarase v. Bainimarama [2009], 3 LRC (Fiji CA).

Qarase v. Bainimarama [2009], 3 LRC (Fiji HC).

Queen v. Rea, [1865], 17 Ir. Jur Rep.

Quincy, Josiah, Miller, Quincy, Samuel and Gray, Horace (eds.), *Reports of Cases Argued and Adjudged in the Superior Court of Judicature of the Province of Massachusetts* (Boston: Little, Brown, and Company, 1865).

R v. Christian (No 2) [2006], 1 LRC [212].

R v. Christian (No 2) [2006], 1 LRC (Pitcairn SC).

R v. Christian (No 2) [2006], 4 LRC (Pitcairn CA).

R v. CIP Inc [1992], 1 SCR.

R v. Collins [1995], 2 SCR.

R v. Godin [2009], 2 SCR 3, 7[6].

R v. Hence [2012], SBHC.

R v. Inhabitants of Thames Ditton, 4 Douglas 300, 301; 99 Eng. *Rep.* 891, 892 (1785).

R v. Jewitt [1985], 2 SCR (SC) (Dickson CJ).

R v. Kalanj [1989], 1 SCR.

R v. Lahiry [2011], 109 OR (3d).

R v. Lahiry [2011], ONSC.

R v. Lee [2010], ONCJ.

R v. MacDougal [1998], 3 SCR.

R v. MacDougall [1998], 3 SCR (SCC).

R v. Mae [2005], SBHC.

R v. Maelisu'u [2013], SBHC 181[43].

R v. Morin [1992], 1 SCR (SCC).

R v. Poitvin [1993], 2 SCR.

R v. Rahey [1987], 1 SCR.

R v. Rahey [1987], 1 SCR (SCC).

R v. Setaga [2009], 2 LRC (Tuvalu HC).

R v. Tangisi [2008], SBHC (Solomon Is HC).

Ramsay, James, *An Essay on the Treatment and Conversion of African Slaves in the British Colonies* (James Phillips: London, 1784).

Re State of Himachal Pradesh v. Parents of A Student of Medical College, Simla [1985], 3 SCC169.

Reid, John P., *Controlling the Law: Legal Politics in Early National New Hampshire* (DeKalb: Northern Illinois University Press, 2004).

Republic of Fiji Islands v. Prasad [2001], 2 LRC.

Republic of Fiji Military Forces v. Qicatabua [2008], FJCA.

Republic of Kiribati v. Teoiaki [1993], 3 LRC.

Republic of Kiribati v. Teoiaki [1993], 3 LRC.

Republic v. Kaiue [2003], KIHC (Kiribati HC).

Republic v. Teoiaki [1993], 3 LRC (Kiribati HC).

Resolution adopted by the Assembly of St Vincent, The Royal Gazette (Jamaica), vol XXXVIII, no.14, 18.

Resolution adopted by the Jamaican Assembly, Journals of the Assembly of Jamaica, vol. XII, 696, 782–283.

Resolutions of the Stamp Act Congress of October 19, 1765. Available at http://www.let .rug.nl/usa/documents/1751–1775/the-resolutions-of-the-stamp-act-congress-october -19-1765.php (last accessed 6 December 2014).

Resolves of the Maryland House of Delegates', printed in The Maryland Gazette (3 October 1765).

Riendeau, N., *The Legendary Past: Michael Oakeshott on Imagination and Political Identity* (Exeter and Charlottesville: Imprint Academic, 2014).

Riley v. AG Jamaica [1983], AC.

Ritz, Wilfred, J., Book Review, 'The Road from Runnymede, Magna Carta and Constitutionalism in America, A.E. Dick Howard', *Washington and Lee Law Review* 26 (1969), 409–14.

Robinson, Nick, 'Cameron sets sight on human rights court', BBC News, 17 July 2014, http://www.bbc.co.uk/news/uk-politics-28339263 (last accessed 10 December 2014).

Robinson v. R [1984], UKPC 3.

Robinson, Tracey, 'Our Inherent Constitution', in D. Berry and T. Robinson (eds.), *Transitions in Caribbean Law* (Kingston, Jamaica: Caribbean Law Publishing Company, 2013) 273.

Robu v. R [2006], SBCA.

Rokoua v. The State [2006], FJCA.

Rothwell, H., *English Historical Documents*, (London: Eyre and Spottiswoode, 1975).

Rummel v. Estelle, 445 U.S. (1980).

Rupprecht, A., 'Excessive Memories: Slavery, Insurance and Resistance', *History Workshop Journal* 64 (2007), 6–28.

Sahim v. State [2007], FJHC.

Sajo, Andras, 'Reading the Invisible Constitution: Judicial Review in Hungary', *Oxford Journal of Legal Studies* 15 (1995), 253–67.

Salzberger, Eli M., 'A Positive Analysis of the Doctrine of Separation of Powers, or: Why Do We Have an Independent Judiciary?' *International Review of Law and Economics* 13 (1993), 340–79.

Samoa Party v. Attorney General [2010], WSCA (Samoa CA).

Santayana, George, *Reason in Common Sense', Volume I, The Life of Reason* (Charles Scribner's Sons, Dover Publications, 1905).

Schuyler, R. L., 'The Constitutional Claims of the British West Indies', *Political Science Quarterly* 40 (1925), 1–36.

Scott v. Sandford, Judgement 60 U.S. 19 How. 393 (1856).

Seel, Graham E., 'Good King John', *History Today*, 62(2) (2012).

Sellar, W. C. and Yeatman, R. J., *1066 and All That: A Memorable History of England, Comprising All the Parts You Can Remember, Including 103 Good Things, 5 Bad Kings and 2 Genuine Dates* (London: Methuen, 1930).

Seru v. State [2003], FJCA.

Seru v. State [2003], FJCA.

Seru v. State [2003], FJCA.

Shanley v. Harvey (Chancery 1762), *ER* 28(2), 125.

Shaw, Danny, 'Police stop and search powers to be overhauled', BBC News, 30 April 2014, http://www.bbc.co.uk/news/uk-27224887 (last accessed 6 June 2014).

Shelley, Percy Bysshe, 'The Masque of Anarchy', 1819.

Sheppard, Steve, *The Selected Writings of Sir Edward Coke* (Indianapolis, IN: Liberty Fund, 2003).

Shuter, Bill, 'Tradition as Rereading', in David Galef (ed.), *Second Thoughts: A Focus on Rereading* (Detroit: Wayne State University Press, 1998), 79.

Solem v. Helm, 463 U.S. (1983).

Somerset v. Stewart, 98 Eng. Rep. 499, 1 Lofft 1 (KB 1772).

Soobramoney v. Minister of Health (Kwazulu-Natal) (CCT32/97) [1997], ZACC 17; 1998 (1) SA 765 (CC); 1997 (12) BCLR 1696 (27 November 1997).

Sorovanalagi v. State [2011], FJHC.

Spierenburg, P., *The Spectacle of Suffering: Executions and the Evolution of Repression* (Cambridge: Cambridge University Press, 1984).

Stamp Act Congress 1765, 5 Geo. 3, c. 12. Available at http://www.ushistory.org/declaration/related/sac65.htm (last accessed at 6 December 2014).

State v. Bowser, 926 S.E.2d (Ohio App. 3rd 2010).

State v. Brooks, 739 So.2d (Fla. App. 5th 1999).

State v. Driver, 78 N.C. (1878).

State v. Farrington, 141 N.C. (1906).

State v. Khanna [2004], FJHC.

State v. Ledua [2011], FJMC.

State v. Pettie, 80 N.C. (1879).

State v. Reid, 106 N.C. (1890).

State v. Rokotuiwai [1998], FJHC.

State v. Stevens [1999], FJHC.

State v. Vunisa [2000], 2 FLR 38, 39(Fiji HC).

Stinneford, John F., 'Rethinking Proportionality under the Cruel and Unusual Punishments Clause', *Virginia Law Review* 97 (2011), 899–912.

Stivison, David V., *Magna Carta in America: A Project of the Magna Carta Research Foundation* (Baltimore: Gateway Press, 1993).

Stroud, D. I., *Magna Carta* (Southampton: Paul Cave Publications Ltd, 1998).

Stuart v. Laird, the Court upheld the repeal of the 1801 Judiciary Act. (chapters 9, 13)

Summerson, H. R. T., 'The Structure of Law Enforcement in Thirteenth Century England', *American Journal of Legal History* 23 (1979), 313, 315.

Sunstein, Cass, *The Second Bill of Rights* (New York: Basic Books, 2004).

Swindler, William F., *Magna Carta: Legend and Legacy* (Indianapolis: Bobbs-Merrill Company, Inc, 1965).

'Rights of Englishman since 1776: Some Anglo-American Notes', *University of Pennsylvania Law Review* 124 (1976), 1089–90

Tawake v. State [2009], FJHC.

Taylor, Matthew, 'Can Funding Reform Stir the Party Animal?' *Parliamentary Affairs* 58 (2005), 621–26.

Teetea v. Republic [1996], KIHC 101[3].

Thomas v. Baptiste [2000], AC 1.

Thompson, Faith, *Magna Carta: Its Role in the Making of the English Constitution 1300–1629* (Minneapolis: University of Minnesota Press, 1948).

Thorpe, Francis N. (ed.), *The Federal and State Constitutions, Colonial Charters, and Other Organic Laws of the United States of America* (Washington, DC: U.S. Government Printing Office, 1909).

Tracy, Larissa, *Castration and Culture in the Medieval Ages* (Cambridge: D.S. Brewer, 2013).

Treanor, William, 'Judicial Review before Marbury', *Stanford Law Review* 58 (2005), 455–562.

Trop v. Dulles, 356 U.S. (1958).

Tuchman, Barbara, *A Distant Mirror: The Calamitous Fourteenth Century* (New York: Ballantine Books, 1978).

Tuimoala v. Public Service Commission [2003], FJHC.

Turner, Ralph V., *The English Judiciary in the Age of Glanvill and Bracton* (New York: Cambridge University Press, 1985).

'Young John in His Brothers' Shadows', in *King John: England's Evil King* (Stroud: History Press, 1994), 29–56.

Magna Carta: Through the Ages (Harlow: Pearson Education, 2003).

Tyler, David W., 'Clarifying Departmentalism: How the Framers' Vision of Judicial and Presidential Review Makes the Case for Deductive Judicial Supremacy', *William & Mary Law Review* 50 (2009), 2219.

UK Foreign Office, 'EU Reform Treaty Abandons Constitutional Approach', 22 August 2007.

UK Parliament, Political and Constitutional Reform Committee, 'A New Magna Carta?' 3 July 2014, report on recommending constitutional reform in the United Kingdom, available at http://www.publications.parliament.uk/pa/cm201415/cmselect/cmpolcon/463/463.pdf (last accessed 24 November 2014).

United Nations Committee on Economic, Social and Cultural Rights, General Comment 14, The right to the highest attainable standard of health (Twenty-second session, 2000), UN Doc E/C.12/2000/4 (2000).

United Kingdom, Observations, Doc E/C.12/GBR/C)/5, 12 June 2009.

United Nations Department of Public Information, UDHR's 50th Anniversary, http://www.un.org/rights/50/carta.htm (last accessed 24 November 2014).

United States' Bill of Rights 1791. Available from the Bill of Rights Institute at http://billofrightsinstitute.org/founding-documents/bill-of-rights/ (last accessed 6 December 2014).

Van Bueren, Geraldine, 'Housing', in Cheadle et al. (eds.), *South African Constitutional Law* (Durban: Butterworths, 2002), 473.

Law's Duty to the Poor (Paris: UNESCO, 2010).

'Socioeconomic Rights and a Bill of Rights – An Overlooked British Tradition', *Public Law* (2013), 821–37.

Vicecontc v. Ministry of Health and Social Welfare, Poder Judicial de la Nacion, Causa no 31 777/96 Judgement of 2 June 1998.

Virginia Bill of Rights 1776.

Virginia Legislation Va. Code 18.2–51.2.

Wade-Evans, A. W., *Welsh Medieval Law: Being a Text of the Laws of Howel the Good* (Oxford: Clarendon Press, 1909).

Waldron, J., 'John Locke – Social Contract versus Political Anthropology', in Boucher and Kelly (eds.), *The Social Contract from Hobbes to Rawls* (London: Routledge, 1994), 54–55.

Watson v. United States, 979 A.2d (D.C. 2009).

Weingast, Barry R., 'The Political Foundations of Democracy and the Rule of Law', *American Political Science Review* 91 (1997), 245–63.

Weems v. United States, 217 U.S. (1910).

Wert, Justin J., 'With a Little Help from a Friend: Habeas Corpus and the Magna Carta after Runnymede', *PS: Political Science* 43 (2010), 475–78.

Weslager, C. A., *The Stamp Act Congress: With an Exact Copy of the Complete Journal* (Newark: University of Delaware Press), 1976.

Wesley, C. H., 'The Negro in the West Indies', *Journal of Negro History* 17 (1932), 51, 54, 55.

Whittington, Keith E., *Constitutional Construction: Divided Powers and Constitutional Meaning* (Cambridge, MA: Harvard University Press, 1999).

'Extrajudicial Constitutional Interpretation: Three Objections and Responses', *North Carolina Law Review* 80 (2002), 776.

Wilkerson v. Utah, 99 U.S. (1878).

Williams, E., *From Columbus to Castro: The History of the Caribbean 1492–1969* (London: Andre Deutsch, 1970).

Winthrop, John, *The Journal of John Winthrop, 1630–1649*, Richard S. Dunn et al. (eds.) (Cambridge, MA: Belknap Press, 1996).

Wishnie, Michael J., 'Proportionality: The Struggle for Balance in U.S. Immigration Policy', *University of Pittsburg Law Review* 72 (2011), 431, 445.

Wishprun Pty Ltd v. Dixon [2003], 77 ALJR (HCA).

Wolfram, Charles W., 'The Constitutional History of the Seventh Amendment', *Minnesota Law Review* 57 (1973), 639, 674–76.

Woolf, Lord, 'Magna Carta: a Precedent for Recent Constitutional Change', available at http://magnacarta800th.com/lectures/magna-carta-a-precedent-for-recent-cons titutional-change/ (last accessed at 10 December 2014).

Worcester, Kent, 'The Meaning and Legacy of the Magna Carta', *Political Science* 43 (2010), 451–56.

Worchester, Robert, 'Why Commemorate 800 Years?' *Magna Carta Today*, 2013, available at http://magnacarta800th.com/magna-carta-today/objectives-of-the -magna-carta-800th-committee/ (last accessed at 21 November 2014).

Young, C., *The Royal Forests of Medieval England* (Philadelphia: University of Pennsylvania Press, 1979).

Zagorin, Perez, *A History of Political Thought in the English Revolution* (Chicago: Thoemmes Press, 1997).

The English Revolution: Politics, Events, Ideas (Aldershot: Ashgate, 1998).

Zylstra v. Corporation of Charleston, 1 Bay (S.C. 1794).

Index

Lightning Source UK Ltd.
Milton Keynes UK
UKOW02f1224300615

254339UK00012B/630/P